EATING VIỆT NAM

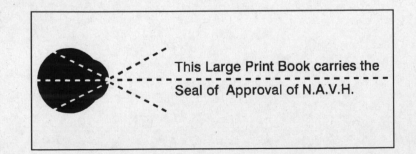

This Large Print Book carries the Seal of Approval of N.A.V.H.

EATING VIỆT NAM

DISPATCHES FROM A BLUE PLASTIC TABLE

GRAHAM HOLLIDAY

THORNDIKE PRESS

A part of Gale, Cengage Learning

Farmington Hills, Mich • San Francisco • New York • Waterville, Maine
Meriden, Conn • Mason, Ohio • Chicago

GALE
CENGAGE Learning®

LIBRARY OF CONGRESS CATALOGING-IN-PUBLICATION DATA

Holliday, Graham, 1969–
    Eating Việt Nam : dispatches from a blue plastic table / by Graham Holliday. -- Large print edition.
        pages (large print) cm — (Thorndike Press large print peer picks)
        ISBN 978-1-4104-7893-1 (hardback) — ISBN 1-4104-7893-9 (hardcover)
    1. Cooking, Vietnamese. 2. Street food—Vietnam. 3. Food—Vietnam. 4. Large type books. I. Title.
TX724.5.V5H65 2015
641.59597—dc23
                                                                2015006176

Published in 2015 by arrangement with Ecco, an imprint of HarperCollins Publishers

Printed in Mexico
1 2 3 4 5 6 7 19 18 17 16 15

for noodle girl
and the toad

CONTENTS

7

FOREWORD
BY ANTHONY BOURDAIN

Việt Nam owns me. From my first visit, I was helpless to resist.

Just a few months previous, I'd been resigned to the certainty that I would never see Việt Nam; that my dreams of Graham Greene Land, that faraway place I only knew from childhood news reports, books, and films would have to wait for another life. This life, I was sure, would finish in close proximity to a Manhattan deep fryer.

So, simply finding myself there, finally, outside the legendary Continental Hotel in Sài Gòn, smelling Việt Nam, hearing it, the high roar of thousands of motorbikes, I was overcome with gratitude and disbelief. Jet-lagged (back when I still got jet lag) and deranged by anti-malarial meds, I staggered happily through the heat to the places I'd read about in the great nonfiction accounts of the French and American wartime years: the Majestic, the rooftop at the Rex, and of course, the very hotel where I was staying. I ate steaming, spicy bowls of phở on the street, and crispy fried quails, and was delightfully overwhelmed by the smells and flavors of Bến Thành market. I ventured out into the Mekong Delta, where I got savagely drunk with an extended family of former Việt Cộng. I explored the islands and floating markets off Nha Trang, had many adventures, and made lasting friends.

And I changed.

My attitude changed, of course. Your eyes can't help but open when you travel — and just to see the places I'd read so much about was surely life-changing. But something else changed — on an almost cellular level, as if my very tissues had been penetrated by the smells and atmosphere of Việt Nam, that heavy air, thick with odors of jackfruit, durian, fresh flowers, raw chicken, diesel fuel, incense. Việt Nam is a country of proud cooks and passionate eaters. And, after experiencing the spicy morning soups of Sài Gòn, the notion of ever settling for a bland Western-style breakfast again was unthinkable.

I was hooked. I wanted more. I needed more. I left Việt Nam that first time determined to do whatever was necessary to keep coming back — even if that involved something as undistinguished as making television.

I have since visited the country many times, always with a television crew. Unsurprisingly, the people I work with have always come to feel the same way about the place as I do.

In the preproduction phase of one of those shows, I came across a wonderfully unusual, deeply authoritative food blog called *noodlepie*, by a British expat named Graham Holliday.

For reasons I would only later come to understand, this man had chosen to exhaustively photograph, write about, explain, and appreciate the kind of street food vendors I loved but still knew relatively little about.

No one I was aware of, anywhere, owned his territory like Holliday. He explained everyday, working-class Vietnamese food from the point of view of an enthusiast: insider enough to have access to, and understanding of, the facts, but outsider enough to thrill at the newness and strangeness of it all.

Holliday's knowledge of the street food landscape in Hà Nội and Sài Gòn was breathtaking. He went deep in his search for every bún chả and phở vendor in Hà Nội, each purveyor of bánh mì in Sài Gòn, soliciting suggestions from xe ôm drivers, students in the English classes he taught, neighbors and strangers. He'd follow each lead, or stop in at whatever stall or shop caught his eye in his exhaustive urban travels, and report back thoughtfully, without bias, condescension, or cliché.

In preparing to visit, my colleagues and I be-

11

gan to piggyback shamelessly on Holliday's extraordinary body of work. In Sài Gòn, his careful-yet-joyous research sent us down an alley to Mrs. Thanh Hải's snail stall. We heeded his advice and found the masterful crepe cook at 46A Dinh Cong Trang, whose beloved ancient pan yields the city's best banh xeo.

I was a huge fan of his blog for as long as Graham lived in Việt Nam, and felt, always, that there was an important book there. A few years later, when Dan Halpern at Ecco Press, in his wisdom, gave me my own publishing imprint, I saw an opportunity to help make that book happen. When asked who in the whole wide world had a story and a voice I'd like to publish, Graham Holliday was one of the first people I thought of.

What would it be like to move to Việt Nam? To actually live there? To both live the dream — and deal with a very steep learning curve — a stranger in a strange, yet wonderful, wonderful land? What would that be like? Surely many of us have wondered about that. I know I have.

Eating Việt Nam provides an excellent account of what that might be like. It takes a special kind of person to move to a country as complicated — with as complicated a history — as Việt Nam, and to let things happen, to let things in, to let it all wash over you and through you. It takes an even more special person to describe the experience so richly and affectionately, clear-eyed —

and yet always with heart.

This is — and will remain — an essential account for anyone considering travel to Việt Nam. But it should be a deeply rewarding read as well for those who won't be getting that opportunity anytime soon. A solid jumping-off point for the imagination. The beginning of a dream.

Because, as I found out, the dream comes first.

CHAPTER ONE:
HÀ NỘI

As the pig's uterus landed on the blue plastic table in front of me, I knew I'd made a mistake.

Not that I understood that the slab of shiny pinkness plonked atop a tangle of green herbs was a farm animal's womb at first. I was certain of only two things:

1. It didn't look good.
2. I was expected to eat it.

It was a late summer's evening in 1997. The air hung like a damp, hot curtain. Mine was the sole white face jammed in among hundreds of cackling, beer-soaked Vietnamese men seated at a grubby intersection on Tăng Bạt Hổ Street in the south of Hà Nội, the capital of Việt Nam.

"I like to come here after work to relax," said Nghĩa, an IT consultant and my student. I taught English at the first foreign-run English-language school in the capital. He wore a white shirt, white socks, black trousers, and black shoes.

The memory of teenage acne streaked across the forty-year-old's face.

Nghĩa bent over the table to inspect the recent arrival and seemed pleased by what he saw. I was not pleased. Dinner's arrival had sent my appetite hightailing it down the street. I was panicked, distressed, and chained by good manners to the dinner table.

Using a pair of wooden chopsticks, Nghĩa picked up a slice of uterus and placed the morsel between his teeth. He left his mouth open as he masticated. Like a washing machine warming up, he churned the offal this way and that, tossing it from incisor to molar and back again. He looked up at me. The crescent moon of his chomping mouth radiated approval.

"It's good. Good snack food. Good for drinking beer. Try some."

I peered down at the sharing plate. The cacophony of howling Vietnamese government officials and office workers that echoed around us was as loud as the voice inside me screaming *Leave. Now.*

Apart from hog's anus, the dish in front of me was as intimate and inedible a part of an animal as I could think of. I found myself wondering, *At what point in human evolution did some guy, somewhere, say to himself, "Hmmm . . . boiled uterus? You know what, that might just work"?*

Taking a pair of chopsticks from the red plas-

16

tic container on the table, I prodded dinner and took a tentative bite.

In the end, it wasn't the taste of the uterus that repelled me — there was no taste. It was the *texture*.

Boiled womb of pig is slightly tough on the outside and spongy on the inside. It's not *good* tough and it's not *good* spongy. Pig wombs have only one true purpose in life, and that is to bear piglets. It's just not something that should grace a menu, or a mouth, or anything other than the interior of a mature sow, I reasoned.

Nghĩa frowned his surprise. "You don't like it?" he inquired. The subtext to his frown was clear in his bulging eyes, which seemed to scold, "What the hell's the matter with you? This is man's food, good for your health, makes you strong, good with beer. What's not to like? Take a chunk of this and you'll be banging the missus into the middle of next week. Are you some kind of loser?"

"It's a little . . . err . . . visceral for me," I replied. I was desperate to skirt offense, push aside loss of face, and avoid any other cultural black hole of misunderstanding I might be about to step into. "And the texture . . . well . . . it's tough."

A tad crestfallen, Nghĩa yelled at the petite, perspiring young waitress. She'd been busy darting between tables with plates of innards, glasses of beer, and cold towels, totting up the

17

beer count on a flimsy piece of paper attached with an elastic band to a sliver of a Marlboro carton ever since we'd pulled up a plastic stool.

Minutes later, she was back at our table with a second dish.

It was less appetizing than the first. An umbilical cord perhaps? It was clearly identifiable as pipes or tubes, but of what animal origin I wasn't certain. Whatever it was, I felt sure that only a vet, hacking away at a poor beast during a lifesaving surgical operation, should ever have to see it.

"Pig's intestine." Nghĩa smiled. His teeth glistened as he hacked into a tube. Flecks of offal pebble dashed the table in the blasted fluorescence. "My favorite." He chomped.

I liked Nghĩa, but something told me our friendship was not really going anywhere.

I shook my head. The waitress zapped back into the kitchen. The pavement was a shambles of plastic tables and men. Hundreds of them. Hunched low, shouting, sloshing beer, tapping cheap flip-flops on the uneven pathway and picking at offcuts between cigarette puffs and back slaps. The teenage waitress returned seconds later bearing a plate laden with something I knew well, something I could eat with abandon, something British: deep-fried, greasy, crinkle-cut chips.

I relaxed, my taste buds returned, and even

the sweat furring my back cooled. As Nghĩa intermittently barked away the persistent lottery ticket sellers, I dug in to my chip supper, sipped beer, and did my best to tune out the cracks and crunches of Nghĩa's teeth sawing through the intestines and the most feminine of pig's parts. I failed to understand in what stratosphere Nghĩa's taste buds operated. Pigs are great. They make some of the animal world's best noises. Pork is divine. Bacon better. But uterus? Intestine? It's not as if Việt Nam was in the throes of a pig drought. Why did Nghĩa and the hundreds of men around us opt for pig womb over pork chop? Why did I move here? For this?

When we got up to leave, Nghĩa passed a ticket and a few hundred đồng to the motorbike-parking valet. He found Nghĩa's bike and gave the saddle a quick wipe with a grubby cloth, nearly but not quite completely erasing the chalk number he'd earlier etched onto it.

Nghĩa sat with his posterior so far back on the sloping saddle that my nether regions could not help but grind into his rear end. He slipped his sleek, black Honda Dream into gear, and off we skedaddled, helmetless of course, into the Hà Nội night, leaving a half-eaten plate of entrails in our wake.

A slew of teenagers cruised around Hoàn Kiếm Lake on a repetitive circuit that took in much of the Old Quarter, turning the picturesque heart of

19

Hà Nội into a groaning, tooting, sticky, fume-filled jam of testosterone, tittle-tattle, and two-stroke.

Short-skirted girlfriends and lovers rode at the rear, elegantly sitting sidesaddle, draped adoringly over their steersmen as I, inelegantly, thrust my groin into Nghĩa's buttocks at every bump, scratch, and trough in the road.

The motorbike came to a halt outside my flat on Cầu Gỗ Street, slap-bang in the center of Hà Nội, adjacent to the capital's busiest intersection. The breeze of the ride immediately vanished and I felt the inevitable return of the tacky, dank air on my skin. Air injected with the scent of blackening maize from a vendor across the road. I thanked Nghĩa for an interesting dinner, said I'd see him next week, and bid him good night. Donning a coat called relief, I turned to face the entrance to my new home.

Between Đinh Liệt Street and Cầu Gỗ market, there was nothing but shops and soup kitchens. A T-shirt seller here, an incense trader there, tofu, chickens, and flowers farther down. At random points, slotted between these businesses, were a series of narrow, covered alleyways. Some were hidden from view at the back of shops, others opened directly onto the pavement. I lived at the end of a hidden one. The alley entrance to my new home was no bigger than a regular door. However, once I passed through, it was more of a secret portal of Tardis-like dimensions than any home entrance I'd ever previously known.

To enter the alley, I had to walk a distance of five yards from the curbside. Circling the sugarcane seller chipping her wares in a basket conveniently placed in the middle of the pavement, I scurried through the photocopier shop, smiled at the copy boy, squeezed past the ancient Japanese paper pumper as it churned out copies on cheap, yellowing paper, stepped over the sleeping teenager, dodged the kneeling eight-year-old in a school uniform doing his homework, exited the back of the shop, and finally began the journey down the darkened, mold-covered bare brick alley, past four or five motorbikes, to my home.

Halfway through the gloom, the fat woman in pajamas, who was *always* downstairs, in the alley, shouting into a phone, was downstairs, in the alley, shouting into a phone. I strode over a two-step incline, pinched my way around another row of Hondas, and headed into the last house at the conclusion of the dead-end alley. By now I was some thirty yards away from the street.

As I took off my shoes and walked through their living room, I paid my respects to the Vietnamese family from whom I was renting a floor, smiling and making the tiniest of bows.

The TV was on, tuned in to a game show. The

grinning, gray-haired, toothless father of the house sat cross-legged on a straw mat. He wore a vest and boxers and held a beer in his hand. Several half-empty bowls and plates, a bag of persimmons, and a tray of green tea and thimble-sized cups lay in front of his crossed shins. The rest of the family — his daughter, son, daughter-in-law, and sole grandchild — all huddled around him, engrossed in the flickering tube. His wife smiled up at me as she cut the persimmons, letting the peels fall onto a dirty dinner plate. She offered me a quarter slice.

I headed up a set of wooden stairs to the second floor of the three-story house. The house was in the capital's Old Quarter, but it had been built within the last five years. A combination of humidity and a bad build had prematurely aged it to look like all the other slim, concrete blocks in the capital. At the landing, I took the door on my immediate right and entered the livingroom cum office. The air was heavy with must. It was ninety degrees Fahrenheit. Over 90 percent humidity. I closed the door and switched on the ceiling fan. There was no air conditioner.

There were two armchairs and a small table in the center of the room. A bookshelf leaned against the wall in the middle of the room and a large desk and chair sat at the far end in front of the only window. Through its iron bars I could see a neighbor's house not three yards away, the

22

washing line on the balcony, the TV glowing, and dinner sitting on the floor.

In truth, I was surrounded on all sides by neighbors, as my new home was smack dab in the middle of a squash of houses, shops, shacks, apartments, and lean-tos.

As I sat down behind the desk, the muffled shrieks, squeaks, and parps of Hà Nội were still audible. It was a persistently random crackle of chattering voices, whining sticky-rice sellers, distorted TV, and machinery that would, around 9 P.M., fade into the infrequent sound of feuding motorbikes and silence.

As I sat there, I knew that at 6 A.M. sharp, the same refrain would crank back into gear, together with the morning variant. Gone would be the sticky-rice seller and in would come the sing-song echo of "Bánh mì, bánh mì nóng," which bounced up to the washing lines, water tanks, and TV-aerial-festooned rooftops. It signaled to anyone within earshot that a bicycle-wheeling bread seller was somewhere in the depths below, navigating the knotted alleyways.

Three books populated my shelf: Lonely Planet's guide to Việt Nam, François Bizot's *The Gate,* and a *Learn Vietnamese* handbook. All were counterfeit copies that I'd picked up on the street for a dollar or two. All were unread.

In my desk drawer I had a shoebox of photos and letters, several journals, a portable CD player, and a pack of CDs. A laptop and two candles sat upon my desk. Apart from clothes, these were my sole possessions. I had no TV, no radio, and the World Wide Web had yet to arrive in Việt Nam. The landlord had said I could use their fridge in the kitchen downstairs. I never needed to.

The rest of my rental consisted of a small shower room on the other side of the landing and a bedroom that was big enough for a double bed, a wardrobe, and nothing else.

I thought of Nghĩa. He would be going home, over the Red River bridge and into the district of Gia Lâm, to a full dinner prepared by his wife and mother, and eaten on the floor with the TV blaring, like every other middle-class Hà Nội family. The uterus and intestines were, as Nghĩa put it, snack food for him, picked up on the way home, the way I might have dropped off for a pint on the way home from work in Britain in the not too dim and distant.

I wasn't an idiot. I knew boiled and grilled offal wasn't the heart and soul of Vietnamese food — although pig's heart was also on the menu that night. I'd heard of their soups, their spring rolls, and their fish sauce, but beyond a few nibbles of an uneventful fried crab thing in a Vietnamese diner opposite Camden Lock Market in London years earlier, I was largely ignorant of the cuisine. My faith in the quality of Vietnamese food remained theoretical, based as it was on almost zero personal experience. I'd kind of heard, you know, *somewhere,* that it was pretty good. As a result, I couldn't help but be a little disappointed that my first meal out on the street in Việt Nam, with a Vietnamese person, had been such an unmitigated disaster.

My introduction to street food that night in Hà Nội was the unlikely beginning of a long-running love affair with Việt Nam and Vietnamese food. It was just unfortunate that I'd gotten started at both the wrong end of the menu and the animal.

But really, it was all my fault.

I'd pushed Nghĩa into a corner. I'd persevered in asking him to take me somewhere he liked, somewhere he *really* liked. This seemingly simple task is far harder than you might think.

It was a lesson I'd learned living in the city of Iksan, in South Korea, for one year before moving to Việt Nam.

The English department at Iri Middle School for Girls consisted of three middle-aged mothers: Mrs. Lee, Mrs. Choi, and Mrs. Hong. From day one, these three women had cornered me in the teachers' staff room. One sat either side of me, while the third sat opposite, facing me. I was the English-language machine and I needed to be installed in the optimum position for adverbial inquisitions, tense clarifications, and spell checks. I decided to turn their attack to my

25

advantage.

They loved their country and they loved their food. But when they first took me out for lunch, we ended up at a train wreck of a restaurant. It was a Western joint of some supposed repute among well-to-do Koreans.

It sat atop a garish hotel, which sat atop a tawdry shopping mall, which sat in the middle of concrete-ville.

This restaurant was all knives, forks, napkins, suited waiters, and piano ballads. We were the only customers and there was not a single metallic Korean chopstick in sight. It was torture-chamber grim.

We ate canned soup and breaded pork cutlets in sauce-du-crap with boiled potatoes and frozen peas. It was awful. It was expensive. And worse: it was as uncomfortable and inedible for them as it was for me. It wasn't just the food. The starched napkins, the foreign clinks of knives against forks, the large heavy white plates, that bloody piano. It was all wrong. My hosts pleaded approval from me, the native-English-speaking guest. I gave it. Falsely. I was just being polite.

My hosts told me that they had had almost no previous contact with foreigners. Each could list the number of non-Koreans they had met on one or two digits of one hand. They wanted what they thought was best for me, but in their eagerness to please, they'd taken a bad turn up the wrong street.

I'd already been eating the likes of kimchi jigae, nakji bokum bap, and mandu guk every day after work, in fluorescent-lit huts near my Jung-Ang Heights apartment, near the city's western limits. I knew Koreans didn't eat breaded pork, canned soup, and frozen peas, and *I* didn't want to, either.

Some weeks after our pork catastrophe, I arrived at school and, as usual, donned my plastic slippers, shoved my shoes in the allotted cubbyhole, hauled myself and my bag up the stairs, greeted the teachers' room with a bow, and sat down at my desk.

The conversation turned to food. I recounted some of my more interesting dinnertime exploratory missions to my dutiful audience of three. So well did it go down, I decided to set this morning mode to repeat as I waited for the Korean culinary cogs to turn in a different direction, away from high-rise hotel nosh and into the Korean shed. I'd traveled halfway around the world and it seemed to me that every Korean acquaintance I made thought that the way to impress me was to take me somewhere to eat as far removed from the Korean dining table as they could find. I wanted to try live baby octopus and sannakji, and to know what agujjim, a spicy monkfish stew, tasted like.

I don't think they really believed me at first

that I wanted to eat their food, not a sodomized version of it. So, I'd talk to them about food. A lot. I'd push them hard to tell me what they liked, until their eyes would light up brighter than any strip lighting in any Iksan restaurant, as one of them described a particular dish in a particular shack in a particular part of town.

Our stomachs would rumble and, inevitably, one of my colleagues would reach for a dusty, crumbling thesaurus, looking for a forgotten English adjective that they'd use to praise this or that soup, some grilled dish, raw fish, hotpot, noodle, or wonton.

It was autumn 1996. There were no guide-books to this province, and very few English speakers, but the places they described were the places I wanted to eat at. To understand this country, I'd decided, I had to begin with what I put in my mouth. Picking at a hotel buffet, grabbing a slice at the local pizza parlor, and eating a fried drumstick wasn't my desired route. It was the kimchi-laden soups and stews that would lead me to where I really wanted to go. And it was infuriating that every Korean I met failed to spot this immediately. Because I knew I would never discover these places without their help, I kept on pushing. *I wanted to eat where they ate*.

By the end of my Korean tenure, my colleagues and I were dining out on a weekly basis in shabby, wee, no-name holes-in-the-wall and middle-of-nowhere farm huts all over Cholla-buk-do province. It was our way of getting to know each other. As we ate, I'd show them photos of my family, my friends, an old girlfriend. Their response: "Can she cook?"

We feasted on kungnamul kukbap with all the hangover sufferers of Jeonju. We drank soju with sam gyeop sal. We gorged on insam tol-sot bibimbap and slurped kalbi tang in each and every granny-run, back-alley shack that they had swooned over since their school days. They loved this food. And they loved that I loved it. It was, as they say in the common parlance, a win-win situation.

The method I used to get the red-chili-pepper-paste-strewn food experience I craved in Korea, and the ones I would later love even more in Việt Nam, was what I called the "Four Questions Theory" of food exploration. It's a concept I have tested with hotel staff, travel guides, colleagues, government ministers, journalists, diplomats, lawyers, bankers, and students. In fact, as I became more and more obsessed with seeking out Vietnamese food experiences, I tested my theory on every single Vietnamese person I met in Việt Nam and abroad. It goes something like this:

Me: I'm not sure where to go for lunch. I want to eat Vietnamese food. Is there anywhere you particularly like that you could recommend?

Vietnamese response: Oh, for sure. You must go to the [insert name of a big, fancy-schmancy hotel, serving Western, "Asian" — whatever that is — or worst of all: the abomination that is "fusion cuisine." Invariably, there'll be an "authentic street food stall" snuck away in one corner, replete with a pristine three-wheeled cyclo taxi and a bored-looking woman in a conical hat. The air-conditioned restaurant will be almost entirely deserted, apart from some sad traveling business type, struggling with the slop on his plate as he simultaneously tap-tap-taps at a laptop. Total cost, with drinks: $50–$100. Fun factor: *zero*.]

Me: Hmm. I'm not so keen on eating in Western hotels. I'd like to eat Vietnamese food. You know, real Vietnamese food. Do you know a good place, a place that you like?

Vietnamese response: Oh, I see. OK then. I think you might enjoy the food at [insert restaurant called something like Golden Lotus or Việt Nam Garden, which is invariably filled with busloads of Western and Japanese tourists. It looks self-consciously antique.

You'll be served faux Vietnamese nosh, with flowers carved from carrots on the side of your plate. "Ambient" lighting is de rigueur, as is the twinky-twanky Muzak. You'll probably find a mystical Buddha water feature somewhere near the entrance. The waitresses are all clad in tight-fitting traditional Vietnamese áo dài dress. Total cost per head: about $20. Fun factor: not zero, but not far off.]

Me: That's not really what I'm looking for. I want to eat where Vietnamese people eat, where they really eat. Not some tourist trap with pretty girls and carved carrots.

Vietnamese response: Really? Are you sure?

Me: One hundred percent sure. No carved carrots for me.

Vietnamese response: I see . . . in that case . . . you might quite like this little place called [insert restaurant called something like Quán Cơm or Quán Nguyễn. It's reasonably comfortable, not too rough around the edges, with fluorescent strip lighting. It's possibly even modern, clean too, and definitely full of well-to-do Vietnamese. The rows of expensive motorbikes outside are a giveaway.

31

It serves decent-enough Vietnamese food, probably focusing on a limited number of dishes. There will be a TV. It will be big. And it will be on. Total cost: no more than $10. Fun factor: tolerable, in short bursts.]

Me: That sounds a little bit more like it, but where do *you* eat? Where do you *really* eat? Where do you go to eat your favorite food?

Vietnamese response: [With an embarrassed smile, nervously glancing around to make sure no one is listening in, possibly whispering to you, not quite sure whether to tell you or not. Thinking that you're not really ready for this, but what the heck, here goes] There's a little noodle stall down the alley, behind the office. I've been going there ever since I was a student. Madame Linh only serves one dish, it's called bún chả. [By now your restaurant recommender's face is alight with pleasure, possibly going slightly red, and getting very excited to divulge their secret spot.] She has the freshest noodles, the best fish sauce, and the finest grilled pork balls in all of Hà Nội. But get there before midday, or she'll be completely sold out. [Total cost: around $1. Fun factor: *ballistic*.]

Me: That'll do very nicely. Thanks.

Vietnamese response: You're really going to eat there? Really?

Me: *Yup*.

Vietnamese response: [Thinking I'm lying] You must tell me if you like it. If you really like it. [With a big smile, looking slightly disheveled, panting and/or giggling, like they've just had a vaguely erotic experience, they send you on your way with a disbelieving look and some directions written on the back of a business card, a scrap of paper, or a napkin.]

The Four Questions Theory, and practice, may vary from person to person, but in essence, those be the guts of it.

And, indeed, guts was what I got on my first night out after employing this theory on Nghĩa in Hà Nội, but I wasn't about to let a uterus and a couple of intestines come between me and a crash course in Vietnamese grub.

To most Vietnamese, it's quite unfathomable that a non-Vietnamese person could ever like the same things, in the same places, in the same ways as a Vietnamese person. I'm foreign. I have money (so they kept telling me). I'm white. Why would I *ever* want to sit on the street and eat, when I could go to a posh hotel? What was *wrong* with me?

Instead of telling you what he really thinks, and with all the best (but desperately misguided) intentions, your average Joe Nguyễn will recommend places he's never even tried, but about which he's heard someone, somewhere, mutter that "foreigners like to go there."

I'm told that the three million or more Việt Kiều, Vietnamese in exile, feel compelled to "teach" their relatives and friends back in the motherland that foreigners must eat "like this": with a "proper table," napkins, respect for hygiene, Muzak, water features, and, yes, *carved carrots*.

However, I wasn't about to blame the Việt Kiều for my trials in prying open the street food secrets locked inside every passerby, colleague, and contact. I'd persevere, in my own way, chaotically, pigs' privates an' all.

CHAPTER TWO:
BÚN CHẢ

It's the smoke you notice first. Not the sight of it, but the *smell*. Meat is cooking somewhere. And it's nearby.

It could be coming from a gutter-level barbecue plopped onto a busy pavement. A Vietnamese woman wearing the flowing, pajamalike blouse called an áo bà ba is crouched, clutching a bamboo fan that she waves at the white hot coals in front of her. A pall of smoke envelops her customers, who are all bent bowlward, slurping tepid sauce, crunching herbs, and gnawing charred meat.

Or maybe it's hidden away down a back alley, off the main boulevard, behind a tree, next to a motorbike, a different woman, with different pajamas, wafting that smoke. Sometimes it's sweeter, sometimes it's more charcoaly, but essentially it's always the same smell.

It was a few days after my uncomfortable evening of the womb that I found myself cycling down Phùng Hưng Street, at the northwestern edge of the Old Quarter, on a clapped-out Chinese piece of shit masquerading as a bicycle, that I began to discover the delights of Vietnamese street food.

I cycled through a curtain of pork in fume form. It danced its way across the street, wiggling its hips, flashing its tits, tempting me to come sit down for a while, to imbibe, nibble, or gorge. It was around midday on a typically hot and humid Hà Nội Saturday in early September.

Although I'd caught the smell as I cycled past, I couldn't quite see where it was coming from, but I knew I wanted whatever it was.

My senses had yet to tune in to Vietnamese street food. I didn't know what to look for. What signs. What smells. What words. I was new in the country, and I was still learning to read my surroundings — a process that would take me years.

As the brakes on my Chinese piece of shit were nonexistent, I dragged my sneaker-clad feet on the speeding tarmac to halt at the Lê Văn Linh Street intersection, just outside the Việt Pháp bia hơi, a beer den where men sat drinking, with their pet birds, chuntering in cages, hanging from the railway bridge above them.

Phùng Hưng Street ran parallel with the single-track railway line that led to the mountains of Sa Pa and on to the border with China, just over 170 miles north. The arches under the railway line were bricked shut and numbered at the peak of each arch.

A passing train chugged along over the rattle-trap bridge behind me. A grating din engulfed the surrounding streets as the train blasted the entire Old Quarter with its deafening horn, drowning out, just for a second, the constant background honking, buzzing two-stroke motorbike engines, roosters crowing and clucking, tiny yappy dogs, the shouts of sellers, buyers, and cooks, and the perpetual *dink-dink-dink* of a man on the corner bashing a small piece of metal against a larger piece of metal for no apparent or useful reason.

I crossed the street. My pinball machine eyes ricocheted around, taking in the riotous scene. A woman was hacking at a plucked and washed chicken down at my heels. Every other house was open to the street, crammed with food and people happily devouring it. Sugarcane sellers nearly crashed into my bicycle at my left, while a knife sharpener got to work a dangerous step away to my right.

A buffet-style restaurant was emblazoned with a sign that, in the ensuing years, I would become all too familiar with: "Cơm bình dân," or "food for the workers." The restaurant anchored my attention for a second with its rows of bowls filled with grilled and fried bony fish, stews with whole boiled eggs, plates of greens, and rice cookers steaming on the floor next to gurgling soups.

A couple of houses up the thoroughfare, I spotted a trickle of charcoal smoke emanating from a vast, churning vat of soup at the entrance to a phở joint. I knew, however, that neither of these eateries was the source of that sweet, charred smell.

A good thirty yards or more up the road, beyond saucepans, orange sellers, static motorbikes, tea drinkers, coffee drinkers, beer drinkers, and cauldrons and vats and pots and pans filled with steaming, bubbling stuff, a wisp of smoke soon became a flood. It streamed from behind a hoa sữa tree with a white ring of paint around its trunk, positioned just as the road began to bend toward the junction with Hàng Cót and Hàng Lược Streets.

I pushed my bike out of the gutter and into the traffic, through discarded and shredded sweetcorn husks, coconut shells, toothpicks, and cigarette butts, as a xe ôm (motorbike taxi driver) hassled me for business.

It was unclear why he thought that I wanted a ride on a motorbike when I already had my own bike in tow. Or how he expected to successfully convey my bulk, and my Chinese piece of shit, on the back of his piddly 50cc.

I tuned out his hassle and locked in on lunch,

which hid behind a tree just yards away.

Coming closer, I was nearly drowned in the thick, delicious-smelling pork pea-souper. Peering round the wide trunk, I saw the white-hot metal tray cum barbecue lying on a scrap of dirt at the base of the tree.

Two trap grills fizzed and popped in the low, fat-fed flame. One was laden with thin cuts of fatty pork belly and the other with what looked like meatballs. Both were being blackened by furious blasts of fiery air driven by the considerable force of a ponytailed woman in her late forties. She was wearing brown and black zigzag-striped pajamas and tattered yellow plastic flip-flops. Incredibly, she perspired not a drop.

A yard or so away from the grill, another woman sat at a shin-high wooden table. Like Captain Kirk commanding the helm of the starship *Enterprise,* she was surrounded, at arm's length, by her crew of ingredients and utensils.

To her right, in place of Spock, sat a large blue plastic bucket filled with fish sauce, another with sliced carrot and chayote, and a tray heaped with pork balls and belly, fresh off the grill.

To her left, also on the pavement, next to her flip-flopped feet, sat a bamboo basket filled with white noodles kept fresh in a phrynium leaf. Another basket was filled to overflowing with four or five varieties of leaves and herbs.

This woman was in command. She dished out

lunch at a rapid pace to the ten or so customers already lined up in front of her stall and seated at the two small plastic tables situated at odd angles on the uneven pavement.

I chained together the rear wheel and red frame of my Chinese piece of shit, rested it on the kickstand, and left it in the gutter where, by rights, it truly belonged, next to a conical-hatted orange seller trying to tempt me into a purchase by forcing a halved, green-skinned orange into my face. Seconds later, she was replaced by a lottery ticket vendor waving a book of tickets so close she fluttered my eyelashes for me.

Slightly nervous, I pulled up a stool whose seat practically scraped the gritty pavement surface. I parked my butt cheeks and tested the give in the plastic. Sensing the stool could take the strain, I relaxed a little and sat down, a foot or so back from the table, my knees hunched high.

A ripple of chatter broke out among the customers. I deduced that it was about me. The two street barbie owners cracked smiles in my direction. I had no idea what anyone was saying, but I was determined to eat whatever it was they were cooking.

I fiddled with a pair of chopsticks and tried to blend in, which was somewhat tricky, being fair-haired and six feet tall with my knees inches away from my chin. With the upended chopsticks, I played dot-to-dot with the cigarette divots on the surface of the table. These welts, I'd later come to learn, marked a hundred heated conversations over beer, where a burning fag end was forgotten, a toilet break was taken, a sleeping drunk slept, or where a police raid had swooped in. History had played out in those burns, dot by melted dot.

Under my T-shirt, the sweat dripped down my chest in the oppressive humidity and met the belt of my jeans, though the tree offered some shade from the harsh sunlight. I sipped from the plastic beaker of iced tea, cooled by one large chunk of ice, which had arrived unrequested at my table. And I waited.

The stallholders brushed off the key ring sellers, cigarette purveyors, and newspaper vendors. They all wore baseball caps and two-sizes-too-big shirts, which hung from their universally slim frames. Having spotted the foreigner, they were gearing up for a lengthy sales pitch.

I blotted out thoughts of dysentery, giardia, diarrhea, of feverish nights loaded on Imodium, and all the other unpleasantness that too many guidebooks had warned against. Instead, I relied upon a simple logic: this many local customers can't be eating here and getting sick. How could a street stall function as a viable business, I rationalized, while at the same time holding a citywide reputation for involuntary bowel loosening?

On another level, it was all so obvious. It just looked like huge amounts of fun. There was no way I could ever experience anything remotely like this back in Europe. In an ever increasingly homogenized, globalized, sanitized world where every developed nation's high street looks much the same whether it be in New York, Paris, London, or Rome, here was something truly foreign. Glorious in its otherness. Something that immediately struck me as unique and valuable. There was treasure on them there streets, of that I was certain.

The anal retentives at Health and Safety would suffer heart failure as they attempted to count the voluminous violations flashing before my eyes. And I'll admit to second thoughts as I looked over my shoulder at the stall next door. A girl, no more than eighteen years old, hacked at a plucked chicken with nothing but a plastic bag between the dead bird and the pavement. Was this standard kitchen prep-practice on Phùng Hưng Street? And if so, how had my pork been slaughtered? I turned back to the smoky stall.

The manner of the banter and the familiarity of the customers with the cooks told me that these diners were regulars. Maybe the paranoid guidebook authors were more worried about ticking public warning boxes than relaying the simple reality from the streets? Maybe.

The pig char mist telegraphed hunger pangs

to all it reached through the hot, gummy ether. Whenever the woman in zigzag pajamas stopped wafting the fire to disgorge the meat, or to rinse used bowls and chopsticks in a dirty bucket bereft of dishwashing liquid, the stall and customers would disappear in a splendid cloud of pig.

I noticed that she would only send smoke in the direction of the street. As I waited, I realized that cumulus porkus was their sole form of advertising, apart from the ragged, faintly felt-tipped cardboard sign hanging from a tree at head height just behind the barbie. Pathetic though it was, the sign did serve one purpose: it told this hapless foreigner that this was a one-dish stall, serving something called bún chả.

My lunch arrived. I didn't have a clue how to proceed. In front of me was a small porcelain bowl filled with blistered pork balls and crispy belly, submerged in warm fish sauce, sliced carrot and chayote, topped with a speckle of black pepper and miniature black char flakes. To my right were two plastic plates; one with the fresh white noodles, the other with a mound of lettuce and various leaves I didn't know the names of.

I sat pondering my next move. Should I play the clueless foreigner and look helplessly into the eyes of Captain Bún Chả, seated across the starship command center from me? Or take a sly glance at the moto-taxi-driving customer next to me and figure out how to proceed?

In the end, I didn't need any sly looks. It was the xe ôm (moto-taxi driver) who showed me what to do, by doing it himself and pointing at things.

The only thing I'd learned in Vietnamese up until that point was "làm ơn" — "please" in English — and I thought it'd be useful for me, but in almost ten years of living in Việt Nam, I never ever heard anyone, apart from me, use it. In the end, I didn't need any linguistic skills. I copied.

I added a chopstick grab of chili, did the same with the garlic, snatched a ball of noodles and a few cut up leaves into the bowl that held the main meaty event. I swirled it around a bit, leaned forward, stuck the chopsticks in, grabbed a bit of everything, and delivered the package into my face.

The whole sweet, salty fish sauce, pork ball, noodly, leafy, charred parcel exploded in one sensational gob-burst. It was fresh. The flavor was alive. This food tasted healthy. It was astoundingly good. *Finally.* This was Vietnamese food.

I looked up, no doubt smiling, radiant — my mouth gently burning as the chopped chili made its presence felt.

Only then did I notice all eyes upon me. My fellow diners with their chopsticks suspended midair, the barbie wafter looking on expectantly, Captain Bún Chả with her arms folded, sternly awaiting the reaction of the big-nosed lard butt who had improbably landed at her stall, from a land far, far away, on a Chinese piece of shit.

I beamed, no doubt spat out some approving words in English, dribbled fish sauce down myself, and/or regurgitated crumbs of garlic as I spoke. I don't quite remember, as I'd been hopelessly lassoed by the atom bomb in the bowl in front of me. And this particular explosive device demanded a thorough dismantling.

The bún chả not only tasted fantastic, it had the power to make the surroundings almost attractive. The filthy floor, the horns, the *yak-yak* of sellers, the fumes, trains, hustlers, chicken choppers, soup-vat maneuverers — and even the *dink-dink-dink* of the metal workers sounded almost musical alongside this ballistic bowl of bún chả, located on the upper reaches of Phùng Hưng Street.

Captain Bún Chả held up a few notes, demonstrating how much she expected me to pay. 8,000 đồng. A little more than a dollar. As I was getting up to leave, she pointed at my unadorned ring finger, then at the grill chef, and then back at my finger, rubbed her belly and let out an unnerving guffaw. As this was the second time in a day that I'd had such an exchange, I knew exactly what was happening.

Earlier that day, I had sat under a low tarpaulin at the tea stall of an old woman with black-stained teeth on a narrow alleyway near Cầu Gỗ flower and fish market. Her teeth had been blackened after her first menstrual cycle to tell the world she was ready for marriage. The lacquer coating also helped prevent tooth decay. This octogenarian still had a full set.

I'd come for a shot of bitter green tea, but what I got was attention. Firstly, from a smiling, slightly out-of-it, fortysomething man squeezing a sticky brown lump of opium between forefinger and thumb. He attempted to offer me a hit, but failed to keep his eyes open long enough to make much of a convincing salesman. And, secondly, from a twenty-one-year-old student of English, who insisted on practicing with me.

There are five questions the single white male gets in these situations.

1. How old are you?
2. Where are you from?
3. Can you speak Vietnamese?
4. Are you married? [Answer no for the bonus question number 5.]
5. Do you want to marry a Vietnamese?

The last question is asked as if there's a wife shop with shelves of them for sale. In truth, somewhere in Hà Nội there probably *is* such a shop, but in any case, I didn't get a chance to answer.

He pointed at the girl at the next stall.

"Why not her? She can cook."

I laughed, but I could tell from his look he was verging on the serious.

"No thanks, I'm good. Single works for me."

Cooking skill, I concluded, was a top requirement in a partner in Hà Nội.

CHAPTER THREE:
IN SEARCH OF A MONSTER

I knew I'd enjoy living on this continent from the first day I stepped off the plane in a different country. A little north of Hà Nội.

I was standing in a phone booth at a busy intersection in downtown Iksan, South Korea, on a hot, clear, sunny day.

It was June 1996. Korean men in suits walked past, smoking and holding hands. Korean women trotted busily along the pavement in high heels, flitting between shops. Like manic bees overdoing the morning pollen collection, they gathered shiny logo-embossed paper bags with braided string handles as they went.

There was a breath of kimchi on the breeze. It fermented its way across town from the fetid alleyway market a block or two up the road. Shopfronts were plastered in garish signs whose language was utterly impenetrable to me. Loudspeakers sat out front and inflicted synthetic, screaming schoolgirl pop tunes on the ears of passersby as a ruse to entice them to come spend some won.

There were no English signs, no English voices, only Korean faces, thousands of heads of black hair. And me. Alone on a street corner, very, very far from home, looking out from behind the glass shutters of a telephone box.

I turned to face the phone and inserted a five-thousand-won prepaid phone card into the slot. I waited for the tone, keyed in the long-distance number, and swiveled back to face the street.

An old woman, an *ajima,* wheeled a creaking watermelon cart in front of me, yelling out her price. A plumpish Korean man in dark checked trousers belted high above his waist, black shirt tucked in tight, stood on the other side of the street, pulling on the charcoal filter of his 88 cigarette. A taxi with one customer already ensconced in the front passenger seat pulled up on the eight-lane main boulevard, and a group of shoppers hopped in the back. At the other end of the line, the telephone rang.

There was nothing familiar for me to grasp onto. Everything I could see, smell, taste, touch, and hear was completely foreign. It was as if someone had pulled back the blanket on my previous life, swished aside the curtains, pranged the window wide open, and filled the air with great gusts of caffeine. I was beyond smitten.

It was not a scene I was supposed to relish. I'd always been a homebody. Not keen to travel. Quite content to stay in the small-town England of my childhood. Simply not that interested in anything *foreign*.

Even the strenuous efforts of my fifth-grade teacher, a severe, busty, bucktoothed, stick-wielding sixty-year-old dominatrix called Mrs. Higginbotham, could not convince me otherwise. I recall how she wagged her baton at the gargantuan pull-down map of the world that spanned the entire length and breadth of the blackboard at Paddox Middle School, in Rugby, in the center of England.

"This is our world," she declared, with a look that could pulverize a fly or a small child at fifty paces. The UK sections of the map were pink; the other nations, other colors.

"But it wasn't always like this." She held our gaze with her unblinking glare, and with a brisk snap of her stick, the map magically rolled up and disappeared into a holder above the blackboard to reveal another map underneath.

This one was identical in every way, bar one: most of the nations were pink.

"This," she intoned, thwacking her rod across the Atlantic, madly jabbing at the Barbie's-bedroom-colored world and spanking much of West Africa, "This used to all be ours. This is the British Empire. This is when Britain truly ruled the waves."

With a final lash of victory across Canada, she jackbooted around the classroom, lapping up the *oooh*s, the *arghhh*s, and the *wowwws* of the rural British youth ensnared in her den.

I sat there. I didn't *wow,* I more harrumphed. *But we're such a small country,* I said to myself. *Why would all these other countries want us to come and take them over? Does the world like Britain that much?* I knew better than to ask this question of that teacher.

With a final desk-trembling thud of her stick, Mrs. Higginbotham zapped the British Empire from view. It rolled up above the blackboard. She returned to explaining decimal division, greater than, less than, and other such important life lessons.

Once a month, this buttoned-up harpy, born perhaps in the wrong century, would perform the exact same ritual with her hidden maps to remind us preadolescents that once upon a time, our country was all-powerful. That Great Britain truly was *great.*

Even with, or maybe *because of,* the Higginbotham brand of indoctrination, I failed to form an interest in anything foreign beyond lions, tigers, and elephants. And we had zoos full of them.

But at some point in my early twenties, everything changed. By accident, as so often seems to be the case with life-changing decisions, I came across something that ignited my curiosity. It was a photograph of Hà Nội in a book.

The photographer had taken the picture while standing on Tràng Tiền Street, looking at the Hà Nội Opera House.

It was a simple street scene. There were no cars in the photograph, no advertising on the shop-fronts. Bicycles plied the street. A motorbike or two carried large cardboard boxes. People strolled, oblivious, through the traffic. A cyclo transported someone or something. A woman with a navy blue chemise and conical hat ped-aled away from the camera, toward the opera house. The street looked busy, but calm. Most of all, Hà Nội looked alien.

I said to myself, quite flippantly, "One day I'll live there." It was 1992.

This picture, from this city, sparked a curios-ity that remained burned in my memory. It was all so . . . *exotic*. Yes, it's an awful, lazy word, used by travelers of all shades, at the same time meaningless and patronizing, sometimes inter-preted as racist. But, at that time, at that age, ex-otic only meant it was very, very different, it was exciting, and I didn't understand it. And, most important, the photo was of another place. Not of where I was.

As the nineties rolled on, friends left for In-dia, Tibet, China, and beyond. I was jealous of their escapades, but I had no money to go with them and I had no interest in following the hippie, dope, and dreadlocks trail they had chosen. I didn't want to travel through somewhere alien. I wanted to live it.

Now, looking back, it's perhaps difficult to understand exactly what this meant in the early nineties. Back then, a news report in Việt Nam would take at least one day to reach the pages of a newspaper. A trip from London to Hà Nội was a very big thing. Phone calls home were prohibitively expensive. I had to reserve a long-distance call slot at the International Post Office next to Hoàn Kiếm Lake. A British newspaper took one month to arrive at my desk in Hà Nội, and was often held up by the "culture censor." A letter could take three months to arrive. I'd never used a mobile phone and I didn't know anyone who owned one. Information came from books, not pixels. Even later in the nineties, when I returned to Britain for a holiday in the summer of 1997, for example, my friends didn't believe me when I said I'd never heard of the Spice Girls. Moving to somewhere like Việt Nam at that time really did feel like traveling to another planet.

And now, in this day, with Twitter, Instagram, Skype, Facebook, 24/7 news, reams and reams of information freely available and everybody connected online, all the time, it is almost impossible for anyone anywhere on the planet today to feel the isolation and deep sense of otherness I felt as I embarked upon my journey to

53

Việt Nam.

And that's why I wanted to travel. To push myself. To escape. For adventure. Because back then, it really did feel like jumping off a gigantic cliff.

I'm not sure why Việt Nam lodged itself within my brain. Maybe incomprehensible, overheard TV reports from the war in Việt Nam had embedded themselves in my infant brain as I dribbled soup with a TV on in the background in 1969, the year I was born. However, after seeing that photo of Hà Nội in 1992, I began to read about Việt Nam, watch travel documentaries, and listen to BBC World Service reports from the region. I picked up a Lonely Planet guide. I read the food section. I bought a cookbook, and I even occasionally cooked from it. The five-spice stewed beef — something I later learned was called bò kho — was a particular hit. The aniseed-laden dish was like nothing I'd ever eaten before. In a good way. There were no Vietnamese restaurants anywhere between my town and London — a distance of a hundred miles.

Like a ship's rope fraying against its mooring, Việt Nam scratched steadily at the back of my mind. It was a grumble that promised escape and adventure, a radically different life, away from the one I was living in Rugby, in the British Midlands, in the middle of the recession-hit early nineties.

Of course, I never for one minute thought I would end up living in Hà Nội, but in retrospect a seed had been sown, one that began to blossom a little farther north, in a phone box, on a street corner in Iksan, in the western province of South Korea, in northeast Asia, in 1996.

The phone clicked.

"Hi, Mum, it's me," I blurted down the line.

"Oh, hi," she replied. "How are things going? Where are you?"

"I'm standing on a street corner in the center of a town called Iksan. This is going to be my home for the next year. I can't read anything. No one speaks English, I can't speak much Korean yet, but the food is amazing. I'm having a great time."

The buzz of living in very foreign places is one that rapidly turns dabblers into addicts. And that was me.

But, back to 1992, to Craven Road, Rugby, England, before I'd seen the photograph of Hà Nội. I was bored, hanging out with my friend Paul in our rented house. It was summertime. I was twenty-three years old.

Paul worked as a binman. He had long ginger hair and a penchant for West Coast sixties psychedelia, and, like regular binmen the world over, he was studying for a master's degree in Continental philosophy. I was a glorified clerk, shuffling paper and inputting numbers for a gargantuan multinational company called GEC Alsthom.

We rented a house together at the crappier end of a crap town, on the corner of Murray Road and Craven Road in Rugby, near the railway station.

"He what?" I mumbled at Paul, lolling in the armchair opposite. "He gave up his home, his girlfriend, and his job to go and hunt for the Loch Ness Monster?"

"That's what it says in the *Radio Times*," he replied without looking up from the weekly magazine. "Must be true."

"Hmm?"

At twenty-eight years old, Steve Feltham had left a life he didn't like — installing burglar alarms on the south coast of England — bought an old mobile library, and drove 640 miles north to a life he was convinced he would prefer: monster hunting. And for one year, he recorded his journey for the BBC. We settled down to watch the program. Nodded at the wisdom. Wowed at the daring. Oohed and aahed at the anti-ambition.

He headed to the banks of Loch Ness to look for whatever it was that may or may not be living in Britain's largest body of freshwater. It wasn't so much the onset of an early midlife crisis as the solution to a lifelong one.

Like millions of office workers who punch the

56

clock from nine to five the world over, Feltham felt snared by the expectations of twentieth-century society. And he'd managed to find a way out. Go off-grid. Leave the matrix.

My own synapses snapped. A light went on. I was reminded of a story about a Chinese master guzheng player who sat strumming just one note, on just one of the instrument's twenty-one strings, day after day, year after year.

"But, Master, you are the most renowned guzheng player in all of China. Why do you only play one note?" asked his student.

"Because I've found my note. You haven't found yours yet," replied the master.

As the weekend faded from existence, Sunday evening and the prospect of another day at the office arriving like an iron yoke, the last words of Feltham's documentary brimmed with a looming portent.

"This isn't just about hunting for a monster, but about having a dream and following it. It doesn't matter if people say you're mad. If you don't go for it, one day you may say, 'Well, I wish I'd done that when I had the chance.' If you don't follow your dreams, the only person who loses is you."

I needed to get myself a monster.

Three years later, in 1995, I found myself in a pub called the Victoria Inn on Lower Hillmorton

Road in Rugby. My father and I entered from the main road, ordered two pints of mild, and sat in the corner on leather seats shiny from decades of bum rubbing.

"I've decided to take the redundancy offer." It hadn't been a difficult decision, but I knew my father wouldn't necessarily approve.

"Are you sure? GEC Alsthom is a big company. You could move up with them," he said. His own thirty-five-year experience slaving at a printing firm was plain in every syllable. "What are you going to do now?"

It was a fair question. Just what was I going to do?

With the return of friends from their own travel adventures and postcards from others still on theirs, the Việt Nam itch had gotten a little more insistent. In fact, by now it had grown into a full-fledged nagging feeling. It appeared I'd found my monster. It was out east and hungry. Still, I wasn't sure how I could make it all happen.

"I don't know," I said. "But, whatever it is, I'll make sure it's better than what I've been doing for the last five years."

He wasn't wholly convinced by this non-plan, and neither was I, but there was no way I was about to spend the rest of my life doing something I already found toxic for my mental health by the time I'd reached a mere twenty-five years old. Statistically speaking, I'd already burned through 31.25 percent of my lifespan. If I couldn't deviate off-piste at this time in my life, then I'd never be able to. In forty years' time, I'd be one of the pipe-and-slippers brigade bemoaning their lost youth and missed opportunities. No thanks.

I could leave. Unlike my friends, I wasn't married; I had no kids, no girlfriend, no mortgage, no debts, no pets, no illnesses, no insurance policies, no commitments, and no excuses. *I could leave.*

As I looked around the office on my last day, I saw the gray faces of those waiting on their pension with a gargantuan ten years left to grind it out, each brow counting every minute of the day in seconds and furrows. And worse were those far younger, who were already graying into the same mold, yet were barely ten years older than me. I refused to believe this was it. That this was what life had in store for me, for anyone.

"You need to speak to Pete," said Richard, the head of the Job Club office situated above a Cornish pasty shop next to a group of empty offices in the Rugby town center.

The unemployment office had forced me to *get my shit together*. I had to join Job Club, a government initiative to monitor how serious the dole queue was about getting back into the workplace. It was October 1995, six months after I'd quit my job. The only official work I'd done in the interim was washing dishes on the European leg of the Formula One tour that season, scrubbing the leftovers from countless meals eaten by drivers, engineers, and journalists for four days straight from 6 A.M. to 2 A.M. I was the lowliest cog in Formula One. It was the hardest job I have ever done. I needed to find an alternative. I needed an out.

Job Club consisted of two rooms: one room where people looked for jobs, talked about looking for jobs, wrote job application letters, printed job-related stuff, and made phone calls about jobs; and the other to practice job interviews and discuss depression and other unemployment-related ailments.

The benefits included free stamps and envelopes, use of the phone, access to computers and a printer, and travel expenses to interviews. But the whole thing was compulsory, and I didn't expect to meet anyone at Job Club remotely like me. They all seemed to force on a superhero cloak of positivity before they arrived in the morning to mask their utter despair at their personal situations. None of them had any interest in anything outside of that small town. And I had no interest in them.

It was my first day, and I'd just told Richard that I was looking into becoming a teacher and moving to Asia.

"I think it's Brazil Pete's going to," said the mustachioed Richard, looking up at me from his swivel chair as he stirred his tea. His mug was imprinted with the phrase "I love Rugby."

"Pete did a teaching course in Coventry a few months back. He'll be in later on this morning."

I took a seat and made at mulling the half-page Careers section in the *Rugby Advertiser,* the local weekly rag. A part-time waiter needed here, a forklift driver there, a double-glazing sales rep someplace else. I sighed. And waited for Pete. Did he really hold the key to my way out? Looking at the jobless detritus that surrounded me, it seemed highly unlikely.

Outside on the street, I could hear the lament of the preposterous red-coated town crier dishing out the day's news — *what kind of a job was that for a grown man?* — and the *dong* of the clock tower and the chatter of people going about their day across the paving slabs of the faceless English town.

At that moment, a tall, slim West Indian guy walked in and headed to Richard's office. I could see them behind the glass as I flicked to the barren What's On section of the paper. Richard pointed at me and the other guy chinned in my direction before coming out of the office and collaring me.

"You Graham, yeah?" he asked in a deep, insistent voice. "I'm Pete. I just done the teaching course. Richard said you're interested in becoming a teacher, right?"

I think my reaction implied fear, but came out as a vaguely positive "Right."

"Come on," said Pete. "Let's go next door for a chat."

Pete had a shaved head and wore a short leather jacket, faded jeans, and a plain red T-shirt. I pulled up a chair in the sterile practice interview room. In front of me on the wall were posters of models in suits, smiling, pointing at impressive charts, sitting in front of computers, and exuding a terrifyingly grim vision of career success. Pete closed the door and turned to sit on the only table in the room, blocking out my view of the depressing posters. He boomed down at me.

"Look around you," he implored, waving toward the room we'd just vacated. "You don't wanna be a part of that. Training to be a teacher is the best thing you could do. You wanna spend another winter in this shithole?"

I hadn't said a word to Pete and he'd already decided upon my destiny.

His confidence was unsettling, but it intrigued me. He didn't know the first thing about me, my work experience, or my qualifications. He only knew that Richard had said I was thinking about *kinda* becoming, *you know,* a teacher, *somewhere,* not here, *somewhere* else, *maybe* in Asia.

Yes, I was that decisive.

"Listen to me, Graham," he insisted. "I can't even speak English proper and I done it." Pete, I realized as our conversation progressed, had *done* a lot. It wasn't so much what he said, but how confidently he said it.

"Look, I'm going to Brazil at the end of the month." He grinned. "Other folks I trained with are going to Russia, Japan, Spain, all over."

"Is anyone going to Việt Nam?" I asked hopefully. He looked at me and was quiet for the first and only time. "Nah. No one done that. Not Việt Nam."

Pete wrote down the name and number of his "main man" at the college in Coventry and frog-marched me to the phone. Within one hour of meeting Pete, and pending a bunch of paperwork, I had a confirmed place in a teacher training course at Coventry Technical College for February 1996. Just a few months away. As I put the phone down, Pete gave me a smile.

"You gone and done it, man. I told you, Graham. Easy. You're gonna love it."

I looked out at the town I'd known for twenty-five years through the windowpane speckled with drizzle. I'd just taken one giant step toward extricating myself from this primordial gluepot.

Seven months later, a thin airmail letter lay under a pile of junk mail at the foot of the front door.

The letter, bearing red socialist postage stamps, had originated in Việt Nam. According to the smudged date stamp on the envelope, it had taken a whole four months to travel from Hải Phòng, in the northeast of the country, to my front door, in the center of England.

It was a response to an inquiry I had made about working in Việt Nam. Not only that, it was a job offer, for an English teaching position at Hải Phòng University. The offer included a room, a bicycle, and $100 per month. The gig was mine. All I had to do was get myself to Việt Nam.

This was *very* tempting, but I had already accepted a job in South Korea, paying significantly more than $100 per month, albeit without the promise of a bike. I decided to write a reply, expressing my thanks to the university for the kind offer and telling them that while I would unfortunately be unable to take the position, I would be in touch again the following year.

By the time it would take my reply to arrive, I figured, I might have already moved to the country. But, in the pre-Internet age, this was the first confirmation I had that there were jobs for people like me, a newly qualified, totally inexperienced English teacher, in Việt Nam in 1996.

I decided I'd do a year in South Korea, save some money, and move to Việt Nam the following summer.

And that's *exactly* what I did.

CHAPTER FOUR:
BEYOND TRÀNG TIỀN STREET

In September 1997, I strolled out of my Hàng Gà Street hotel and shoe-leathered it across town.

An hour earlier, I'd stepped off a Singapore Airlines flight from London Heathrow, waded through the clammy air of Hà Nội's Nội Bài International Airport, bent myself into a groaning taxi, and skirted rice paddies on my way toward the creeping metropolis of almost 1.5 million people. "That's Why (You Go Away)," by Michael Learns to Rock, a group of Europop ballad nobodies who were massively, and inexplicably, popular in Southeast Asia, crackled from the taxi's cassette player.

I walked around parked motorbikes and people crouched peeling vegetables, changing bike oil, smoking, wagging jaws, and tipping half-eaten bowls of noodles into buckets in the gutter. I zigzagged tentatively through the Old Quarter and on into the shoe-selling district, under the myrtle trees alongside Hoàn Kiếm Lake. I made my way past the International Post Office, fought off the street-dealing moneychangers, and continued en route to the lake's southeastern edge, and the corner of Tràng Tiền Street.

"I am home," Steve Feltham had declared as he finally arrived on the banks of Loch Ness in his BBC *Video Diary*. While I wasn't about to announce that — I was 8,447 miles from home as the crow wriggles — I felt there was cause for some kind of inner celebration. I had *finally* made it.

I stood under a tree, next to a wooden traffic police pillar box, outside a pharmacy with windows full of sliced Korean red ginseng and boxes of silkworm drinks, at the intersection of Hàng Bài, Hàng Khay, Đinh Tiên Hoàng, and Tràng Tiền Streets. I was at the same spot where the photo I'd come across years earlier had been taken. The long-lost image was still clear in my mind as I looked down toward the opera house.

There were bicycles, conical hats, cyclos, and motorbikes, just as there were in the frame embedded inside my head.

At the traffic lights there stood a traffic cop in a uniform with a distinctive badge with the letters "CSGT" — Traffic Police — on his shoulder. He had a short truncheon in his left hand. I frowned to myself, wondering what kind of country was this that required a man with a stick to make sure drivers stopped at a red light and remained stopped until it turned green?

I walked around the officer's big white Honda motorbike and traipsed into the scene I'd only ever known as a photograph.

Halfway down, opposite number 12 Tràng Tiền, was a narrow alleyway. It was covered from the elements by a mess of rusted metal supports, chipboard, corrugated iron, and plastic sheeting, from which hung maps, calendars, and red good luck signs with gold lettering in Chinese and Vietnamese.

A bookshelf leaning against one grotty, peeling wall contained photocopied sheaves of all the tourist hits: *The Quiet American,* Lonely Planet's guide to Việt Nam, and Michael Herr's *Dispatches*. I bought a thin, foldable, color-coded map of Hà Nội for less than a buck, and carried on.

Farther down the alley was a tea stall with filthy walls, eaten by humidity and blackened with soot from a nearby charcoal fire under a large kettle.

A steamed-sweet-corn seller pushed a cart in the direction of the lake. A state-run newsagent and stationery store sold two- or three-day-old copies of the *International Herald Tribune* with sections related to Việt Nam blacked out with marker. Day-old copies of the *South China Morning Post* and the weekly *Far Eastern*

Economic Review were nested in among Việt Nam's torpid government-speak sheets; the headlines, which rarely changed during my entire stay, read: "Việt Nam boosts ties with Laos." "Việt Nam strengthens ties with Myanmar." "Việt Nam renews ties with Burkina Faso." "Việt Nam cements ties with This-is-not-news-istan." And on it went.

Halfway down the left-hand side of Nguyễn Xí Street was a house. Two cages, each containing a single red-whiskered bulbul, hung above the shuttered windows. They tweeted occasionally. The doors to the house were wide open. Inside, a moneychanger dished out đồng for dollars and dollars for đồng.

Whenever a customer in need of hard currency arrived, the money changer would head up a set of ladders into the attic to retrieve the stash: big bricks of the preposterously named đồng, tied together with thin bamboo string. I imagined an attic insulated with the world's major currencies and Việt Nam's own, less-important notes. Outside a man arrived with a pair of green scales and set about weighing plucked ducks hanging off the front of a Honda Cub.

Closer to the opera house, and across the main Lý Thái Tổ Road, stood the Metropole Hotel, where Graham Greene had stayed, and where every wannabe-Greene since then has sipped a cocktail or two.

On the opposite side of Tràng Tiền was a small side road. It led to Ngõ Tràng Tiền — literally "Alleyway Tràng Tiền." I decided to explore this detour rather than continue to the opera house. An explosion of food sights and scents greeted me as I turned into the ngõ.

The blast of beef bones, fish sauce, fried tofu, and shrimp paste fumes sent my nasal dials juddering into the red zone.

Mopeds parped and puttered around me. A faltering car alarm whirled like an air raid siren in the distance, mingling with the chuntering of street diners and the agonizing wail of a Viet-pop-star-wannabe strangling a karaoke machine somewhere nearby.

On the cracked, crumpled, and dusty pavement corner next to me sat five men on those all-too-common blue plastic stools, in front of an impromptu tea stall with a low table, a Carlsberg bucket filled with ice, a line of plastic beakers, a large flask of jasmine tea, and a neat row of individual Everest cigarettes for sale, one stick at a time.

A man wearing shorts, like me, and flip-flops tugged on a bamboo water pipe. The pipe produced a whistling sound as he filled his lungs, and he made a face as the rough tobacco struck the roof of his skull. Satiated, the smoker let out the noxious fumes in sizable smoky gusts.

Two women served bún đậu from four tin-can

charcoal burners hunkered on the pavement. At that time, of course, I didn't know what this dish was, or any of the others I could see stretched out toward a street food horizon in front of me, as I took my first stroll down this food-filled street. The tofu fizzed in the pan. Plastic bags filled with herbs hung from nails slammed into the cracking, piss-stained concrete wall. It was an alley path strewn with the unfamiliar. Back then, I knew nothing. I'd never heard of any of the dishes on offer. The variety overwhelmed me. The unfamiliarity spooked me.

At first, it's a battle. What I saw chafed uncomfortably against a lifetime of cellophane-wrapped supermarket meats, perfectly shaped, shiny vegetables, and restaurant hygiene certificates. Sure, South Korea had shaken away the frayed edges of Western expectations. I'd grown accustomed to seeing food at pavement level. But as I'd just set foot in Việt Nam for the first time, Hà Nội looked, to me, like a baffling board game without a rule sheet: hardcore, aggressive, difficult, yet intriguing. I still believed, as I did in South Korea, that the doorway to understanding any foreign country was through its food, but what had I gotten myself into? How could I ever adapt to a place like this? How could I ever sit at the blue plastic table?

Blobs of potent purple shrimp paste — mắm

tôm — sat in tiny bowls, awaiting each order of bún đậu. Việt Nam's mắm tôm has muscle enough to beat any other cuisine's pungency, plus it has the ability to transport food to another dimension. In time, I'd learn that adding it to any dish is the equivalent of slotting a supercharged V-8 engine into a Honda Civic.

The smells and sounds intrigued me, but it would take me more than twenty-four hours in-country to overcome these overriding and rather pesky perception problems.

Motorbikes lined one side of the alley like leaning soldiers about to domino-fall the length of the street. Four feet above my head, cables and wires resembling jungle vines choked the entire length of Ngõ Tràng Tiền.

Fuse boxes hung exposed from electricity pylons, their countless connections just out of arm's reach. Every spare bit of concrete wall was stenciled in red and black spray paint with telephone numbers advertising concrete-cutting services.

Another stall, another dish, this time inside a shop. More noodles with the fish-filled bún cá, and the southern beef classic, popular in the north, bún bò nam bộ. A little farther along, at number 15, more noodles, bún chả, bún riêu cua, and the glass noodle stir-fry miến trộn. At number 8, a phở gà shop, selling the chicken version of the famous Hà Nội soup.

And people. People. *Everywhere people*. Eating. Cooking. Chopping. Frying. Boiling. Steaming. Serving. Shouting.

Time would teach me that whether it be served in a bowl, on a plate, inside a sheet of rice paper, wrapped up in a mustard leaf, on a spitting hot metal plate, in a jar, a cup, a banana leaf, a plastic bag, a newspaper, an old electricity bill, or a sheath from the Hà Nội Yellow Pages, Vietnamese food could be exceptional in all forms. The price of entry was low. I just needed to get over my inhibitions.

I'd just arrived. I hadn't discovered bún chả yet. I didn't know where to start. I needed time. I needed a sandwich. I headed back to the lake. I had an appointment.

Nhà Hàng Thủy Tạl restaurant café was at the northwest edge of Hoàn Kiếm Lake. The state-run establishment was popular with young, well-to-do Vietnamese couples looking for a romantic view over the green murk, and among expats who needed shelter from the streets, a cooling lake breeze, and a comfy chair.

I'd arranged to meet Alessandra in the café that afternoon. Outside of work, she was my only contact in the country. She was Italian, same age as me, and was a former volunteer worker who'd slugged it out in a rural school, teaching English, for a year before moving to the capital to take up a paying job as a secretary for an Italian-run firm. She was the friend of a friend. We'd met a few times in London, many years previously.

She could speak Vietnamese and was well connected. I was confident she could help quickly propel me into the Vietnamese scene, where I'd make friends, explore stuff, and build a social life.

I arrived at the café early. A waitress in a brown skirt, sensible black shoes, and white blouse spotted me sitting at a table under a parasol in a corner of the deck. She plodded over, handed me a menu, and stood and waited, staring blankly out across the lake as I scanned the contents for something familiar.

"A croque monsieur, please. And a mango juice," I said.

Without saying anything or making any facial movement to acknowledge my order, she took the menu back, and with a swing of her ponytail, clippety-clopped back across the wooden deck.

Nearby, a few briefcase-toting, balding white men sipped iced coffees and tugged on cigarettes. They were deep in German-accented English conversation with a couple of slick-looking Vietnamese men, whom I guessed were business folk.

Two sunny backpacker girls with floppy hats, shades, sandals, and the eternal glow of the persistent holiday maker "doing Asia" for a year sat smiling and chatting as they sipped fruit juices.

My first taste of Việt Nam, a croque monsieur, arrived with a thin paper napkin and two slices of tomato. I consumed it without any particular joy. I'd soon hit the streets for eats, but I needed time and local knowledge. I was nervous. I figured my Italian connection with the local lingo, now arriving, would put me straight.

"I just can NOT fuckin' believe it," blasted Alessandra as she did that full-on, Continental European hugging and kissing thing under the parasol, after pulling up on her rented Honda Dream and darting into the café. "I've had it with this fuckin' place."

Alessandra wore a pretty, knee-length, red and white floral dress, as well as big sunglasses and white sneakers. She sat down, flipped her long curly brown hair over her shoulder, and reached into her small bag for a pack of Marlboros. She lit a cigarette with a loud suck and let it dangle from her lips, jerking up and down, as she cranked up the rant factor.

She was pissed off, it was clear. Every pointed gesture, flail of the arms, and jag of her fingers as she fired ashes into a helpless ashtray conveyed *Fuck it.*

For forty minutes she spewed vitriol in the direction of Việt Nam, Hà Nội, Hanoians, Asia, Asians, the traffic, the hassle, the rip-offs, the landlord, her Vietnamese colleagues, her Italian boss, *and* the guy who looked at her the wrong way on the street just minutes ago. *It was Alessandra against the planet.*

"What happened?" I asked.

"You cannot trust anyone. No one," she blazed, ashes flying. "I put a pencil on my desk, I went out to the toilet, I came back, and the pencil's gone."

Her face twisted into a "You understand me, right?" shape. This was not the Alessandra I'd met previously. I thought she might be losing it.

"And they lie to you. 'No, there wasn't a pencil there. No, no pencil. You're imagining it.' Un-be-liev-able. Lies, lies, lies. All the fuckin' time. Lies. I've had it."

All that. Over a pencil?

You see it. Expats lose it. Hit a wall. They have to get out. South Korea was full of casualties. I guessed Việt Nam was no different. Little things become big things. The fact that things just don't work in quite the same way as they do back home becomes all too much. And you lose it. Sometimes justifiably, sometimes not. I'd done it. I'd do it again.

"I called the airline and booked a flight home," she sighed. "I go back to Genoa in ten days' time. Thank fuck for that."

"I guess you're not gonna miss this place, huh?" I asked.

"Fuck, no," she snorted, her voice husky. She managed the feeblest of eye-smiles through her sunglasses before slouching back into the chair, one arm hanging lifelessly over the armrest.

She lit another Marlboro to feed her post-tirade glow and breathed out a succession of smoke-filled sighs.

"Ach . . . the food, maybe. Some of it. The street food. But no, there's not much I'll miss. I didn't wanna leave this way, but there you go. Shit happens. Fuck it."

And with that, over my first-ever lunch in Việt Nam (which was not very good, and not at all Vietnamese), my only decent contact in Hà Nội was leaving the country. *Is this how a long stint in Việt Nam ends?* I wondered. *Disillusioned, depressed, and not a little bit mad?*

One of the (admittedly few) significant burdens of the long-term expat is the constant necessity to start over again. This was only my second restart. I could already see the negative side of the lifestyle choice.

Friends, colleagues, and girlfriends known over a year or more in one place are left behind when you move on, alone, to start all over again. It's a brutal, self-inflicted wound that unnaturally cuts through any semblance of normal life. I wasn't sure the perpetual restarting thing was for me. I was already missing my life in Korea, but I was in it now, for better or worse. And here I was in Việt Nam, finally, left to my own devices to figure out how this place worked. To find out what Vietnamese food was all about. To find out if the grub was, as I seemed to have gotten into my head, so very, very special after all.

Binh provided an alternative introduction to Việt Nam. In between offering me drugs, girls, a room in a house that doubled as a fully functioning knocking shop, giving me a criminal exchange rate on U.S. dollars, taking me to buy books and electronics, and pocketing my change, he also offered me a ride.

Binh was a skinny twenty-year-old bellhop and odd-job man in the hotel on Hàng Gà Street where I lived for my first two weeks in Hà Nội. The red, rusted Chinese bicycle was a steal at $15. And Binh robbed me blind when he sold it to me. I dread to think how his other deals might have turned out.

The Chinese piece of shit, as I christened the machine less than one hour after buying it, was barely functional for the full four weeks I owned it.

I absentmindedly left it in a back alley one night, forgot about it for twenty-four hours, gasped a little when I remembered, before shrugging off its loss with a sense, predominantly, of relief. Easy come, easy break down, easy go.

In that short time, the bicycle, although it

pains me to call it that, had become a bit like a glorified handbag, in that I held it and/or pushed it more than I ever rode it. Whenever I bumped into Binh around town, he would point at the bike and laughingly ask, "That thing's still going?" And then he'd tell anyone nearby who would listen that it was he, with the smile of victory, who had sold it to me.

Not far from the hotel, at one end of Hàng Bông Street, lay a narrow passageway called Ngõ Cấm Chỉ. This, Binh confidently informed me, was a "street food street." It was not quite a street and not quite an alleyway, barely big enough to ride two Chinese pieces of shit side by side down the length of it. And it was impossible to do so without banging handlebars.

The first time I turned into the ngõ early one evening, I was grabbed by the forearm mid-pedal, forcibly extracted from my bike, and led to a table.

As kidnaps go, it was opportunistic and aggressive, but essentially well meaning. They demanded a small ransom. I'd get my arm and my bike back if I paid to eat. I caved in to their demands instantly.

All I had to do was choose: a bowl of rice porridge; a plate of fried rice; a ladle of thick, pungent crab, tofu, and tomato-filled soup; or something with snails and coconut.

I opted for cơm rang, the fried rice, and got my

arm back. The bike, as far as I could tell, was still negotiating its terms of release.

I leaned back into my blue plastic chair. It creased at the hinge. I judged it too dangerous for a full lean and instead readjusted my movements, leaned forward, and put one elbow on the sticky acrylic tablecloth as I scanned the ngõ.

A mosaic of unimaginative red, yellow, and white signs advertised food. A single font was in use throughout the entire ngõ. And there was blue plastic furniture. Always blue plastic furniture.

I imagined the millionaire with the monopoly on the manufacture of blue plastic restaurant furniture, reclining in one of his own ubiquitous products, in his blue plastic mansion, somewhere in the mountains, dispensing blue plastic knowledge to his son.

"One day, my blue plastic empire will all be yours, my son. The earliest designs were passed down from my father's father's father by a Nguyễn dynasty prophet. He said, 'Go forward and prosper. In blue plastic.' And so it was. And so it shall be. For you. But, beware," he added, wagging an index finger. "The blue plastic giveth, and the blue plastic taketh away."

At which point, the back caved in on his chair and he fell onto a blue plastic crate full of empty beer bottles, one of which shattered, piercing his liver. The blue plastic emperor of Việt Nam died of his injuries soon after.

Back in the alley stall, still held hostage, I watched as a cook set about marshaling my com rang order. The diminutive woman in regulation pajamas thwacked the gas on with a loud whoosh that sucked the oxygen from the street before plonkin' a yard-wide blackened wok on top of the vicious blue flame that was roughly the size of a small forest fire. The base of the wok flared lava hot.

Oil fizzed. She threw in some onion, slices of Chinese sausage, a dose of ham cubes, and finally the rice. The clatter and clang of the metal spatula against the wok sounded like a spluttering Model T Ford backfiring its way up a steep incline.

Within a minute, she'd slopped the fried concoction onto a hard plastic plate and doused the flame. Dinner arrived steaming.

On the table were a broken pepper dispenser, a salt dispenser with uncooked rice inside to keep the white granules dry, soy sauce, and a bright orange chili sauce in a squeeze bottle with an indecipherable Vietnamese label.

I dolloped a healthy gob of the orange stuff on one side of my plate. Upon release it appeared to throb, winking in my direction and whispering, "Go on. Just try me. Dare you. You should see the last guy who released me. We haven't seen him round these parts for quite some time . . ."

The rice was mouth-burningly hot, but taste-less. I squirted on a jet of soy and tried again. Still nothing. I edged my fork toward the crack-ling, radioactive orange splodge, extracted a mi-nuscule sample, and added a load of rice.

The burn flew through the rice and stabbed me in the tongue. The heat I could handle. Hell, I could even enjoy that section of the perfor-mance. It was the synthetic nature of its taste that made me recoil. Chemicals were involved, and my tongue told me they were bad chemicals.

In fact, there were four observations I took away from this meal:

1. Never go near the hot orange bottle ever again.
2. Chinese sausage (lạp xưởng) is sweet, and, much as I prefer not to take salt in my coffee, I don't care for sweet in my sausage either.
3. I'd done better fried rice at home in England.
4. *That* was Vietnamese food? THAT?

Disappointment bonged like a tolling bell at a funeral. I'm not sure exactly what I expected from a plate of fried rice, but it should have at least been better than that bland slop. That was not the all-singing, all-dancing symphony of Eastern spice I'd traveled halfway around the world for. To be perfectly frank, *that was shit.*

Very soon after that, I went from the shit pan to the entrail bin. Nghĩa's night of the throbbing womb took me on a porcine ride, far from fried rice, to a place called disgust.

In between, I tried cơm bình dân on Đinh Liệt street. It's fried fish, rice, and rau muống, a vegetable that's nearly impossible to translate into English. It's either morning glory, water spinach, or . . . pondweed. It's green, it's quite delicious, and it's everywhere in Việt Nam.

It came served on prison plates in a garage-sized, white-tile-lined, fly-ridden front room a step off the pavement. I was still looking for rocket-propelled Vietnamese bites, something that would sparkle inside my mouth and detonate inside my head. What I got was varying shades of *Hmmm . . . it's OK . . . I guess . . . but, really . . . is that it?*

Without the fish sauce dip and, possibly, the rau muống, you'd be hard-pressed to call this remotely special on any decent international good-taste barometer. This was no diamond in the rough. To find a Vietnamese muse, I'd need to try a lot harder.

Three months in, after many a basic, bare-bones rice restaurant, and much of Ngõ Cấm Chỉ — "street food street" — explored, I found it difficult to reconcile the stratosphere-breaking high that was a bowl of bún chả with the magma-piercing lows of fried rice, chemically enhanced chili sauce, rubbery uterus, and intestines. I pondered this one morning while sipping green tea at the boiled-chicken-feet stall next to the office.

I knew that Vietnamese food was famous. People were constantly lauding it. And yet here were the Vietnamese, eating chicken feet. *Boiled* chicken feet. My dog would turn its nose up at that, if I had a dog. I hadn't seen that in any *Cooking with Mrs. Nguyên: Vietnamese Food You'll Love at First Bite* tome in the library. What was wrong with Việt Nam? *Where was all the bloody Vietnamese food?*

What I found in Hà Nội in those weeks was not what I had been expecting. This was not the Vietnamese food of the sepia-toned, soft-focus, rustic images of the few recipe and travel books I'd managed to purloin, buy, or borrow. This was rough at best, disgusting at worst, but Việt Nam hardly had a patent on that. Clearly I was going wrong somewhere.

And it wasn't just me. The office was a travesty. The ten twentysomething Vietnamese women I worked with at an English-language school all took their lunch order from the mysterious "food delivery company." What this venerable institution delivered was a three-partition tray dolloped with rice, meat, and veg. There was also a canh, a thin pork and vegetable soup. The meat, when it was (I think) pork in origin, came with hairs. All meat, regardless of type, came with gristle. But it was the hairs that finally broke my relationship with the "food delivery company." It was a ridiculously cheap lunch, a dollar or less. The unseen cost was to your taste buds and sense of self-respect. I canceled my order after week one. No more pig hair or gristle for me. Or, at least, not cheap hair and cheap gristle.

It wasn't until that first bún chả lunchtime, soaked in smoke, on Phùng Hưng Street, that Việt Nam began to reveal herself in all her shapely glory.

However, it seemed to me in those first few weeks in the capital that as soon as I found a ravenous temptress on one street, on the next she'd morphed into her spotty, swotty half sister from the countryside, with a dribbling nose and tape around one corner of her glasses, her matted hair rendered immobile with grease.

I didn't fancy the half sister. I wanted the other one, the more elusive one. I needed to track her down. *Pronto*.

CHAPTER FIVE:
FOOD SAFARI

Once I'd entered, it was the decapitation ritual I noticed first. It was certainly not what I'd expected to find in an eel restaurant. Not that entering an eel restaurant was high on my list of expectations in life, but neither was bearing witness to a decapitation.

I should note that it wasn't the eel being decapitated, but a bowl of fruit. As I sat down at table number four, one of nine tables with red plastic numbers stuck onto the white-tiled walls alongside, in Nhà Hàng Miến Lươn at 87 Hàng Điếu, in the capital's Old Quarter, I surveyed the stainless steel surface in front of me.

Vinegar, chopped chilies, chopsticks in a holder, a tissue rack. It was then I noticed the girl in a yellow top sitting at the table next to me in the less than half-full restaurant at midafternoon. She had a red basin full of small fruits.

"Small tangerines, not lemons," she told me.

With a blade, she very carefully lopped the top

of each green-skinned fruit so that the stalk end held on by a slim slither of skin. The customer could then grab one from the bowl on the table, pull back the decapitated "head," and squeeze it over a spoon. The trick is then to pour the juice into the soup, but keep the pips on the spoon to discard (onto the floor, naturally). The decapitation detail was ingenious, pretty, and time-saving. I never ever saw this particular method anywhere else in Việt Nam.

The small tangerines, it turned out, were actually calamansis, which have a slightly sour yet sweet orange flavor that injects zappy power into eel dishes, whether they be rice porridge, glass noodle soup, or a stir-fry of vermicelli and eel. Calamansis, it seemed to me, were the ideal supercharger for any eel dish.

How I found this joint is another matter. It was the dark brown fried stuff in the glass cabinet at the entrance that first caught my eye.

"Foreigners come here in the evening sometimes. They think it's worms they're eating, not eels," Lê Hoàng Hà, the manager and son of the original owner, told me with a big laugh.

The restaurant, situated on a prime piece of turf opposite Hàng Da market, had been in the Đồng Thịnh family, at the same location, since the mid-eighties. They started out as a bánh cuốn shack before introducing miến lươn.

"The customers preferred our miến lươn, so

87

we ditched the bánh cuốn end of the menu," Hà explained to me on one visit. Although, when I asked him if that meant his bánh cuốn was total dross, he ignored me.

"My aunt still makes bánh cuốn outside on the pavement every night. In fact, we have four relatives in Hà Nội who still make and sell bánh cuốn."

Hà was one of six siblings, all of whom worked in the food trade. The eel on which this restaurant built its reputation was cooked elsewhere in Hà Nội, somewhere downtown. He would never tell me exactly where. It was as if he thought I'd go and muscle in on his order, set up a rival joint, or just plain mess with things.

It was always when you got to that line of questioning that the Vietnamese would clam up and you morphed from an interested, curious, oddball foreigner who appeared out of the ether with an obsessive interest in their food, into a threat, a competitor, someone not to be trusted.

I experienced this same suspicion more acutely while wondering what to order at a seafood, snail, and offal restaurant on Trúc Bạch Lake in the north of Hà Nội one evening. The "English Menu" I was given went beyond comedy on a headlong journey toward travesty — "Fried crap" and "Testicles in medicine" being two memorable, mouthwatering highlights. I was so enamored of the menu I asked for a copy of it as a souvenir. The manager came over and politely but firmly said, "No. What if you want to copy it and open your own restaurant with the same menu? I can't allow it."

At that point I wasn't sure what was funnier, his menu or the seriousness with which he defended it. His restaurant closed within the year. And, in a time before digital cameras, I never did get a copy of the menu.

The eel cooks, wherever they were hidden, would deliver the precooked brown shreds to the restaurant and deposit them, pouring the fish from their sacks like grain into the glass cabinet for all passersby to see and inspect.

"Having them cooked elsewhere saves us a lot of time," Hà explained. "To remove all of the bones, to clean them and then cook them is a long process. Quite laborious."

Nhà Hàng Miến Lươn opened at 6 A.M. and closed at around 9 P.M. In a day, they'd go through thirty or forty kilograms of cleaned, boned, and fried eel.

Hanoians, so I'm told, tend to eat eel dishes mainly in the evening. The small front room at Nhà Hàng Miến Lươn could become packed very quickly, with customers often spilling out onto the street alongside Auntie's bánh cuốn setup.

There was never a huge amount of flavor involved in any of these eel dishes, hence the need

89

for the ever-present calamansi to tickle its underbelly and the rau răm (Vietnamese coriander) to propel it along. What eel and noodles did do well together was texture. The fried and crispy coupled exceptionally well with the slippery and noodly. It was a winning combo that kept me coming back, whether to pull up a stool or to sit on my motorbike, engine left putt-putting like a true Hanoian, and order a mang đi về (take-away order) like umpteen others every evening. (Actually, that bit about the engine isn't true. I'd turn it off. Honest.)

I was repeatedly warned not to eat too much of the rau răm herb, which I always found curious. Why? I asked one day.

"You won't be able to perform if you eat too much," said Hà.

"Perform what?"

"You'll become impotent," Hà told me with a completely straight face.

To balance my impending lack of virility, Hà explained the benefits of eating eel.

"Eel is very good for your back bones, and even better," he said, "if you take a shot or two of snake alcohol with it." I never quite subscribed to this theory, but then again, I never had a bad back in Việt Nam.

When the bill came, it was always on a yellow Post-it note. They'd jot down what you'd had to eat and drink and stick it on your table. That way, the four wall-mounted fans that continuously circulated, cooling customers and soups, would not blow the tab away into a bin, onto the tissue-laden floor, or off down the street. Notices on the wall even told customers, in Vietnamese, to take their yellow ticket to the counter at the end of their meal.

An old woman, the original owner, was in charge. Like a slightly friendlier version of Jabba the Hutt, the women in these places never seemed to move very much, but always appeared to be in total control. Decked out in a flowery brown áo bà ba, this particular silent, blobby maître d' would take my yellow slip, take the money, and hand back the change without so much as a sniff, a grunt, or a thank you.

Hà Nội. Old style.

It was at this joint, back in 1997, that I first jotted down a few notes. The address, the dish, the cost, what it was like, the ambience, how packed it was. It was a habit I continued throughout my tenure. At the time, I had no idea I'd compile a food guide to the city, eventually sell words for a living, or start a blog. Blogs did not exist. I'd only just registered for an e-mail account.

I could e-mail a limited amount of text at a time over the barely-a-kilobyte-per-second connection. The paranoid theory doing the rounds was that the authorities couldn't read and monitor more than a page of text at a time, and therefore limited the amount you could send. The wider world of the Internet was, for the time being, prohibited by the government.

You see, I'm not one for jungle treks, whitewater rafting, traversing the Andes on sustainably bred albino llamas, or swimming with disabled lesbian dolphins off the coast of the Bahamas. If a year in Korea had taught me anything, it was that I liked trying interesting food. I couldn't think of a better locale than Southeast and Northeast Asia to just plain gorge. Food was safari enough for me.

CHAPTER SIX:
VINA-LAND

Shortly after my Italian friend Alessandra's blunt exit from Việt Nam, and her dire warning of lies, misery, and impending psychosis, I received warning number two from a more level-headed source. And I was still mulling it over.

"Whatever you do, get yourself a hobby," said Chris, a long-term Australian expat business-man who'd been based in Hà Nội since the early nineties. We were at a tiny pavement tea stall on Lê Văn Hưu Street. Chris was referring to the relative lack of entertainment available in the early-to-bed capital. It was an easy place to get into trouble.

"If the girls don't get you, the booze will. If the booze doesn't get you, the drugs will. If the drugs don't get you, you're already psychotic and an alcoholic and you're probably on your latest in a very long line of dodgy girlfriends."

We were at Mrs. Ninh's, where I'd gotten into a habit of coming for tea. She'd opened the place in 1986. I say "opened," but it was really more a case of moving a bunch of stuff from her living room into a vacant spot on the pavement.

The nearby five-street intersection was manned at each angle by a xe ôm motorbike taxi driver. They perched on their passenger seats like vultures waiting for a carcass.

When I first started coming to Ninh's stall, I'd often wondered about a persistent and pervading smell, but I'd never had enough gumption to put two and two together. It was just as Chris advised me to get a hobby that Ninh piped up and I figured it out.

"My customers mostly come after they have breakfast at the phở restaurant next door," Ninh said as she wagged a finger over our shoulders. "But it's closed this morning. Someone died. That's why my stall's quiet today."

Behind us was an upturned sideboard. "What's that I can smell?" I asked

"It's the phở," said Ninh.

Hang on, I thought, *you just said the phở restaurant next door was closed today.* Chris sipped his tea. The leaves had sunk to the bottom of the small, thin glass.

I stood up and looked around the other side of the sideboard. Three large cooking pots sat on a brick stove that was filled with burning coals. The pots were chained together across the lids, through the handles, and padlocked with

94

a substantial-looking lock. In parts of Tokyo, some people pay to have themselves trussed up like that, I thought. But why padlock these things and how the hell would you nick one of them, even if you wanted to?

There were pots like this all over the city. Cooking was constant and everywhere. Food, Vietnamese food, was everywhere. I sat back down and turned to Chris. "A hobby, you say?" The beefster joint next door had gotten me thinking. "How about food? Does that qualify as a hobby?"

"The Vina-stuff?"

Every expat (and a few funky Vietnamese) were in the habit of describing anything Vietnamese with the prefix "Vina." "Vina-nosh" was used to indicate Vietnamese food. A hot chick was a "Vina-babe." An argument with a hot chick was a "Vina-drama." A cool male Hanoian was a "Vina-dude." And on it went. It was, of course, a prefix borrowed from the Vietnamese themselves. Main cigarette brand: Vinataba. Ceiling fan manufacturer: Vinawind. Steel company: Vinasteel. Milk: Vinamilk.

"Well, yeah, the Vina-stuff." I nodded. "I just can't believe there's nothing much decent beyond bún chả in this town." The simple barbecued pork dish was the easiest and most obvious street food dish for foreigners to start off with. You could tell what it was by sight and smell.

95

Perhaps it was that reassuring scent of grilling pig that made this dish the one that so many foreigners would begin their journey into the Vinakitchen with. Conversely, a poke inside a random street soup vat and the inexperienced diner, lacking essential Vina-knowledge, wouldn't have a clue as to what was going on inside.

Chris had some advice to help me navigate the territory I'd decided I wanted to explore further.

"Look out for the women walking around with two bamboo baskets attached to a pole and slung over a shoulder," said Chris. "But steer clear of the meat and shellfish in the afternoon."

"Why?"

"The heat. You dunno how long it's been festering in the sun."

I never forgot that simple piece of advice, even if I didn't always stick to it. However, I was grateful when, one evening, I did.

Some friends and I were three-quarters of the way through our second bottle of lizard rice wine — rượu tắc kè — during an overlong evening in a tiny rượu bar cum shack called Rượu Lý, south of central Hà Nội, when my mate Patrick suggested we hit an "oyster bar" he'd spotted earlier in the day.

Patrick, it would be fair to say, was an enthusiastic drinker. His doctor had told him that if he didn't stop drinking he would kill himself — not necessarily from the alcohol, but from driving his motorbike just as enthusiastically as he drank, and generally after he'd been drinking.

The four of us bumbled over to Tô Hiến Thành Street. Sure enough, the oysters were there, on display, in a green plastic basin, out front at one of several seafood shacks that stayed open reasonably late for Hà Nội, which is to say until about 10 P.M.

They were big. Already shucked. Patrick, who spoke respectable Vietnamese, even after the sun had long since sailed past his yardarm, ordered without a thought. Sat down. Followed up with a shout for beers. The oysters arrived at the same time as the booze. Everyone tucked in — but not me.

"Why are you not eating? When was the last time you saw an oyster in this town?" Patrick's eyes drooped at the sides. Like a large herring gull, he popped his neck back and slung a tongue-sized oyster down his gullet.

"How long have they been outside? You said you saw them earlier today, yeah?"

"Yeah, I cruised past at around eleven this morning."

"I'm not risking that. They've been outside all day long. It was baking hot. They've been sitting there baking, too."

Patrick and my fellow diners questioned, for one split slow-mo second, the wisdom of their decision, but then the alcoholic bravado kicked logic out into the street, and they quickly devoured the plate.

Regardless of any serious health issues, these specimens were enormous. Definitely more of the chew variety than the swallow. More suitable for grilling. A nice wee grating of cheese maybe. Some bread crumbs. But *raw*?

Patrick and the others were violently ill the entire night.

"Food? As a hobby? Why not?" said Chris, back at Ninh's tea stall. "It doesn't matter if it's food hunting, bird watching, mountain walking, or flower arranging. Get yourself a hobby and stay sane. That's my advice for living in this town."

Chris was outlining the expat white guy cliché. While I'd never heard it quite laid out in these exacting terms before, the evidence for its existence was littered in all its sad glory across every bar in Hà Nội. Expat alcoholics, bums, and weirdoes were as common as conical hats in the capital.

Of course, Chris hadn't exactly followed his own advice. Two years earlier, he'd divorced his Australian wife and taken up with his Vietnamese maid. Plenty of others we knew had taken a similar path, but divorce, robbery (by wife), assault (by wife's friends), or "visa issues" (organized by "business partner") had blown their hopes and dreams of a happy Vina-ever-after soundly out of the water, expelled them from the country, launched them into a lonely life of long-term debt, rendering them unable, in many cases, to reenter Vina-land ever again.

Chris got up to leave. He had a meeting deep in a blocked bowel of a government department, "the office of fuckwittery," as he called it, somewhere in Hà Nội.

I was left to ponder hobbies. Nhũ, Chris's second wife, had led him to numerous fantastic stalls over the years. He gave me a lead: an eleven o'clock tofu woman on a pavement in the outskirts of the Old Quarter. Part of the appeal was that at that time, very few foreigners were eating street food. Yet all the Vietnamese were. I felt sure we were missing out, and I wanted to find out if we were.

As I checked my watch, I had half an hour. I could make it to the tofu woman easily. I ordered another glass of tea, and Mrs. Ninh told me how she made it "my way."

Having been shown the tea ceremony in South Korea, I was half-expecting prayers, incense, green smoke, and a floating Buddha to accompany her directions. Alas, no.

Add 30 percent hot water to the tea, she explained, and only use Thái Nguyên tea, because "it's the best, everyone knows that." Leave it to steep for five to ten minutes. Then continue adding hot water to keep the tea tasty. Make sure you leave the teapot lid slightly ajar when you add the hot water. If you don't, the smell won't be good and the tea turns brown or red, not green like it should be.

Chris's words of advice concerning the tofu woman were still hanging in the beef-stock-scented air as I slurped the tea.

There was never an awful lot to do at these stalls, beyond people watching and chatting. But it was never dull. I could stay in these places for hours. Sometimes I'd write notes to myself — snippets of potential stories. I'd attempted short stories, which were short, yes, but they were also bad. *Very bad*. I'd tried to write a novel, too. I'd gotten seventy pages in before I tired of my cast of angsty Canadians, marooned in Korea, spiritually bereft, stricken by a collective kimchi allergy and plagued with incestuous love lives. These attempts had failed, whereas I'd kept up taking notes at street stalls, jotting down snippets of life. From front-room restaurants to street sellers, I recorded their prices, places, names, and dishes.

The fiction was useless, but the food notes were useful: not only for me, but possibly for others, too. Later, I compiled my favorite places into a printed guide, which I gave to friends and colleagues. And in my notes, I'd hammer away and strive to articulate this place, this city, this food.

To make any attempt to describe Vietnamese food in Hà Nội, you must first begin with sound. If there's one thing Vietnamese food in Hà Nội is not, it is silent. Whether it be gobbled down in a brightly lit diner with a karaoke singer howling out a hearing-aid-destroying lament, in a family living room in front of the TV, or on the street, Vietnamese food in Hà Nội comes with a "must be eaten with loud noises" label. At street level, that noise is very specific.

Push-button motorbike horns, once aroused into action, were like a gaggle of intermittently disgruntled geese caught in the middle of a very large swarm of fat and lumbering bees: a rumbling engine noise. The bees lurch, barge, and buzz. The geese grumble, natter, and quack. Every day the geese and the bees wake up in the *same* mood and in the *same* place.

A tea order at Mrs. Ninh's stall was always accompanied by this Vina-street symphony. Despite that, to my mind she had one of the most interesting jobs in town. On the surface, it also seemed to be one of the most simplistic: she made and served tea. But she wasn't just in the tea trade. She was a cross between a psychotherapist, a marriage counselor, and an intelligence agent. Ninh was the hub for all the local gossip.

She knew who was banging who. Who'd left who. Who gambled. Who'd lost their job. Who'd been to prison. Who'd died and who was nearly dead. She could map the local wife beaters, junkies, and drunks, pinpoint where the real money was on the street and where it used to be. She knew who was up and who was down. Everything.

Ninh, and hundreds of women like her, were the gossip conduits of the city. Unlike, say, a phở stall, a tea table is a place to linger. To talk. And you might not always talk directly to a woman like Ninh at a place like this, but her sonar-powered ears would pick up your conversation regardless. Fortunately, my conversations were mostly in English, with Chris.

In later years, I decided that if I could ever choose a street stall job in Việt Nam, it would be Ninh's job. There was, I reckoned, a novel (or ten) in the tales she must have picked up while serving tea and petri dishes filled with pumpkin seeds.

I declined Ninh's offer of another glass of tea, paid the paltry tab, and headed across town. I had a tofu seller to find.

There are blue plastic stools and there are *blue plastic stools*. If you're lucky (or in an actual brick-and-mortar restaurant), you might find yourself on the almost-comfortable variety, at almost-normal chair height. It might possibly even have a back to it.

More commonly, you'll find yourself on a

"croucher." Tolerable for a short time, but comes with an osteopath's warning for loiterers.

Then there are the "ultras." You really don't want to find yourself on an ultra. Commonly found surrounding a two-basket mobile vendor, they can be blue, red, yellow, or white. They are small, *very* small. *Uncomfortably* small. *Annoyingly* small. Bone-creakingly awfully small.

Ultras, per Chris's recommendation, are the price you pay if you want or need to go and eat at a double-basket street vendor. And on Hàng Trống Street, that's what I had to do if I wanted a nibble at Mrs. Nhung's fried tofu lunch on the pavement midway along the street.

The best line of attack with an ultra is to first understand that, no matter what, unless you're a dwarf, you're gonna be bloody uncomfortable.

The second is to vehemently not copy the Vietnamese. Don't go for a crouching position, knees hunched, chin at your heels, spine snapped, neck bent crooked forever more, your health insurance groaning at the premium-busting seams.

No. Sit on the ultra, by all means, but cross your legs in a kind of prone, legs wide open at the knees, bending, sitting position. This, after years of practice, is the only way I have found to sit for any length of time at these places.

Why provide such bloody uncomfortable seats? I cynically assumed that the likes of Nhung, the tofu woman, purposefully used this streetside furniture to deter foreigners.

The explanation was, as ever in Việt Nam, more pragmatic.

Nhung had only recently started in the street-food-selling business. She chose to sell fried tofu — bún đậu — which comes with sticky white noodles cut into bite-sized square bundles, two kinds of herbs — kinh giới (Vietnamese balm) and tía tô (perilla) — and a mắm tôm or nước mắm dip. She chose this dish because it's dead easy to make. Plus, the villagers of Hưng Yên province, where she came from, were known for tofu. Nhung made the forty-mile, ninety-minute journey from Hưng Yên by bus every morning.

Bún đậu was normally a breakfast and lunch-time dish. During the post–American War subsidy era, the dish was known as "food for the poor." In the morning, Nhung sold her tofu deep in the Old Quarter. At around 11 A.M., she moved to Hàng Trống Street and set up on the pavement in front of a tea stall. Her position was strategic.

The tea stall cum cubbyhole at number 58 also acted as the entrance to an electrical repair shop. The tea stall had been there since 1985. It was nothing more than a tiny wooden cabinet with a glass front, set on a windowless alcove, under a bunch of fuse boxes and electricity meters. Inside the cabinet were packets of yellow Thành Long cigarettes and warm bottles of Bia Hà Nội.

On the floor was a tea cozy with hot green tea, and the toothless and very old woman who sold the tea from the cubbyhole. At night, she slept where she worked.

If it rained, like a cornered mouse with nowhere to go, Nhung would scurry off the pavement inside the tea shop to occupy a tiny corner so that she could continue her trade. If it was dry, she stayed on the pavement under the shade of a banyan tree to protect herself and her vat of oil, which she placed between the tree and a metal electricity distribution box, with the words Tủ Điện Phân Phối on it. Nhung would rest her conical hat upon the large box.

The combination of Nhung's stall, the tree, a concrete telegraph pole, the box, *plus* the parked motorbikes, lingerers, and tea drinkers, meant that anyone trying to traverse the pavement would, more often than not, need to make a detour onto the road, into the traffic, to continue their journey.

Every day, seven days a week, after the last of her ten kilos of noodles and one hundred pieces of tofu had been consumed, Nhung cleaned her kit. Then she packed everything and stored it in a small space she rented at an inn in the center of Hà Nội.

All of this is to say: the size of the ultra stools came down to practicality. They simply did not *need* to be any bigger, and as she was transporting them around town much of the day, every day, she really didn't *want* them to be any bigger.

She did this every day of the year, apart from a few days off at Tết, and for family anniversaries. Her goal in life was to pay for her son's education. After morning class, he would come to help her serve customers, clean up plates, and check on the noodle supply.

Bún đậu is one of the most simple, yet most electrifying, dishes in Hà Nội. And it's a Hà Nội dish, a true original. This is how Nhung made it:

Rectangular portions of tofu and globs of young green rice, called chả cốm, were fried to order in a small, coal-fueled aluminum vat filled with oil. That was one basket.

In the other basket was a large metal tray, upon which sat a smaller bamboo basket, lined with phrynium leaves. This is where she kept her noodles. Under that tray was the fresh tofu. Herbs and cucumber could be found in thin plastic bags hanging from the top of her pannier pole.

One thing I noticed with sellers like Nhung over the years was the degree of pride they had in the food that they served. Especially when serving it to a foreigner. And then there was the level of care they took to make sure it was done properly and served properly. Either the way you wanted it or the way it *should* be done.

If you liked it crispy, she'd fry it a long time for you. If you preferred it very soft in the middle, she'd be quicker. Or maybe you liked it hard in the middle, but not crispy. Nhung would cook it to your taste. Before serving, she let the tofu drain a little on a small grill above her frying vat.

Traditionally, you eat bún đậu with mắm tôm, shrimp paste. Nhung always bought hers from Hàng Bè Street because, she said, "it's the most famous mắm tôm in Hà Nội." Some customers, admittedly very few in number, preferred a bowl of fish sauce, known as nước mắm.

Lunch would come on a plastic tray, which Nhung would set on an ultra. There were five components on the tray: the bundle of herbs, a small bowl of chopped red chilies, a plastic plate of fried tofu, another of fresh, white sticky noodles, and a bowl of mắm tôm — for me, anyway. Always the purple stink monster for me.

As far as I'm concerned, mắm tôm is vital to bún đậu. Sort of like the tiny computer that parked the Apollo lunar landing module at Tranquility Base on the moon on July 20, 1969. A piddly seventy-four kilobytes of memory controlled a spaceship weighing thirteen thousand kilograms, orbiting the moon at twenty-two hundred miles. Without that box of techwizardry, Armstrong and friends were going nowhere. With it, they got to moonwalk and get back home after picking up some rocks. Much like a lunar lander, mắm tôm adds cosmic power to your lunch, whereas, to my mind — and to most Hanoians' too — nước mắm could never give this dish enough gas to escape gravity.

Nhung squeezed a quarter of a calamansi through a tea strainer and into my mắm tôm to wake it up. I'd always add a glob of chili, as I liked my tofu with a bit of a snap to it. I'd then give it a good stir with my chopsticks, and I was ready to start dipping.

Nhung would keep topping up my plate with a fresh supply of tofu, which she cut with a snip-snip of her scissors, as and when it was ready, until I groaned "No rồi," signifying, "I've had enough, I'm stuffed, I'm satisfied, and I cannot possibly eat one more morsel."

As is the case at all good street stalls in Việt Nam, when it's gone, it's gone. It took a little time for me to learn this. Many was the day I'd arrive at Nhung's, even before noon, only to hear the words "hết rồi," meaning, "it's all finished," delivered with a twist of a hand, like she was shaking an empty salt cellar, and an expression that said, "It's not my fault, don't blame me, you showed up too late, buster."

Why, I wondered, did seemingly very success-ful street vendors like Nhung not get tempted to set up a shop? She had, of course, thought about it. And she'd done the calculations.

"It's the cost of the rent," she'd tell me. "It's too high, and there's no profit in it for someone like me. It's easier to make money on the street."

Nhung had enough stools to cook for eight to ten customers at any one time, particularly eager customers who were willing to stand and wait, and stand and eat, if necessary.

The hardest thing about this life, Nhung told me years later, was the police. When they came, as they did regularly, they took everything. The panniers, the stools, the food.

Before the 1986 government policies of đổi mới ("renovation") and mở cửa ("open door"), the streets and pavements were relatively free of traders. In the fledgling, renamed "Socialist-oriented market economy," collectivized agriculture was abandoned, rules restricting the right to engage in foreign trade were relaxed, and private enterprise was encouraged. The impetus to implement these radically new economic policies accelerated as the USSR imploded in the early nineties.

With the beginning of these new policies, street sellers became a regular phenomenon and an unintended consequence of the more relaxed rules. And, as time went on, these street sellers became a pain for the government. Different cities responded differently to street traders. Some were loose on enforcement, some not. But whenever the cops did go in, as they always did eventually, they went in hard and fast. In more recent years, đổi mới and mở cửa have been supplemented by a state discourse around hiện đại hóa ("modernization") and văn minh ("civilization"). And, in 2014, vendors like Nhung are increasingly seen as being associated with the backwardness and underdevelopment that these modernizing and civilizing policies were brought in to bolster.

"I've been fined many, many times. I pay a few hundred thousand a year in fines," she'd tell me between servings. "Once you pay, you get all your equipment back, but of course the food is ruined."

Regardless of the cops, there was no way that Nhung could keep any leftover food for the next day. It's not like her panniers were refrigerated, and she didn't even have a fridge at home. Moreover, her customers simply would not have come back if she tried to serve them day-old food.

Freshness in everything was absolutely key to Nhung's business model, and indeed, the business model of every vendor plying the byways and alleyways of the capital, day in, day out.

When Nhung got home at 5 P.M., she would prepare dinner for her family, clean up, and sleep. And at 4 A.M., she started the whole cycle over again.

CHAPTER SEVEN:
MOVING OUT

It was dinnertime. I groaned as we entered. *Oh no, another abattoir.*

I was with Hưng, my landlord's son, whom I'd slowly gotten to know over the previous month. We turned a corner behind the opera house and entered the large, iron-barred bia hơi (beer bar), known as the Tiger Cage, at number 2 Tràng Tiền Street. Supposedly, when the French ruled the roost in these parts, they kept the tigers for the local circus in here, hence the nickname.

I eyed the jumble of entrails, half-grown chicken eggs, tofu, and deep-fried scorpions on the buffet spread at the entrance. There was the regulation tiled floor, and a row of low plastic tables lined one side. Customers nattered, supped, and peered through the bars onto the street.

We crouched into eating position on red plastic chairs. Yes — *chairs* — we had the rare luxury of a back to lean on. A fan with years of cobwebs trailing off the exposed motor whirred above us. A group of geckos hunted around a fluorescent light in the humid, darkening air, already thick with bugs. Three large trees grew inside the bar. The corrugated iron roof had been cut to accommodate their unchecked growth.

A uniformed waiter came over. He had on a T-shirt that advertised the brand of beer at the bia hơi, which was the common name for both the restaurants like this and the brews served within. He deposited a hardback, laminated folder with the words "English menu" taped to the cover.

What was inside stretched the definition of English beyond its linguistic limits. Any possible enticement within was more than lost in translation — it was obliterated:

"Beef fried by shaking the saucepan"

"Cattlefish stirfried with mixed various meats"

"Sea crap spring roll"

"Beef testicle steaming boat"

Hưng told me he was an architect. He wore a white shirt, black trousers, shiny belt, and sensible shoes. He had the face of a teenager, yet he was the same age as me, though a good foot shorter, with a jet-black mop of hair, parted low on one side, in a style more common to Hanoian males over fifty.

An architect this young couldn't be blamed entirely for the plague of ugly late-twentieth-century buildings across the city. Hà Nội was a rash of pointy, jagged, crumbling communist-era concrete houses and apartment blocks. These architectural horrors lined every cramped alley in the city. Each was three, four, or five floors high and boasted one room per floor. They were simple structures that always felt temporary to me.

By the time beer number three had arrived, Hưng's cheeks had bloomed a bright shade of red. I was worried his head might pop a blood vessel and paint the Tiger Cage bia hơi a deep crimson.

We were here together because the landlord was having issues with my rental, and he'd bravely sent his son on a mission to ply me with booze and put me straight.

Good, I thought, as I was having issues with my rental, too. My list already had ten points:

1. Everyone used the shower on my floor — the floor that I rented, and that no one else lived on, or should have had access to.
2. They showered with my toiletries. And brushed their teeth with my toothpaste. I crossed my fingers that they brought their own toothbrushes, but I wasn't 100 percent sure they did.
3. The landlord had been through my personal photographs and diary.
4. He listened in on my private phone calls on the upstairs line. I heard the

113

telltale click and the sound of his beery breath whenever I used the phone.

5. He wouldn't give me a key. Let me repeat that. He wouldn't give *me* — the renter — a key to the house that *I* rented.

6. He key-locked the door, from the inside, at 9 P.M. sharp, went to bed, and snored like a walrus. On two occasions, a friend had to stay the night because we couldn't open the door. No key.

7. This constituted a breach of several health and safety regulations, surely?

8. What if there was a fire? Imagine that? I tried not to.

9. On an all too regular basis, I could hear the aging landlord beating his aging wife.

10. I arrived home early one day and caught the maid asleep in my bed.

"You must understand my father," the dutiful son implored after a few more sips of Bia Hà Nội, a nibble of fried tofu, a munch of sautéed pumpkin flowers, and several flicks of his flop noir. "You must respect him."

Understand? Respect? The landlord wasn't my father. He was a wife beater. I paid money for a floor in his house. He showered in my shower, he wouldn't give me the key, and it seemed to me that he didn't understand the basics of a formal rental agreement.

"Look, I don't even have a key. I want to go out. I go out late. You know, I have friends, and I need a key." I prodded the tofu, ordered a side of mực chiên bơ, or fried squid, and guzzled the beer in my glistening half stein.

It was an open-and-shut case. How could it not be? I was the one paying — U.S. $250 per month — and yet I was the one having to put up with an unsustainable living situation.

"They've never rented to foreigners before. They've never even rented. This is the first time. You have to understand them." His face throbbed like a wobbly, overfilled bloody balloon. It was hypnotizing. It was breathing. Red. Deeper red. Red. A deeper and deeper red.

Could a human head *actually* explode? I wondered as I frowned at him, twizzling my chopsticks thoughtfully. From a few beers? Was that humanly possible? I had to research this.

My attention returned to the tofu between us. "Well, I don't think they're going to be renting to too many more foreigners if this is the way they think it works," I added before disrespectfully grabbing the first piece of hot squid from the plate as soon as it arrived, and dipping it thoughtlessly into the cheap chili sauce in the small plastic dish, having momentarily forgotten how terrible it was.

Hưng paid the bill. We walked out of the Tiger

Cage and strolled back to Cầu Gỗ Street. He hiccupped, made small talk, smiled, and laughed in a Vietnamese way I would come to know.

Every facial expression and bit of his body language said, "I'm attempting to ease a 'situation' here. C'mon, work with me, do what I'm telling you to do — not because it's in your best interests, but because it's in my best interests, and I'm banking on you being just about dumb enough a foreigner to go along with me, OK?" That smile was an attempt at ironing out those stubborn crinkles of misunderstanding.

He hadn't put me straight on anything, but he'd succeeded in helping me make the decision I'd already half made before his attempt at beer and tofu bribery. I told him I would find somewhere else to live. I'd move out of his father's house at the end of the month.

I had a new baseline requirement for renting. I needed a place where the landlord would deign to give me a key.

Bang, bang, bang. On my last day in the apartment, I was awoken early. Gone were any remains of politeness. I was told by the landlord to vacate the bedroom.

"Very important work to do."

At 7 A.M. on a Saturday?

In walked three men with equipment. They brought the never-ending sound of building work in from the street and chucked the whole gig live and direct at one end of my bedroom. Great.

They set about destroying the only wall with a window in it, on a mission to install a brand-spanking-new air conditioner. To do so, they had to tackle the windowpane. They tore down those ubiquitous iron bars, lugged the outdoor part of the contraption through the window, and put it in place, fixing it to the indoor section, before replacing the bars.

By the time I'd exited the shower, they'd all but installed the great, groaning new machine where there had been none before. There was no new tenant coming. I was their first and last-ever foreign lodger. I was still packing in the living room that formed the other part of my quarters, but was told to make space so that the workers could come and do a repeat job in there, too.

Drills drilled, circular saws whirred, and before too long, and in typical Hà Nội fashion, the second air conditioner was installed, while several other things were broken in the process, and a building site full of shit remained. But, hey, they were quick!

To escape the mayhem, and grab breakfast, I left my half-finished packing and went downstairs out onto Cầu Gỗ Street to a bún thang stall I frequented, and ordered this grocery store in a bowl. Here's what goes into this one bowl of soup: shredded turnip, sliced fried eggs, slivers of chicken, slices of Vietnamese pork roll called chả lụa (in the north) or giò lụa (in the south), pork, mushrooms, white noodles, and pork stock.

There is an awful lot going on inside a bowl of bún thang. But, wait, there's more.

"It's the dried shrimp and the sá sùng that makes it special," Hương, the thirty-year-old wife of a bar-owning American friend told me one day. Try as she might, this virtually English-fluent woman hadn't been able to translate "sá sùng" to my satisfaction.

"It's kind of a worm. It comes from the sea."

"An eel?"

"No."

"A sea slug?"

"No, no . . . Ôi giời ơi," she sighed in Vietnamese, using the oft-heard expression used to signify exasperation at, well, everything. Kind of like "Oh my god," "Jesus Christ," and "Oh, for crying out loud, you have GOT to be kidding me," all rolled into one.

She took me to the market around the corner to show me the bag of dried worms, with the label "sá sùng" stuck on the outside.

"They're very expensive, these ones. They make sure there's no sand in them."

I was still none the wiser. Only years later, after copious amounts of research and countless dead ends, bad leads, and just plain wrong turns,

I discovered that, in English, "sá sùng" means "peanut worm." Any wiser? No, me neither, though I do now know that peanut worms live under the sand and are harvested at low tide.

I used to go looking for lugworms at the beach in Britain to use as fishing bait. I'd never for one moment considered using them in a dish.

The Vietnamese dig them up, clean them and dry them, and, in one bún thang stall on Cầu Gỗ Street, at least, add them to the stock.

"It's this that adds the sweetness you can taste in the bún thang," said Hương, poking the bag, which hung on an elastic band from the iron shutter gates. "We don't use sugar."

The bowl of bún thang on Cầu Gỗ Street was always beholden to a deep and balanced sweetness provided, apparently, by the worm.

I tapped my toes on the tiled floor, took a restorative sip of the remainder of the bún thang, and thought about my rental on Cầu Gỗ Street.

Had I been forced out on purpose? Had the old couple rented to this foreigner for just long enough to pay for the air-conditioning units, but — crucially — not long enough to pay the commission to the guy who set up the rental for me?

The agreement stated that the "rental agent" would only get his payoff if I stayed in the flat for three months or longer. No chance of that now. The rental agent's name was Binh, otherwise known as the guy who'd sold me the Chinese piece of shit bicycle. I smiled inwardly at his lost commission. *Karma*.

I slurped from my chipped bowl right down to the gritty bottom, paid the meager fifty-cent tab, and went next door to the howling market to buy the landlord's wife a bundle of flowers. She'd made me ginger rice soup when I'd caught a cold, and I knew the beating she was getting upstairs, though of course flowers hardly helped with that.

The couple looked ecstatic as they watched me leave, squeezed into a cyclo. My meager possessions were stuffed into two large rucksacks, one on my lap, the other under my feet.

Soon after my move into a new four-story, one-room-per-floor home, I began teaching Vietnamese government ministers, senior officials, and their favored underlings in the cultural attaché's office of the British embassy, just down the street from the uninviting, closed, and wooden-shuttered windows of the North Korean embassy. The office of the cultural attaché, which would later become a fully fledged British Council office, was desperate for qualified teachers. They headhunted Brits at the foreign-run school where I was teaching and asked me to cover some lessons. After a two-month evaluation of my abilities was over, I was offered a contract.

My eldest student at the embassy was eighty-seven years old, a decorated war hero with a heart condition. One minister always came to class by bicycle. This impressed me enormously — how very communist — as did my students' ability to come to class three times per week for three hours at a time. For students who were also ministers, deputies, or in other ways "senior," this seemed like a huge amount of time to be away from their other, more important, desk.

If I found myself at the office working on a Saturday morning, I sometimes got my kicks drinking tea, eating peanuts, and attempting something close to chatting with the locals. There was a tea stall just down the road from my office. It was located next to a street hairdresser. The barber (or "the butcher," as I nicknamed him — I never did learn his real name) first set up shop next to a wall outside the Vietnamese Ministry of Foreign Affairs, opposite the North Korean embassy, on Cao Bá Quát Street, in 1995. I only ever let him cut my hair once. I kept a distance from him after that.

At the tea stall, I had a good view of the embassy opposite. I'd wait to see if the North Korean ambassador's car would appear. It was a 1960s four-door black Mercedes-Benz 220S, the exact same model that Blofeld's henchman drove in the James Bond film *On Her Majesty's Secret Service*. I only ever spotted it a couple of times, but when I did, I'd down my tea, kick my navy blue Belarusian Minsk motorbike into gear, and trail the Mercedes around Hà Nội until it came to a halt, at a Korean restaurant or a nondescript house in the suburbs. And that was the end of the pointless game.

When I originally signed the work contract with my then boss Jasper, a large Brit with a black mustache and stubby fingers that he would use to batter a poor, defenseless laptop, I hadn't examined the bit of paper very carefully. I figured it would be all right. British embassy connections and all that. I was in for a shock.

"So, that's your salary, insurance, flights, and shipping allowance all taken care of," Jasper said, spinning this way and that in his black leather swivel chair. "There's the rental allowance, but don't worry if you don't spend it all, it's nonaccountable. Oh, and of course, there's your hardship allowance."

"Hardship?"

"Yeah. Việt Nam's classified by the British government as a hard place to live. You get an allowance to live here."

"You're kidding."

I was genuinely bamboozled. The noise, the dirt, and the pollution might be a pain now and again, and the roads a bit dangerous, but to call living in Hà Nội a hardship? Who drew up the hardship ranking? How did they rank countries?

And which other ones were on that list?

"So, how much do I get for my sufferance?"

"It converts, at the moment," Jasper said, tapping away at his laptop, "to about U.S. $800 per month."

My rent was less than $300. Utilities were $50 or so. I ate street food every day for pence. The reality was I didn't even need my salary. I could never spend it. With the leftover from my rental allowance, I had $1,000 to spill on the streets before I even touched my salary.

There was a story making the rounds about a former British ambassador to Việt Nam who went to one of the few minimarts in the capital in the mid-nineties and blew his proverbial gasket when he saw that everything in the shop, from yogurt to orange juice to chocolate bars, was past its sell-by date. The poor, deranged diplomat chucked the groceries on the floor, screamed in upper-class English, and stormed out to his chauffeur-driven, air-conditioned car. Ah, the hardship. Nay, the horror.

"Oh, and there's forty days' holiday a year," Jasper called to me as I was leaving his office, making my way across the balcony, befuddled at the ridiculousness of it all.

"And don't forget UK holidays," he shouted to me as I continued away. "And the Vietnamese ones too, naturally."

I'd hit the most ludicrous jackpot of my life.

And, yet, less than a year later, I'd decide to give it all up.

CHAPTER EIGHT:
TẾT

It was the second-worst toilet I had entered in Việt Nam.

The first-worst wasn't exactly a latrine: it was a wall. It had been used as a toilet through the millennia, and had gained a certain reputation as a piss magnet, but by any accepted dictionary definition, it was *not* a toilet.

The one and only time I used the first-worst toilet in Hà Nội was toward midnight, halfway through a warm beer and a dish of peanuts at a sidewalk stall. The stall was a short motorbike hop from the three-story, three-room house I was now renting in a cash-in-hand, no-contract-and-no-questions deal on Lý Nam Đế Street, which ran parallel to the eleventh-century citadel, west of Hoàn Kiếm Lake.

I'd taken over the rent from a friend who had worn out his tenure in Việt Nam after a two-year quagmire of failed relationships, lost money, and drunken brawls. He'd shipped west, to Bangkok, to repeat the process.

Where the path jags at right angles on Ngõ Trung Yên is a small tea stall. It sits, as all good tea stalls do, at knee height. A banyan tree provides a canopy, and extra cover comes from sheet tarps and the tall houses, hotels, and shops that seem to continuously grow higher and higher, a floor at a time, five, six, seven floors up, in this part of the capital.

In the morning, the local men bring out their thrushes and bulbuls — one or two to a cage, seven or more cages in all. They hang them on the tree, or on the edge of a tarp. The birds sing to each other, to no one, to everyone. The idea is that the birds socialize with other birds, from behind their bars, in between pecking at seeds and quarter lemons jammed into the gaps in their cages. Hanoians sip tea, gobble bún cá — fish noodle soup — at number 5 opposite, and buy fruits from the seller in front of a house called Triều Nguyễn. And the birds sing from behind their bars.

That was the daytime scene. By night, there was little more than the tea stall open.

"Nhà vệ sinh ở đâu?" I asked the tea-, peanut-, beer-, and cigarette-selling matron, who conducted business by the light of a paraffin lamp on a wooden table. *Where is the bathroom?* She directed me down a soot-black alley.

Upon reaching its soiled conclusion, I entered

126

an eight-by-five-yard concrete quadrangle, open to the sky and pegged in on three sides by a series of fraying apartments. The enclave reeked of ammonia, but I couldn't find the toilet, or any unlocked door that might lead to a toilet.

I padded back along the alley and asked the lady again.

"Có nhà vệ sinh không có, phải không?" *There isn't a toilet, right?* I asked.

In truth, my Vietnamese never really got more sophisticated than that: soliciting directions, navigating menus, deciphering street stall signs, and telling a dangerous driver or two to go and do something unsanitary, and most definitely illegal, to their mother. I knew enough to know that much of the dialogue during the Russian roulette scene in *The Deer Hunter* was not Vietnamese, but not enough to know what it was the Thai actors playing the Việt cộng should have been saying if they really had been Vietnamese.

As Vietnamese women are wont to do, this kindly soul took matters into her own hands. She got up, left her stall, and marched me back down the corridor. We reached the courtyard and, radiating satisfaction, she raised an arm and gestured at the wall, as if to say, "*Voilà*. It's still there, where it's always been, dummkopf. Don't you know a toilet when you see one?"

Even under the glow of a quarter-moon, I could tell it was a very stained wall, and by God it stank, but it was not what I'd been expecting when I asked for the vệ sinh.

The matron retreated back to the street to continue the conversation with her one other client. Instinctively, I held my breath, pinched my nose, and stood a good half-yard back from the wall before letting go. Even so, the stench coiled around me like a chemical snake. It permeated my clothes, my hair, and my skin. I finished my midnight beer, then puttered home and into the shower for a thorough decontamination.

After experiencing the first-worst toilet in Việt Nam, it would only be fair to acknowledge that the second-worst toilet in Việt Nam did at least resemble a toilet, albeit one from the nastier end of the medieval era.

There were no lights to illuminate the cavernous labyrinth leading to the second-worst toilet, at the bít tết (beefsteak restaurant) on Lý Thái Tổ Street. It was not labeled, but the reek behind one chipped and battered wooden door revealed my target. The door had once been painted white, but had since matured into a half-yellow, half-brown shade of speckled splendor.

The door was stiff on its rusted hinges, and had to be forced back into place with a screech of warped wood on wet concrete before I could swing the bolt home. Behind this was a light switch.

The filament was luridly dim. It would have

been more appropriate to find it hanging from a brothel ceiling than inside this john. It was nowhere near sufficient for this communal privy. However, the less than half-light afforded a faint view of two things:

1. A shit-filled hole in the floor; and
2. A heavy plastic barrel full of water with a plastic thermos flask cup bobbing on top.

I stood over the hole, held my breath, pinched my nose, and peed. I attempted a "clear up" with a couple of cups of water directed into the abyss, but my efforts did nothing to budge the resident floaters.

That was one busy WC, I thought as I made my way back into the restaurant. This one toilet served the restaurant clientele, plus the legion of residents who lived in the firetrap apartments stacked above, behind, and to the side of it.

Back in the restaurant, there were three lines of tables. The ones nearest the wall fans were the most sought-after. A revolving breeze was the best form of attack against the persistent drizzle of fat generated on the furnace out front, which took on a cloud form just under the ceiling and drifted gently down like snow upon the diners ensconced inside, drenching all in a close-fitting, sticky layer of beefy lube.

Bít tết is like walking into a coronary. It is Hà Nội comfort food bar none. A thin slice of beef comes with three (count them) potato fries, a token sprinkling of green onions, a fried egg, and a ball of peppery coagulated cow blood.

Bít tết arrives spitting at you on a fiercely hot, cow-shaped metal plate with a baguette and a side dish of pickled cucumbers. It's the greasiest dish in the east and, despite the condition of the washroom, this restaurant had fast become both my regular after-work dinner stop and a weekend hangover cure, such were bít tết's addictive and curative properties.

A student called Lâm first introduced me to the place after a long day traveling together through northern Việt Nam, chatting about his future and my future, but mostly his future. He had more important things on his mind than hunting down decent street food shacks.

He was a short man with a wispy mustache and hair neatly cropped at the back and sides. His piercing eyes darted this way and that, either to aid his thought processes or to spy women passing behind my back. He spoke rapid-fire English, delivered with the slightest of stutters. Lâm's mother expected him to marry next year. The fact that he didn't have a girlfriend, in the latter half of 1998, was not an issue. He would be married in 1999.

Enveloped in the bít tết's greasy fog, we discussed premarital relations between men and women, both in England and in Việt Nam. I said it was most likely, even highly preferable, that I would end up living with someone long before the possibility of rings entered the arrangement. I may even live with someone and never marry her.

"We want all of that. We want that kind of freedom, but we can't have it," said Lâm. As the spitting subsided, he hacked his cut of cow.

He grinned, shook his head, and glanced to the street and the 50cc river flowing by.

"It's not just a money thing."

Vietnamese culture dictates that you live with your parents before marriage. After marriage, the wife moves in with her new husband and the in-laws. The first son is seen as the security, pension, and well-being of aging Vietnamese parents. The daughter-in-law must do what the mother-in-law desires. Failure to do so would be — well, it would be undesirable.

"Wife and mother-in-law relations are one of the biggest problems for newly married couples," Lâm told me. "If they don't get on . . . it can get tough."

Standing up to leave, I looked up at the dwellings on the first, second, and third floors on the opposite side of the street. Each and every one of them was barred with iron railings. I was reminded of those birds at that café. The Vietnamese — rich, poor, or avian — lived life behind bars.

The following year, I ended up spending Tết, the Vietnamese New Year, with Lâm's family in their small two-story house in Lệ Mật, over the Red River. It was February. He still wasn't married, but had until December. And his mother had an eye on the clock.

"Tết hasn't been as much fun since they banned fireworks, after the local authorities set off a twenty-foot-high rocket," Lâm lamented. "The explosion could be heard all over Hà Nội," he added, flicking through a small scrapbook full of photographs. "Some houses were badly damaged."

We were in his cubbyhole of a bedroom, a nest carved ingeniously out of the tiniest of roof spaces. The walls were lined with faded color clippings from foreign newspapers of an eclectic selection of movie stars, singers, and politicians: ABBA, Pamela Anderson, Boney M, JFK.

If you'd chopped my legs off at the knees, I'd have been able to stand in Lâm's bedroom and fit snug in his bed. As things were, his room was a bit of a doll's house for my frame.

"Didn't anyone think a twenty-foot-high rocket filled with gunpowder might be slightly dangerous?" I asked as he passed me a photo of himself as a teenager with his classmates at

Hoàn Kiếm Lake.

"Oh, they put it in the middle of the street, to be safe. It was a bit more powerful than they imagined."

We could smell the nem (spring rolls) bubbling in the wok downstairs. "She eats too many of those," said Lâm of his mother. "That's why she's so fat."

The nem were good — packed crispy-tight with black mushrooms, glass noodles, minced pork, crabmeat, carrots, and garlic, and seasoned with nước mắm and black pepper. It was Tết eve. We supplemented the spring rolls with steamed bamboo, Bia Hà Nôi, and an entire bottle of Chivas Regal, quite an upgrade from the usual Johnnie Walker Red Label.

"I know a guy in customs." Lâm smiled. "He helps with things like this."

We talked all night. One sentence in particular struck me during our conversation.

"When I was growing up, there was no meat," said Lâm, a child of the mid-seventies. "It was very rare that we ate it. Only on very special occasions, like Tết. But we kept it secret, in case the neighbors wondered where we got it from."

I'd heard a variation on this story a number of times before from other acquaintances, most notably from Hương, my American friend's Vietnamese wife.

We were sitting in a crammed, enormo-dining

133

warehouse on the eastern shore of Hồ Tây, known as West Lake, eating grilled snakehead fish, boiled chicken, and medicinal snails. The snails, ốc hấp thuốc bắc, were loaded with traditional Chinese herbs, stems, roots, branches, dried sea horse, ginseng, and the like, which all contributed a thick, heady aroma to the sauce and an earthy, dark depth to the flavor. This combination was a folk remedy and cure-all, said to help with coughs and colds. Hanoians also believed it to be particularly good for pregnant women. I found the same potion in use at a popular chicken restaurant. Any time I visited the "black chicken" — gà tần thuốc bắc — restaurant on Tống Duy Tân Street, I'd be greeted by row upon row of expectant mothers uncomfortably crouched on stools, supping at their folk remedy chicken soups.

The noise of diners in the West Lake warehouse, loud and loaded on beer, was excruciating — like the caterwauling twang of piano strings snapping, feline pain, and power struggles, liquidized into something unsavory. Hương and I were shouting at each other just to have a conversation.

Bellowing, I asked, "Why do they always have boiled chicken in Hà Nội? It's everywhere. It's way harder to find roasted or grilled chicken."

"We had chicken maybe three times a year when I was young. We always boiled it. I guess this reminds us of those days. That taste, you know," she bellowed back, dipping a chunk of tender white chicken breast into the tiny bowl of salt, lemon juice, and pepper.

"But why boiled?" I quizzed her. "Grilled is pretty damned good too." I'd become a bit sick of the sight of an unadorned, unimaginative boiled chicken. You'd see them lining the street-side front-room restaurants as the sun went down, inexplicably drawing in the motorbike-driving passersby: forlorn, simply boiled chickens. I didn't get it. Where was the imagination? As it turned out, the reason, or at least one of the reasons, had a hardcore communist-era tinge to it.

"We couldn't grill it or roast it back then," said Hương of her early-eighties teenage years in Hà Nội. "We lived in a very small apartment on the ground floor. If we had grilled the chicken, the neighbors would have smelled it, got suspicious, and informed on us. We had to contain the smell, cover the pot completely, cook it slowly, and close all the windows and doors."

Another friend, a secretary called Lý who worked for an import and export company, told me the same story.

"We had money, a villa, and we lived in a rich part of Hà Nội, but we were rationed like everyone was back then. The only chickens we ever ate were sick, old, or had died naturally. You didn't kill a healthy chicken. It was too valuable."

As the Tết evening steamed ahead on a steadfast course toward insobriety, Lâm and his family were lying, sitting, or slouched on the floor. We were on to envelope handing-out time. This was when the elder generation dished out the red envelopes filled with crisp, clean đồng to the younger generation.

"I should get you back," slurred Lâm, his eyes Chivas-red, at 11:30 P.M. "It's bad luck if you're not in your home before midnight."

I reminded him that, as my home was thousands of miles away, I doubted I'd make it in time. Maybe travelers and expats get a waiver, I proffered. In any case, I fancied a bicycle ride home, across the river, to catch the sights and sounds of my first Tết. Lâm didn't need to give me a lift. After a bottle of Chivas, I thought better of risking both our lives. Safety in fewer numbers.

"And tomorrow," I said, "I have my bánh chưng to enjoy." Lâm made an "Mmmm . . . delicious" murmur in anticipation of the traditional rice, pork, and bean dish served at Vietnamese New Year. And, with that, I was on my way.

I had been looking forward to three things at Tết:

1. My mai tree flowering
2. Eating bánh chưng

3. Seeing the action on the streets

I'd heard so much about Tết from my students. As they talked about it, they'd go dreamy and enter some kind of mystical state. It was the one sentiment that united all the Vietnamese I had met. Tết freakin' rocked. And I was gonna love it.

When I awoke on the morning of Tết, the first thing that became apparent was my throbbing head. Lâm's whiskey was exacting its revenge in a series of repetitive dull thuds, aches, pains, and groans.

I sauntered two floors down into the kitchen. I wanted to see my mai tree. A group of students had rallied together to buy it for me.

"Put it in water," they told me. "It has beautiful yellow flowers. If it flowers on the day of Tết, you'll have good luck for the coming year."

It stood there, leaning against the window in the cold, humid air, jammed inside a large plastic water bottle with the neck cut off. I checked the buds. There were signs of life, but not a spot of yellow on the entire branch.

That's me screwed for the year then, I thought to myself. *And I never ended up buying the carp for the kitchen god either. Oh deary, dear.*

On the twenty-third of December, I was told, I had to buy a live carp for my kitchen god. He was called Ông Táo. And he would, apparently, use the carp to travel back to heaven to report on the goings-on at my stove over the previous year. Whether I'd been a good cook or not, how many plates I'd smashed, dishes I'd burned, and bad deeds I'd conducted within the cooking space.

I figured Ông Táo had long since left. I'd never so much as turned the stove on.

So, my mai tree spelled doom. My kitchen god was likely furious with the philistine he'd been dumped with. What was left? Ah, yes, my bánh chưng.

My students had rhapsodized about bánh chưng.

"It's SOOO good," said one. "You must get one for Tết. You'll see. It's delicious."

In the weeks running up to Tết, bánh chưng was difficult to avoid. Shops and markets were full of them. Women trundled trays of the things all over the city, alongside the pretty kumquat fruit trees — another Tết essential — you could often see being transported on the backs of motorbikes.

I was skeptical about my students' praise of bánh chưng. On paper, it seemed like a hard sell: glutinous rice cooked into a mulch, mixed up with mung beans and fatty lumps of pork. Season it and squash it into a brick, wrap it up inside a banana leaf, and tie it with a red ribbon. It weighed about the same as a pudgy baby.

I bought mine from a bicycle-pushing seller I bumped into on Tràng Tiền Street. She was surprised that a foreigner would want to buy such a thing, but pleased at the same time, I figured. I didn't even have to bargain. I got it for the price my students had told me to pay for it.

On the other side of my bánh chưng skepticism sat curiosity. Could they be serious? Could this thing actually be good? If it was so popular, why didn't they eat it year-round? And, why had I never seen people eating it on the streets? They eat everything else on the streets, why not this? Was it that sacred?

I'd arranged for two friends to come over for the grand opening. They were both American. One was doing doctoral research into something technical — something to do with mapping, and something I didn't understand. The other was a teacher and an aspiring writer, like me. They were both called Matt.

I dropped the bánh chưng on the small metal kitchen table and proceeded to unwrap it. There were layers upon layers of leaves, as if an entire tree had been used to wrap the stodgy square. There were enough leaves to fill a bin bag.

As the last leaf fell away, what greeted us was a lumpy, unappetizing brick. We looked at each other.

"Well, you bought it. You should go first. It's only fair," said one of the Matts.

I took a spoon and spaded out a corner. The spoon bent under the weight as I raised it to take a bite. As I was expecting, it was chewy, gloppy, and heavy. What I wasn't expecting was the taste. There was none. Zero, just a stodgy texture, the faintest whiff of pepper, a hint of bean somewhere far away in the distance. I chewed some more. The two Matts looked at me, their spoons still lying on the table.

"Well?"

I swallowed the reduced lump.

"It's great, guys. Dig in."

The two Matts took a spoon each and extracted a lump from the dead weight plopped upon the sagging table. They chewed, screwed up their faces a little.

"Sheeze, that's crap," said graduate student Matt. "What the heck is the big deal with that?" said teacher Matt. "I've heard nothing but bánh chưng this and bánh chưng that for weeks from my students. That's it? This, this . . . *blob*?"

We put our spoons down, and I opened the bin and jettisoned the bánh chưng. We needed an alternative lunch plan.

"The R&R should be open," said one of the Matts referring to the bar named after both rock and roll and military slang for "rest and relaxation. "They do a pretty good burger."

Without another word, we put on our coats and headed out onto the street.

140

The silence. That's what struck me first. So deafening and unexpected was the silence that my hangover immediately fled in surprise as my brain adjusted to the alien environment. Then there was the emptiness. It was almost midday. Where there were usually hordes of street vendors, there was a barren pavement, bereft gutters, and shuttered doors. I'd never seen Hà Nội like this before. I thought, *My students were right, I am gonna love Tết. It's peaceful.*

We arrived at the R&R. I explained our bánh chưng catastrophe to Hương, whose Grateful Dead–loving husband was working the CD player in a cloud of cannabis.

"But no one eats it like that," she said. "You have to slice it and fry it and eat it with small pickled leeks. It's kinda gross to eat it straight out of the leaf."

The two Matts looked at me.

"Anyway," said Hương. "Most people just put it on the altar. For the ancestors. They don't eat it."

The two Matts looked at me again.

"Well, I didn't know. No one told me you had to do anything with it," I said. "Or, even, nothing with it."

We ordered a burger each, and three cold Halidas. We clinked bottles with a "Chúc mừng năm mới" (Happy New Year) and let the burgers lay their calming Western food opiates over us

141

as Bob Weir wondered aloud what in the world ever became of Sweet Jane.

CHAPTER NINE:
TAKING THE VINA-PULSE

I spent most of the eighties, most of my life, riding around in somebody else's car, in possession of, or ingested of, something illegal, on my way from something illegal to something illegal with many illegal things happening all around me," a famous, reptilian rock star allegedly once said.

Those words spoke to me. And this is how I later interpreted them to fit my reality:

"I spent most of my time in Việt Nam riding around on somebody else's motorbike, in possession of, or ingested of, something delicious, on my way from something delicious to something delicious with many delicious things happening all around me."

And, while the lizardlike rock star and I had a rather different line in recreational pursuits, we both found ourselves existing in a habitat that we navigated purely on the basis of the next fix. In my case, it was the next delicious thing. And, increasingly, I was writing about those fixes.

Noting down where I ate, what it was like, and whether or not I would recommend it. I had no outlet for these notes. At least not yet.

And the Vietnamese, as I very quickly learned, were more than happy to feed my habit. The streets were lined with pushers, pimping a variety of food highs.

Vietnamese people were always preparing something to eat, cooking something, buying something to cook with, talking about what to cook, eating something they'd cooked, eating something somebody else had cooked, talking about how good or bad what they'd cooked was — always eating, cooking, and talking about eating and cooking.

It was an intense, ongoing bombardment, although it appeared to have done little to expand the national waistline (with the possible exception of the phở sellers, who often packed a paunchy fold or two). Eating well and often, but not too much, always fresh food, and rarely from a packet, probably helped keep the nation lean. I've yet to see a Vietnamese person in Việt Nam shove a maxipack of Cheetos and a box of Oreos down their gob of an evening. Conversation over and about cooking and eating only seemed to extend an appetite to seek out the very best stuff to cram down the collective gullet.

The national food obsession extended itself to restaurants, but while the Vietnamese would hold loyal to street stalls and their resident chefs, where quality was the norm, restaurants were a different matter. Their reputations would wax and wane with word of mouth, and there was no guarantee that the current flavor of the month would still be the hot new thing in four weeks' time.

A distasteful serving of tofu one week, a dismissive "Oh, no one goes there anymore," and the hordes would already be on to the next big tofu thing on the other side of town by the end of the following week. "This is where everyone goes now. Not that other place. That's total garbage now."

For a foreigner like myself, this meant I had to keep my finger on the ever-shifting Vina-pulse and accept a sudden change of direction whenever one was suggested to me.

Take one of Hà Nội's most famous dishes, chả cá — fried fish with turmeric, dill, and cold noodles. The dish became so synonymous with one family on one street that the street was named Chả Cá Street. The family name was attached to the dish — Chả Cá Lã Vọng. Chả Cá Lã Vọng was then recognized as an official legal trademark in 1989. Ever since, most fish-eating visitors to the capital have found themselves at some point winding their way up the rickety stairs of number 14 Chả Cá Street to sample the famous fried fish dish.

I did it myself, and the food was excellent: chunks of catfish, sloshed in yellow turmeric oil, bag full of herbs, chopped peanuts, chilies, nước mắm, and mắm tôm, all mixed in a bowl with some cold noodles. It's an astounding dish. A true Vietnamese original.

However, there was a dark side to Chả Cá Lã Vọng. Or rather, several dark shades to the same dark side.

1. It was expensive.
2. The owners were stinkin' rich, and didn't make the slightest effort to improve the already shoddy restaurant.
3. And the service. The service. It always felt like having my toes stamped on, my face punched, and my nipples twisted. Eating at Chả Cá Lã Vọng was never something I looked forward to. The endurance test took away any pleasure the food itself held.

As one Hà Nội–based blogger called Teddy later put it, "There is no love inside that place."

This was a shame. I loved the dish, but soon after first trying it, I just couldn't bear going to the restaurant anymore to face the misery of the owners. I mentioned my grouch to Hương. She was one of the few Vietnamese women I knew who would speak her mind and lampoon the bullshit-infused elegies of her brethren.

"Pah, that bunch of dogs. No one goes there anymore." She laughed at me. "Everyone goes to Chả Cá Thăng Long now."

It was the first time I learned that surly service pissed off Hanoians just as much as it did non-Hanoians, although they were obviously far more used to it. Rather than put up with it, they found somewhere better and went there instead. And gradually, word spread.

But (and there's always a "but" in Việt Nam), go ask any Hanoian where the best place to eat chả cá in Hà Nội is. And they will almost all, to a man, woman, and child, point you up the stairs to Chả Cá Lã Vọng, even if they can't stand it themselves. Why recommend it? Because that's where all the foreigners go to eat chả cá. It's a vicious circle that feeds itself and profits only the owners, those gatekeepers to one of the more miserable corners of Hades.

Live a little longer in the capital, ask a few more questions, don't ever take the first answer to those questions, and you might just end up somewhere else. Somewhere like Chả Cá Thăng Long.

The "famous ones" folly is so very difficult to steer a safe course around. Even the educated youth of Việt Nam have been indoctrinated to give you a bum steer.

One day in spring, Hải had been unsuccess-
fully quarreling with the wires under my desk
for the best part of an hour.

"It's nearly lunchtime, Hải, let's finish this
later on, yeah?" I suggested to the twentysomething errand runner, screwdriver man, and
all-around go-to guy at the British Council offices. Hải held the keys to the fax machine. He
was also, by all accounts, the office's resident
spy. Ten dollars was the purported charge the
authorities paid him for every fax that exited the
building via his hand at the photocopier.

Spy stories were common. If you believed all
the tales, we were surrounded by hordes of secret agents. The bloke who gets on the bus, walks
around, looks at everyone, and gets off at the next
stop: spy. The neighbors: spies. The Vietnamese
intelligence officer who was, apparently, running a fake spy agency in Washington for years
and billing the Vietnamese government for his
fictive cables was my favorite yarn. Whether or
not it was true, I have no idea. Every diplomatic
office or foreign company had at least one member of staff who was known or believed to be the
resident spy. And Hải was apparently ours.

I didn't necessarily believe this slander, but
was given pause some years later, as a Vietnamese girl in the office announced she'd been
offered a job in London. I had helped her with
her application. Within twenty minutes of the

proud announcement — she was the first-ever Vietnamese recruit to a British government organization in an office outside Việt Nam — the Vietnamese secret service were in the office to interview her. Hải was the suspected informant.

Hải continued working the cables under my desk. It was a power connection issue, he'd told me. I wondered if he was fixing a frazzled wiretap.

Hải agreed that it was time to take a lunch break. From under the desk he asked, "Where are you going to eat?"

"I dunno, a bún chả nearby," I offered.

When I felt the need to get out of the office for lunch, I'd often end up at a street vendor's stall. Nine times out of ten, I chose a bún chả joint. I was addicted. In four years in the capital, I must have tried at least twenty-five different bún chả.

"Ah . . . You like Bún Chả Hàng Mành? Mmmmm . . . " Hải's voice had gone all dreamy under the desk. "Delicious."

This annoyed me. There are a small number of famous Hà Nội dishes that originate from the city, or nearby. They are:

1. Phở, the city's beef noodle soup
2. Bún ốc, snail noodle soup
3. Chả cá, fried fish with dill and noodles
4. Bánh cuốn, pork and mushrooms wrapped in a gloppy rice crêpe

5. Bún chả, the astounding lunchtime BBQ pork and noodles
6. Bánh tôm Hồ Tây, prawns and sweet potato fried in batter
7. Bún đậu mắm tôm, Nhung's simple fried tofu with stinky sauce
8. Bún thang, a sophisticated, light pork noodle soup
9. Tiết canh, raw goat, duck, or pig's blood soup. Visceral.

It's not a long list, but it is a proud one. And for each of these dishes, there is a designated "famous place" that serves the dish embedded within the psyche of each and every Hà Nội resident.

When it comes to bún chả, the one and only recommendation you will get will be Bún Chả Đắc Kim on Hàng Mành Street. At number 1, to be precise.

Bún Chả Đắc Kim was one of the first such restaurants in the capital, having originally opened in the 1960s. Some say it was the first. It was massively successful, and it was massively overpriced — almost double what you could find elsewhere in Hà Nội. Admittedly, the bowls were bigger, the helpings too, but the soul had drained from the lifeless restaurant's veins long before I ever arrived on the scene. It just wasn't very good. And Hải the spy knew this all too well, which was what annoyed me.

"Bún Chả Hàng Mành?" I spat the words at him, to emphasize my contempt. "That place is crap. They got lazy. I wouldn't eat there if it was the last bún chả in Hà Nội." (That last bit is not true. I would eat there, but I'd grumble about it.)

Hải came out from under the table with a smile on his face. "Yeah, you're right," he agreed. "It used to be the place everybody went, but no one goes there anymore."

"So, why the hell did you ask me if I was going there?"

"Because it's the famous one."

"It's famously shit."

"But everybody goes there."

"You just told me no one goes there anymore."

"Oh yeah, but it's the famous one."

Hải and I were stuck in an infinite feedback loop. We were going nowhere. I changed tack.

"Where do you eat bún chả?"

"My favorite is a small place halfway along Hàng Trống Street. It's not so popular, but to my taste, Mrs. Nga has the best sauce."

"Then why on earth didn't you recommend that one to me in the first place?"

"Because it's not the famous one."

We took my crotchety Minsk motorbike and sped out of the office grounds. I wanted Hải to show me his favorite bún chả. We rode down the

151

long Lê Duẩn Street, which led past the train station, took a left on to Hàng Bông Street, zoomed alongside all the art galleries, printing shops, and boutiques. Halfway through the Old Quarter, we took a right onto Hàng Trống Street. It was less than a ten-minute ride.

This was Nga's bún chả, just down the road from Nhung's tofu dispensary. Nga was a plumpish thirtysomething woman who had been selling bún chả in a corner here, next to an alleyway with bird cages hanging in the arch that led to her house, since 1993.

In the morning, from 6 A.M., she sold the Hà Nội breakfast powerhouse, bún riêu — a tofu, tomato, and crab noodle soup — in the same spot. Then, at midday, she switched to bún chả. It was good bún chả, but it wasn't cosmic, wave-parting bún chả.

I told Hải what I thought of his favorite.

"You've been eating too much of that bún chả on Lò Sũ Street," Hải would tell me. "It's too salty over there. Nga keeps her bún chả clean and light. You won't need two glasses of trà đá [iced tea] to wash her bún chả down."

Hải was right. I had become a little more than addicted to the bún chả on Lò Sũ Street. During my first encounter with the manager there, I didn't know whether to be impressed or depressed by the way she treated her clients.

One memorable lunchtime as I was just tucking

into my bowl of bún chả goodness, she turned to one straggler who, at least in her eyes, was taking way too long to eat his lunch. She told him, "Eat up and get out. I have people waiting. Can't you see?"

The old boy didn't say a word, but bolted his food down and did what the matron told him to. *Clear off and make way for more customers. Can't you see I'm trying to make a living here, scumbag?*

Whenever I related this scenario to Vietnamese friends and colleagues, I always came from a Western perspective, which in hindsight was quite wrong. Wasn't the customer always right? And if he wanted to dawdle over his noodles, grab a coffee, have a smoke, then couldn't he jolly well do so?

"No, of course he can't," came the response from a colleague one day. "It's not polite to just sit and talk, just smoking or something. You must leave. Other people are waiting. The stallholder is trying to make a living. She's not running a bus stop, you know. He should go somewhere else for a coffee and a smoke."

Years later, I asked the same question of the Hà Nội–based street food blogger Mark Lowerson, of the excellent *Sticky Rice* blog, who replied, "I really respect that attitude of, you know, 'eat the fuck up and piss off.' There's none of this grab-your-toothpick, faffing about, dillydallying, hanging around. It's a very no-nonsense approach."

And Mark had seen plenty of this approach after ten years in the capital, devouring anything and everything he could find that was tasty, whether it be from a street stall, front room, or double pannier carrier.

"That's what I like about going out with Vietnamese folk," said Mark. "There's no hanging around when the food's finished. You just get up and piss off."

There was a certain brutal honesty to dining out in Hà Nội. For all the work that went into the soup, spring roll, or sauté — twenty-four hours' preparation and cooking in many cases — the eating experience was the exact opposite — the bullet-train end of dining culture. Shovel it down, grab a thin bamboo toothpick, pay the bill, and, as Mark quite rightly said, piss off. It's an honesty that is at first jarring, but one I very quickly came to respect.

Madame Nga's bún chả was never one of my top ten favorites, but over the years of returning to the formidable woman's stall, I would probe a little into her thoughts on her trade and the future of street food in the capital.

As far I could tell, from a gut feeling more than anything else, we were living through a bit of a golden era. A time before an inevitable collapse. Things couldn't last, I thought. With increased wealth, things could never stay quite the same as they were. Or could they?

"This food will never leave the street," Nga told me emphatically, her raised voice approaching annoyance, like I'd just stabbed her kitten. Her customers all turned to look at me with faces that seemed to say, "Are you some kind of idiot? Of course, the food will never leave the streets."

To them, it seemed not to be a question, a possibility to ponder, a worry, a concern, or even an interesting intellectual diversion to discuss over fish sauce and grilled pork. It simply would not happen, and that, in Nga's mind, was the end of that particular conversation. Well, almost the end. I withdrew the knife from her kitten and looked back at her with a "Sorry I did that" look on my face.

"But . . . surely you have to concede, with development, with money, the government will probably want to smarten up the streets and turf the likes of you back inside?"

One customer chirped up. "OK. Maybe it'll be like Singapore one of these days. But not for one hundred years, mark my words." She then stuck her head back down under the bún chả manhole and waited for Nga's counterpunch.

And Nga was far from finished. She wasn't about to concede. As far as she was concerned, Hà Nội was not about to do a Singapore. Some of her customers weren't so convinced, and a heated argument erupted. Well, I say argument, but I'm not really sure what was happening. It was loud and long and drawn out, but seemingly good-natured under the surface. And Hà Nội is loud: the streets are loud, and so are the people. There's a Vietnamese proverb, which I quoted to them midfight:

"One duck and one woman is not a market. Two women and a duck is a market."

This seemed to calm the heat and they all — well, the women, anyway — burst into laughter.

"It's true, it's true, I confess," said one woman. "We're noisy. But, we like to talk. And WE LIKE TO BE HEARD."

Nga's bún chả always came with a small silver plate of minced garlic and red chili, along with garlic and chili vinegar, served from a plastic jug more suited to dispensing orange juice. I took a mouthful of noodles as Nga, her hair tied up in a bun, returned to the topic of the conversation while reaching down to ladle nước mắm into the bowls of two recent arrivals at her corner.

"Look, even if Hà Nội gets richer and richer — beyond our wildest dreams, even in one thousand years, the food, the streets. Will. Never. Change. *NEVER*."

I liked Nga's confidence. Then I looked at my watch. Hmmm . . . it was around 11 A.M. She was just getting started selling bún chả for the day. The Vietnamese, I'd been repeatedly told,

156

have a great belief in auspicious dates, numbers, and, at restaurants and street stalls, customers. Especially the first customers of the day. Of which I was one.

Did Nga think I was jinxing her day? Was my cloud-of-doom prophecy for the street food business of Hà Nội a curse she wanted to lift for the rest of her day? Would she have to send someone down to the temple to place an offering to cast out my foul words?

I doubted it. She had a good wee spot in the Old Quarter, surrounded by offices and shops. There were a good number of passersby, and it wasn't too threatening a spot for the occasional foreigner to drop in. Though some foreigners more than dropped in, she told me.

"One American, he loved my bún chả so much he asked me to teach him how to make it."

Nga showed him. He picked it up quickly. He was good, she told me. So good, in fact, that one day he took over the barbecue in her house, where all the meat for her stall on the street was cooked, and delivered it to her whenever a new batch was ready.

"Oh, he was good. He knew what he was doing."

In between doling out the fish sauce into bowls and adding grilled pork belly and burger bites into the mix, Nga told me how easy it was to get a permit. "Dead easy. Anyone can get one." The only problem was the cops.

"You have to pay them off. Not officially, you understand. But, if you want to keep working here, it's a kind of a tax."

The brutality of the police raids was the thing that always struck me. At that time there were no laws, only "guidance" pertaining to street food sellers. It was the kind of guidance whose enforcement was based on the whim of whoever was in charge of whichever sector. The cops would kick over stands, pots, and baskets, grab everything, and sling it into the back of a truck. The show was over within ten minutes. There was a clearly demonstrated dislike of street sellers, a yearning from up on high to scrub the streets of the life I'd come to love. It was action like this from the authorities that also gave me pause when considering the future for the likes of pavement dwellers like Nga.

"But what makes your bún chả special?" I asked her. "There are so many all over Hà Nội, but they're all a little different from each other. What do you do?"

"I'm not telling you that."

And, true enough, she never did tell me, though she did share her view that there were four key elements to bear in mind when creating and consuming quality bún chả.

"First, you need your own way to make it. A way that's suited to your taste. If you like it, the

158

chances are that other people will, too. I have my special tricks and ingredients.

"Then, you have to make sure that the meat you use is fresh and fatty. It has to be fatty.

"Don't use too much sugar in the nước mắm. Be careful how you balance what you put into it, and keep it warm. If the nước mắm isn't warm, the fat will rise to the top in little greasy globules. It doesn't taste good, and it looks bad.

"Lastly, make sure you eat it while it's still hot."

To look at her, she was all aglitter. Her blue-and-silver-painted fingernails were bright and shiny, and she wore a dark gray top with a silvery, glinting flower motif around the neck and down the center of her chest. Magpies woke up dreaming of targets like Nga. Was she the most glam bún chả stallholder in Hà Nội? I suspected she might be.

As she talked, Nga served another four customers.

"I've never changed my recipe and I never will. The only thing that changes is the price. The cost of the ingredients changes. So, my costs go up and down with the market."

So, does Nga have a great love for bún chả? For cooking in general?

"Oh, I'll never change my job. Cooking is what I do. I'm happy with that. Bún chả is popular with everybody in Hà Nội. It's the most logical thing to serve here."

If there was ever any left over at the end the afternoon, she'd eat it herself, with her family. If it was all gone, which was a good thing, then she'd go and eat at the cơm bình dân (food for workers) cafeteria on the floor above and behind her stall.

Just one woman helped Nga at her stall. She'd do the menial tasks: clear the decks, wash the plates, and sling the leftover noodles and fish sauce into the gutter. If Nga had to shoot down the alley to grab a new fix of meat from the grill and the helper was busy, a regular customer would take over the helm, dish out the food, and handle the cash.

I got talking to one woman who took over the helm one day. I asked her what her job was.

"I'm an accountant. I work in a small office just around the corner. I've been coming here for years."

Imagine this in New York, Paris, or London, or anywhere else outside of Southeast Asia:

1. An accountant eating at a street stall to begin with; and
2. An accountant deigning to take over the running of the business for ten minutes while the boss nips out.

But, that's Việt Nam.
Nga told me she served one hundred or more

customers per day, but she had never kept count, and had never thought to keep count. The bún riêu–bún chả stall, plus the income from a front room she rented out and the wage from her husband's job, paid enough for her eldest daughter to study hotel management in New Zealand.

I still didn't believe that Nga could look at all the wealth around her every day and still believe things would not change. I kept pushing her.

"Look. OK. The environment might change. The food might, one of these days, go indoors, but I'm telling you what will not change, what will never change, is the food. Never. Ever."

Short-term visitors to Việt Nam don't have the luxury of time to explore, make mistakes, eat bad meals, get bad service, and ponder the future of Vietnamese street food. The lifers and long-stay patients can afford to mess up and make mental notes of the good and bad places.

Like anywhere else, you learn your surroundings, know what signs to look out for, and follow your nose.

The other thing that can put visitors off eating in a place is, bizarrely, the presence of other foreigners.

Read any online forum, blog, or book and the foreign food explorer will always qualify a particularly good find with the fact that they were the only foreigners there. (Hell, I've done it in this book several times already, and I'll do it again.) Like modern-day Livingstones, we like to stick the flag of discovery in first.

"There were no foreigners there," screams the confident blogger. "Only locals. It's the best [insert name of dish] in Việt Nam."

Thus, we bestow upon the shack, shed, cart, or ignominious front room the blessed hallmarks of foreign authentication. Hallelujah.

There's a very specific look that foreigners like this give each other when they bang elbows over the blue plastic table. And to describe it accurately, we need to go back in time.

You're in the Antarctic. It's December 1911. It's rather cold. You are one of Roald Amundsen's team of men who had raced Robert Falcon Scott to be the first to the South Pole. Powered by a legion of huskies, you've won, and you've just planted the Norwegian flag at the South Pole. You're one of the first humans to make the journey. You have time to take a photo at the Pole and down a glug of brandy before you must head back to the ship. Midway on your return journey across the snow- and ice-blasted continent, you pass a befuddled Captain Scott and his doomed and exhausted team of four other men. For one second, across the white waste and crystallized air, your eyes meet with Scott's.

Yeah. It's that look.

CHAPTER TEN:
NOTHING WORKED

It was soon after my first Tết that the disillusionment began to set in with a weight similar to that of the bánh chưng block I'd binned. I'd begun to see glimmers of Alessandra, the enraged Italian, in myself. Mistrust, distrust, how I could take nothing at face value. Friends who appeared to be "in it" for something more than just friendship. There always seemed to be a predetermined goal in relations with people. Everybody seemed to want something from me, and from anyone foreign.

I helped an expat French friend pack to leave and go home one day. She had a bed and a wardrobe left over that she wanted to sell. The landlord arrived and understood the dilemma.

Rather than offer to buy them, he said, "It's better for you if you leave them here."

"How so? Are you going to pay for them?"

"No," he replied, a look of shock flashing across his face. "They're so big. It's better for you."

"Hang on." The French girl was shifting into turbo-pissed-off gear. "How can it be better for me to give them to you than to sell them to you?"

Smiling and giggling, the graying landlord could only reply, "It's better for you, surely you can see that?"

She had been all set just to leave the items in the house, but instead she got on her motorbike and woke up two friends who came and took the items off her hands and out of the reaches of the landlord. He had underestimated the power of peeving her for his own selfish gain.

But, it wasn't just that. It was the food, too. Oh, don't get me wrong, it was good. Well, it was pretty good. It just lacked imagination. The Asian food in my head was fed with nitrous-oxide-fueled spice. Food in Hà Nội was all a bit bland. Maybe I wasn't looking hard enough. But I think I was. Unhelpfully, I had Korea to compare Hà Nội to. And Hà Nội got trumped at every turn. I didn't know it at the time, but I'd need time away from Hà Nội to really appreciate what the city had to offer.

Work, too, was better in Korea. The people were fun, odd, interesting, and tough. To quote P. J. O'Rourke, "They don't like anyone who isn't Korean, and they don't like each other all that much, either. They're hardheaded, hard-drinking, tough little bastards." Or, "The Irish of Asia." Everything worked in Korea. In Hà Nội, everything was broken. Once repaired, things would work for a short time until they broke all over again. And the food. Oh, the food. I adored Korean food. Hà Nội kept shoving the swotty half sister from the countryside, with a dribbling nose, in front of me, while Korea had sumptuous delights on every corner.

I knew there was a better place. I'd been there. I'd lived there, and I'd gotten round to thinking that I wanted to go back.

Two events collided to make me decide. The first happened at the bít tết one night. It was as I fought back the fat spray from the black metal cow-shaped plate that Lâm told me of his dreams.

"Just to touch those stones in Oxford and Cambridge," he said. "To feel the history between my fingers. And to see Manchester United play at Old Trafford. Just once. This is my dream. This is my fantasy."

My dreams were not dissimilar, but were not sporty. To travel and live abroad was as sophisticated as I got. I'd done Korea and Việt Nam. I fancied Buenos Aires and St. Petersburg in the near future. Prague was of interest. Beirut had a certain gnarly pull and Japan also loomed in my thoughts.

Each week in the office, a bulletin arrived. The boss would attach it to the pinboard in the teachers' room. The British Council had offices all over the world, and vacancies aplenty. I scanned them and recalled what colleagues had said of each place: Burma (Not allowed to talk politics in the teachers' room), Saudi Arabia (Don't. You'll go mad), Bogota (Only cokeheads need apply), and South Korea. Lovely, concrete-filled, noisy, nutty South Korea.

The Hà Nội office was overstaffed as it was. I sat back at my desk and reread the e-mail I'd composed that morning, making an inquiry at the Seoul office. My hand hovered over the mouse and, tentatively, I hit send.

The reply came the same day. There was a job for me. I could move, if I wanted to. I asked my boss for a week to decide.

Unlike Lâm's dreams, mine were tangible. At my fingertips. By accident of a British passport and a postcolonial, global cultural institution, I could, within reason, go and work pretty much anywhere on the planet.

The second event happened when the power went out. It cut suddenly, as it always did. With no warning. One minute I was on an uncomfortable, dusty chair, watching a film alongside a young Hanoian couple who were romantically feeding each other strands of flattened dried squid. The next minute, a black blanket smothered me and everyone else as the clanking ceiling fans wound down in the makeshift cinema.

A short burst of involuntary squealing was

166

followed by a muttering ebb as the realization kicked in that this was just a power cut. I sat there in complete darkness, surrounded by strangers. Waiting for power. Waiting for someone to change a fuse somewhere behind the big screen, or to connect a generator, or just to reconnect a plug that had become disconnected. Or, perhaps the longer wait, for the power station to reconnect the entire district.

There was not much in the way of cinema in Hà Nội, and even less when it came to international films. The annual Hà Nội International Film Festival, such as it was, was convened in a shedlike structure on Trần Hưng Đạo Street. Tickets to the films were highly sought-after items about town. I'd managed to snag only one ticket, for the offering from Seoul, given to me by a diplomatic contact at the South Korean embassy. The power had cut out at about thirty minutes into the story, which was:

An unhappy housewife. An overworked husband. He always came home late, if at all, and he was having an affair. The wife didn't know what to do, so she did what she always did. It was a wretched tale. Every evening, she prepared a standard Korean dinner: meat, soup, rice, kimchi, and side dishes. She laid it out on a low table and waited. He never came home. At least not in time to eat.

Just as the camera panned across the dining

table, groaning with uneaten food, the power evaporated.

As if a blacksmith had branded the scene upon the back of my eyeballs, the Korean table scene remained firmly etched in my mind as darkness descended on the makeshift Hà Nội cinema.

I could see each dish clearly. I could name them. Smell them. Taste them. I could feel the warmth of the heating under the silky, flat floor cushion. Hear the gentle tap of metallic chopsticks clicking together as I picked up a shred of kimchi from the communal dishes and wrapped it around rice, as was my wont. And I could hear the loud exclamation of "Mashita!" (Delicious!) from my fellow diners.

In the five minutes it took for the fans to whir once more, for the film reel to ratchet back to life, and for the impression of the Korean table to gently fade, I had made my decision.

I desperately missed Korea. I wanted to go back.

I approached my boss. She'd been in the post for only a few months. She was in her late forties, but her skirt was about thirty years too high for her legs. Her severely pockmarked, deeply nicotine-creased face had earned her the rather unkind nicknames of "Noriega" and "Old Pineapple Face."

I was determined, confident, and, above all, decided.

"I'm gonna take it," I said. We both knew what the subject matter was.

"You're sure about this? There's no going back once it's agreed."

"Sure. I've given it plenty of thought. I'd be happier in Seoul."

"OK," she said, hacking and drawing on the dregs of her cigarette stub before tossing it over the balcony, into the car park with all the diplomatic and ministerial cars. She strode back into her office and picked up the phone to Seoul.

Later that day it was agreed. I would leave Hà Nội in two months. The process was unnervingly smooth. I had little in the way of stuff to off-load. I had accumulated few possessions. Everything I owned still fit into the same two rucksacks I'd moved to the country with. The only thing I would have to sell was my navy blue Minsk. I'd bought the Belarusian motorbike from a colleague who'd moved on the year before. I put a message on the sole, tiny e-mail discussion list for expats in Việt Nam.

I knew I'd be able to sell the bike without difficulty. Even if I didn't have time to organize it, I knew Cường — everyone's Hà Nội Minsk mechanic — would take it off my hands for a fair price and either sell it himself or rent it out. A good Minsk was a desirable bit of expat machinery in 1998.

The first reply, from someone named Sophie,

came the following day.

On that November morning, as I clambered down the office stairs on Cao Bá Quát Street to meet the "Vietnamese woman waiting in reception for you," I had no idea my life was about to alter tack. I was leaving Việt Nam. The DHL guy had collected my signed contract for a position at the British Council in Seoul not ten minutes earlier. I'd depart Hà Nội in three weeks, and I had no intention of returning.

I greeted Sophie in the reception area with a shake of the hand. Hoa, the heavily pregnant receptionist, gave me a cheeky smile. It was the smile of a Vietnamese woman seeing two single people of the opposite sex meet, and mentally fitting them out for marriage, a mortgage, kids, and a down payment on a joint headstone in a rice paddy.

Sophie wore a short black coat to ward off the chill, tight denim jeans, and shiny black leather boots. Her long, straight black hair betrayed her Vietnamese ancestry, but her manner was altogether European: calm, confident, and worldly. I was immediately attracted to her, which caused something of a problem, as I was about to leave. For good.

Next to food, the Minsk was my biggest pleasure in Hà Nội. I'd been nervous about learning to ride it. I'd left it at the office for two nights before braving the pedals for the first time proper.

Frank, an old Hà Nội hand and a British Council colleague, was half-German, half-British, fluent in Vietnamese, but too unhinged for his numerous, more stable, and ever fleeting Vietnamese lady friends to handle. He had agreed to teach me to ride the Minsk.

He expressed surprise at how quickly I picked it up over the course of one evening (although I felt distinctly wobbly for a time). To celebrate, we drove around the corner to Bia Tươi Hoàng Đạt at 124 Hai Bà Trưng Street for a drink. Almost as soon as we entered the Bia Tươi and ordered the first round of bò lúc lắc — shaking beef — the rainy season, unannounced, started. It poured and didn't stop. It was torrential. The streets were flooded. We were marooned on the upper level of the bar. We stared down at our sodden Belarusian machines.

By the time the shaking beef arrived, the ground floor was more than a foot under water. We had on our work clothes. We drank until midnight, hoping for it to stop. It didn't. We decided we had to leave. Neither of us had a change of clothes ready for work the next morning. Which is why, the first day I ever rode a motorbike in my life, I was drunk, in my boxer shorts, in the rain, navigating flooded streets at one in the morning, with my work clothes in my rucksack. It was quite the driving lesson.

It was a wrench to give the Minsk up. I'd priced

it at U.S. $500. Minsks had a bad reputation for breaking down, but young expats loved them — something to do with the allure of failed, or failing, communist states that I could never quite fathom. I just liked the look of the thing, and the choking *plut-plut-plut* it made as I sat at the traffic lights, belching lung-destroying fumes at my fellow bikers mounted on far more sensible and modern Japanese machines.

My Minsk, however, was a rarity in that it was reliable. It rarely broke down and, if it did, it was always something simple that even I could fix — the spark plug needed cleaning, tank needed a bit more oil, piston head needed a shake, back wheel required a kick, that kinda thing.

Sophie wanted to try riding it before buying. She'd never ridden one before. I offered to show her.

Unbeknownst to me at the time, her Belgian colleague, who had appeared and wanted to "vet" the bike with his superior mechanical know-how, had also offered to teach her to ride. Sophie, for some reason, chose me, the stranger, to teach her.

We agreed to meet for a Saturday morning lesson on a quiet side street running parallel to Kim Mã in the west of Hà Nội. It was quite possibly the only quiet stretch of road in the city.

After a couple of false starts — too many revs, trouble finding gears, the usual first-timer issues — she managed to pick it up. Once the lesson was over and she had, in principle, agreed to buy the bike for the asking price, I offered lunch, despite thinking, *No, you shouldn't, you're leaving. This could mess everything up, you moron.*

By now I knew that Sophie was the Laos-born daughter of a North Vietnamese mother and a South Vietnamese father. Sophie spent her earliest years in Vientiane, the Lao capital, and the family escaped Laos at the end of the war in Việt Nam, when Sophie was just seven years old. They settled in the south of France. She'd studied English at university. French was her first language, English a pretty good second, and Vietnamese was the "language of the family." She was single.

While I knew far less of the Vietnamese language than she did, and bucketfuls less of the culture, after a year exploring Hà Nội's back alleys and markets, I felt I had, by now, a fair handle on the nosh. I figured we were a safe bet for a street food lunch. I decided to take her to Captain Bún Chả's.

"Bún chả?" said Sophie with a quizzical look. "I've never tried that before. I've never even heard of it."

This didn't surprise me. Bún chả is a northern specialty, and here I was taking this French-Lao Việt Kiều, with a southern bias, into uncharted territory. After her six-month stint in Sài Gòn

173

working for a Francophone education project, a remnant of a faded empire the French refused to believe was over, Sophie's job had moved north. She'd only been in Hà Nội for a month or so. Her mother had been more disappointed about the move north than Sophie was, and I found out some years later that her mother had given her one piece of advice (really more of a threat) before she headed north.

"Whatever you do, don't bring back a Hanoian." This advice was not uncommon among a diaspora community that had known war.

Meanwhile, back on the street, I knew my ground. I was onto a winner. This clueless Brit at least knew his bún chả. And, although the captain could be a little erratic on the quality front, she usually managed to serve up a blinder.

"They're twins," Sophie said as we dismounted the Minsk and walked toward the stall. "The way she's talking, the twin at the grill must be the younger one."

I'd visited this stall at least once per week for over a year. I'd tried my ever-so-slowly evolving Vietnamese vocabulary out on them. They knew my name, that I preferred meatballs to the pork strips, that I liked plenty of crunchy rau muống curls in among my leaves, and that I took trà đá (iced tea) during the week, but if I popped in on a Saturday lunchtime, they should order me a bia hơi from down the road. I was a regular. Yet I'd never noticed that the bún chả women were twins. What appalling powers of observation I had. When I looked at them again, with these fresh eyes, I could see it. They were almost identical. Only their hair was different. The twin at the grill had a ponytail, while Captain Bún Chả let it all hang out. For Sophie, it was the language that had been the first giveaway: how the elder sister addressed the younger sister, born moments after herself. The order of their births dictated how they would address each other for the rest of their lives.

On that day, their bún chả did not disappoint — at least, to my mind, it didn't. Sophie, however, proceeded to pick the meal apart in a scarily analytical manner, like a coroner peeling back a cadaver's skin and working through a checklist of common ailments, looking for palpable cause of dissatisfaction.

"They should have used more sugar in the nước mắm, but that's the way they tend to do it in the north," she noted. "Plus, there's too much water in with the nước mắm for my taste. The meat could be fresher, too."

I was impressed, if confused. My analysis of bún chả up until this point had gone as follows: meat + herbs + noodles + nước mắm = good.

I couldn't intellectualize it, analyze it, understand it, or even taste it properly. In fact I didn't want to, but I was impressed that I'd met someone who could, with confidence, explain what it was I was eating.

Meanwhile, one of the twins had engaged Sophie in conversation. She turned to me.

"She's asking me if I can cook, and do I cook for you."

"Well, can you cook?" I asked her.

Not only could she cook, but she came from a family full of great cooks. Her parents, two brothers and a sister all had serious skills.

Why her, why now? I asked myself.

Years later, in Sài Gòn, we were at a friend's house in Bình Thạnh district for a dinner party. We were enjoying aperitifs. Olives, crisps, and cashew nuts had been arranged on the black lacquer dishes that every expat seemed to own. We sat down on the wicker sofa that every expat also seemed to own, and sipped and nibbled and bantered about the latest cultural misunderstandings that every expat seemed to have experienced.

"This gin and tonic tastes of garlic," announced Sophie as I grabbed a fistful of cashews and glugged from my 333 beer.

Every other G&T drinker in the room glanced at Sophie. Drinks were re-sipped. There was a collective shaking of heads in Sophie's general direction.

"No, I swear I can taste garlic," she repeated, a ring of confidence in her voice.

By now, she had headed to the kitchen with the host trailing behind her as Sophie went about her inquisition.

"Which knife did you use to cut the lemon?" she inquired.

Our host picked up the blade on the chopping board. Exhibit 1: a sharp knife with telltale lemon pips still clinging to the blade.

"And which knife did you use to chop the garlic for dinner?" Sophie followed up.

Exhibit 2: the same knife.

Every Vietnamese woman I have ever talked to about food has told me that she was taught to cook from a young age. None learned to measure ingredients, but rather to taste until, well, it tasted just so. I never once observed a shelf stacked with recipe books in a Vietnamese home or kitchen.

It took me a while to figure it out, but the concept of a Vietnamese recipe was entirely different from what I had grown up with. For each dish there is a set of ingredients, a method of combining and cooking them, and a tongue. The tongue dictates how much of what goes in and when. And the tongue tells the cook when it's ready.

Vietnamese tongues, I concluded, got to go to the taste gym for a workout from a very young age. As a result, they were extremely well trained and tuned in to the task of tasting. A lesson lost on many other cultures, not least my own.

One October, almost fifteen years after first meeting Sophie, I happened to be in Inverness, Scotland, at the northern end of Loch Ness. I took a taxi to the tiny village of Dores, on the B862 road, south of the Highland capital.

There I found Steve Feltham, monster hunter, in his now-stationary mobile library, surrounded by pebbles and a simple decking area made of disused wooden pallets. Some twenty years after his search began, the first year of which I'd watched in his condensed BBC TV video diary back in England in 1992, Steve was still hunting monsters.

We sat in his home and talked for three hours. Steve occasionally prodded the wood stove, in between molding the plasticine models of Nessie that he sold to tourists to keep him in food and beer.

"There are two types of people," said Steve. "There are those who meet a crossroads and take the predictable path, and there are those who take the unpredictable path. The former are the ones I met in my job installing burglar alarms in Bournemouth. I didn't want to end up like that. I knew what my dream was from when I was a very young child. It's about having a dream and following it, come what may."

It was with this same frame of mind that Sophie and I took a risk, took the unpredictable path, to see what, if anything, would happen.

Yes, I went to Seoul. I'd known Sophie for about a month. She visited me in Seoul twice. And four months after leaving the Vietnamese capital, I left the South Korean one to head back to Hà Nội, where I had no job.

Between us, we had one main point of common interest. Food. Vietnamese food.

The only friend I had in Seoul was a British guy called Andy Salmon. He was the restaurant critic on the *Korea Times* newspaper. His Korean wife, Ji-Young, was a chef and a food consultant. I went along with him whenever he reviewed a restaurant. He had originally moved to Korea to study hapkido. He knew Seoul well. His wife had the insider's view. By going along with them, I got an insight into how he worked, what questions he asked, and what details she would pick up on, and I'd collect little dabs of Korean culture that were new to me.

We ate stone-grilled samgyeopsal (pork belly), drank soju, and swallowed oysters well into the evening in Namdaemun market. We did an all-nighter upstairs in the sashimi rooms of the stupendous wholesale Noryangjin fish market, and made a habit of sitting stoolside for soup and booze inside the many orange-colored tents, known as pojangmacha, that magically popped up along Seoul's walkways come darkness.

Andy knew I was moving back to Hà Nội. He appreciated why. He'd met Sophie.

"Why don't you write a book about Vietnamese food?" he said. "You're always saying how good it is."

I looked at him.

"What?" I said.

"That barbecued pork you keep going on about. All the soups, the tofu thing, and the stinky purple stuff."

I hadn't noticed it until he said it. I was constantly proselytizing Vietnamese food to him in Korea, the same way I would preach Korean food in Hà Nội.

CHAPTER ELEVEN:
POISONED

A year or so earlier I had turned down the opportunity to work as the editor of the weekly *Time Out* magazine in Hà Nội. The writing I had been doing was very simplistic. Not something printworthy, at least not in my mind. But my friend Chris's advice echoed in my memory. *Get yourself a hobby.* I had my hobby. I just needed to resuscitate it upon my return.

I was fortunate. Sophie made a superb companion, willing to seek out anything interesting. Our life in Hà Nội rapidly became one long hogfest. Each evening began with the question of what to eat and where to eat it.

From Chả Cá Thăng Long on Đường Thành Street to Mì Hoành Thánh on Mai Hắc Đễ, we ate everywhere. In the winter, we'd head to a cháo gà shack on Hàng Bông Street, take in miến lươn xào on Hàng Điếu, nibble on ca nương and bánh tôm Hồ Tây on West Lake, slurp down bún ốc on Trúc Bạch Lake, and crack open tamarind crabs at one of the many seafood stalls on Tô Hiến Thành Street.

During our tenure in a two-room apartment on the middle floor of a three-story house at 78 Tuệ Tĩnh Street in central Hà Nội, we cooked at home a grand total of two times, once with devastating results.

We had decided to prepare a papaya salad one morning. We bought the fleshy fruit at Hàng Da market. We had everything else we needed at home, including a jar of mắm tôm that hadn't been opened for several months — the last time being the only other time we'd cooked at home.

I unscrewed the mắm tôm lid, and the contents, perhaps having been invaded by an ambient strain of something pernicious all those months earlier, immediately exploded up the kitchen wall, onto the ceiling, over the floor, and onto me. The kitchen was a massacre of fermented prawns. A scene from prawn hell. It was as if the largest and most evil prawn of the pack had picked up an Uzi and wasted his brethren in one breathtakingly stinky mass killing. I didn't envy forensics the investigation.

What was the point of cooking at home? Street food was always readily available. We were surrounded by the stuff. Not only that, but it was actually more expensive to cook at home than to eat the same stuff out on the street.

Last, and most important, we simply couldn't

match the food on the street with anything we could rustle up at home. We weren't good enough cooks, and we didn't have the time.

Vietnamese food, most of it, involves a lot of preparation. Sometimes it's cooked quickly, sometimes it's cooked for a long time, but in either case the preparation is always lengthy. And sometimes the cleanup operation is just as lengthy, too.

I was still mulling Andy's suggestion to write more about street food when my former boss at the British Council in Hà Nội asked me not only to come back to teach at the British Council on a part-time basis, but also to help produce an induction pack for new arrivals. Included among the information would be suggestions about what to eat in the city and where. It was sorely tempting to go down the "freak out the newbies" route. There was plenty of material, if you knew where to look.

I had done the fresh cobra blood thing, eaten a still-beating heart, drunk snake bile, ingested snake bones and snake penis whiskey, the whole seven, eight, nine courses. It was more of a challenge than a pleasure — a rite of passage for the dumb twentysomething in Việt Nam. However, my only residing memories of those evenings (five or six in total, I am ashamed to say) are as follows:

First and foremost, the look of utter horror on

Nghĩa's face as our group of eight foreigners proceeded to get stupidly wasted, blood pouring down our faces, like amateur thespians doing Dracula, badly.

Nghĩa, one of my first-ever students, the one who had first thrust a uterus in front of me, had recommended the place in Gia Lâm ("It's better than the famous one. There are more animals to choose from"), but he didn't touch a drop of the crazy juice all night. He drank a single bottle of room-temperature Heineken beer.

Second, the shakes. The morning after one of these foul, debauched nights, I woke up shaking. Not the DTs. This was different, something new and unexpected. It was as if someone had lit a fuse inside my arteries. They were on fire. I drove down to Mạc Đĩnh Chi Street to meet Frank, my motorbike-riding instructor.

"Oh, you've been poisoned," he said nonchalantly, like a bush doctor brushing off a patient with an inconsequential crocodile bite.

"What snake did you eat?"

"A cobra. A big one," I replied, the shock of what he'd said only just beginning to sink in.

"Have you spoken to anyone else this morning?" he inquired as he stirred a heaping teaspoon of sugar into his miniature, tar-black coffee. "The people you ate with? Are they OK?" A look approaching stern passed over his face for all of half a second.

"I haven't seen any of them."

"If your friends are still conscious, you'll probably be OK," he said reassuringly. "At least it wasn't a sea snake. I was off work for a week after drinking something with one of them in it."

"But, my blood. It feels like it's on fire," I replied, increasingly concerned at the convulsions wracking my body.

"If it were serious, you'd be dead already," he said, taking a large bite of his bacon sandwich. "Have a can of Coke and a bit of toast, you'll be fine."

Frank went on to bemoan the shocking state of the snake restaurant and alcohol trade in Việt Nam.

"Why can't they just wash the bloody snakes properly? God knows how many people die from eating and drinking in these places."

No. When it came to writing the induction pack, I decided to steer clear of the shock factor. I was over that phase of my life in Việt Nam. It wasn't big, it wasn't clever, and it wasn't (always) fun. Certainly not for the snake. But I did include one suggestion, a bar called Quán Béo at 74 Triệu Việt Vương Street, south of the lake.

It ended up being the unlikeliest popular drinking hole for the teachers. We'd go at least once per week for the dubious goat, bee, crow, and maggot brews. However, one evening at the rượu bar stood out in my mind. And there were no teachers involved on that night.

Haruko was a friend who was visiting from Japan. I took her to Quán Béo for an after-dinner nightcap at around 9 P.M., not foreseeing her distress.

We hitched the Minsk over the high curb and rammed it tight against the jaundiced wall, under the window of Hà Nội's most notorious rượu bar.

Haruko waited on the street as I kicked the bike back onto its stand, wiggled the stubborn key from its rusting slot, and popped it into my trouser pocket. She stood with her feet pointed inward in that endearingly cute or just plain weird Japanese way, her hands held in front of her as she stared up at the one-room bar.

Nghĩa had introduced me to Quán Béo one evening. Foreigners were still a novelty in these parts. Rượu — moonshine, often made with animals, herbs, and roots — was popular all over Hà Nội. It was mostly homemade, with every household seeming to have a vat-full rotting in the front room. Bars serving exclusively rượu were less common, but they were far from being a rarity.

Inside the bar were eight tables — three on one side, three on the other, and two in the middle. The side walls were lined with large glass jars filled with animals, insects, tree bark and the like, and alcohol. Next to one of the middle tables was a murky eight-foot-high tank. Behind the bar, at the far end, were lines of old Hennessy, whiskey, and cognac bottles. On the side of each bottle, the name of the particular concoction within was written in correction fluid.

We took one of the two spare tables in the house, right next to the imposing vat. At first, Haruko didn't notice the bear. It was a full-grown, mummified specimen, standing on its hind legs inside the tank of alcohol, mouth open, teeth flashing, tongue hanging out.

Methodically, Haruko's eyes scanned the shelves that cocooned us inside this grim alcoholic cave. From the middle of the room, she screwed up her face to focus more closely before it widened in surprise as she mouthed the words: "crow," "baby deer," "sea horse," "lizards," "bees" . . . and on it went.

"The lizard and sea horse is the best one I've tried," I offered, glancing through the menu that the waiter had slung upon our table. "I haven't tried the bear one, though. And I have no intention to."

I pointed at the vat behind her. She turned and looked through the murk, at the fur, before tilting her head back until her bob haircut hung at a forty-five-degree angle to her skull and she was eye to eye with the bear. She let out a squeak and drew her hands to her face, as if sweeping up her instinctive shriek and putting it back from where it came. It was clear her mouth remained wide open under her reddening knuckles.

She took some time to compose herself, released her hands, attempted a smile, and turned to face the other side of the room, away from the bear. More bottles, more alcohol jars, more men, cackling and cracking one shot after another of the dubious potion inside the opened Hennessy bottles on the table.

Pointing at the only other spare table in the joint, Haruko stood and insisted we move there, closer to the exit, away from the bear. She sat opposite me. Now she had a commanding view of the entire room from her far corner seat, but essentially she was nearest the exit.

I ordered two bottles of La Vie still water and a bottle of lizard and sea horse — rượu tắc kè, cá ngựa.

The bottle arrived with two fat shot glasses and two cold towels. On the bottle, barely legible, were the words "tắc kè cá ngựa." We wiped our faces and hands. I pulled the thirteenth-hand Hennessy cork and poured us a modest shot each.

Haruko looked at the shot sheepishly and twizzled the plastic covering to the water bottle top. She took the bottle in both hands, clipped the plastic off with her manicured thumbnail, unscrewed the cap, and took a long glug of water. She declined a shot of the firewater with a quick shake of the head. I took a sip.

And there it was. The taste. Like ethanol laced with tree bark and unwashed socks. The urine-colored moonshine was unlikely to ever make any cocktail-of-the-month shortlist.

I drank my shot, refilled my glass, and planted the cork back into the spirit bottle. Haruko was constantly looking over my shoulder, clearly out of sorts. I glanced at the shot left in my glass, determined that it would be my last before I took her back to her hotel on Trần Nhân Tông Street. She had to get up early the next morning to catch the 6:30 A.M. train to Huế. I moved my chair to one side in order to get a better view of the bar for myself.

Two Vietnamese men walked in and took the table we had recently vacated. They had on winter coats. Without looking at the menu, they muttered something to the waiter, then both folded their arms and sat still. Waiting, not talking.

I'd never noticed the cages at the back of the bar before. Inside were two large tắc kè lizards, which were commonly employed in a peculiar Vietnamese betting game. I'd write the following about the game some years later for the *Guardian*:

Somewhere in the rafters above a packed Vietnamese restaurant in Sài Gòn's district 3, a lizard clears its throat with a loud rattle. Down below, a small band of sozzled office workers picking at grilled chickens' feet and gizzards down chopsticks and begin shouting numbers from one to five. The unseen lizard, known locally as a tắc kè, begins its customary series of rhythmic croaks. It hits four and stops. A drunken roar goes up, cash is exchanged and the eating and drinking resumes.

However, no one in Quán Béo was betting on these tắc kè, one of which was seconds away from its own death. The waiter lifted the beast from the cage by its tail. The two-foot-long lizard wriggled from side to side in big, waving motions. The waiter lifted the reptile high in the air and thrust it down hard and fast so that its head landed with a dull crack on the bar. He raised it a second time, and again the lizard thudded into the mock marble counter to the soundtrack of a slow, sickly, lovelorn Vina-pop tune.

Just two punters, Haruko and I, took notice of the slaughter. She sat openmouthed, this time not covering her shock with her hands. And she didn't emit a mere squeak: she let out a full-grown yelp.

The barman placed two shot glasses on the counter as the waiter held the slumped lizard on its back. He used a sharp blade to cut an incision into the reptile's throat. He turned the dead beast over, its head pointing downward at a forty-five-degree angle a couple of inches above the shot glasses. Warm dark crimson blood poured into one glass until the waiter clenched the lizard's neck tight to stop the flow, releasing his grip above the second glass. When that glass was also full, he handed the corpse to the barman and delivered the two gruesome drinks, along with two glasses filled with đặc biệt rượu bìm bịp — special crow spirit — to the waiting customers.

Haruko fidgeted with the La Vie bottle. The two men caught our gaze, but without hesitation, they raised their glasses of what looked to be a particularly gruesome vintage of claret. They swallowed the fluid down in one gulp before gently returning their glasses to the table, picking up the measure of crow, and repeating the ritual.

One of the men, with his straight face looking into mine, reached into his pockets for a few đồng, placed them on the table, hollered to the waiter, and got up to leave. The man's scrunched-up nose telegraphed, "What the hell are you staring at? Have you never seen two grown men stop off after work for a couple of shots of fresh lizard blood and a crow whiskey chaser? What planet are you from?"

191

I've since lost touch with Haruko. I hope she's okay.

CHAPTER TWELVE:
NEVER MIND THE BOLLOCKS

The entire length of Lê VAn Hưu Street and the surrounding area was food central in Hà Nội. Sophie and I lived together on Tuệ Tĩnh Street, just a couple of blocks south of Lê Văn Hưu. To my mind, we were living close to Hà Nội's most replete street food court.

Lê Văn Hưu Street had not been written about in guidebooks, nor in the travel sections of the middle-class Western press (nor the Vietnamese press, for that matter). But it was the place that Vietnamese friends who'd gotten to know me and gotten to know what I liked to eat would point me to again and again for good food.

At lunchtime, women crouched on the pavement at floor level, washing rice bowls and chopsticks, blocking the pedestrian walkway. Grotty holes-in-the-wall served up food under peeling posters of smiling Vietnamese teenagers clutching bottles of Fanta.

I'd drop by the moldy, rat-ridden phở shack at

number 74. A small fan would constantly whir into the coal-powered inferno under the soup vat. A creaking extractor fan would attempt to clear the beefy air.

A tiny old prune-faced woman was hunched outside the phở shack entrance with a bucket of fresh tofu, waiting for buyers who would ride up onto the pavement. They'd leave their engines running, purchase a plastic bag of the stuff, and zoom back into the brawling, bike-filled street.

At number 46, a hủ tiếu seller would churn out "the works" from behind a cheap, shiny stainless steel cupboard on wheels, laden with bowls, pork, noodles, and steamy stock.

At 96, the coffee bean boys would grind me a fresh bag of nerve-jangling Vietnamese arabica.

Under a yellow sign and a paraffin lamp at number 82, I'd duck down a narrow alley, lined with several framed photos of Hồ Chí Minh and a Bruce Lee calendar next to two cabinets filled with various liquors, for a snort or two of rượu, that potent Vietnamese alcoholic spirit, at Quán Rượu Lý.

The bún chả and nem cua bể at number 36 were exquisite. Bowls were piled ten high and fifteen wide, waiting to be filled for lunchtime diners, a testament to the popularity of this stall. The standard white-tiled room, with red plastic numbers denoting rows of seats, was always packed at midday. Customers stood and hovered over you until your seat became vacant. As soon as you sat down, one of the legion of teenage girls working the floor would swash the detritus off the table from the previous diner, take your order, and zap it onto the stainless steel surface in front of you faster than a case of clap could circumnavigate one of the seedier establishments along the same road.

Farther down the street, in Cơm Lý's shop front, a tray of pig's trotters, lá lôt leaf-covered meatballs, deep fried fish, boiled chicken, and sautéed rau muống all lay waiting on an order or ten.

If you dropped a reasonably large bomb in the middle of Lê Văn Hưu Street, it'd be fair to say that the blast zone would cover much of the area where I served my informal Vietnamese food apprenticeship.

Not every stall or restaurant was a shitpit, but among the shitpits I'd eaten in, there were some shocking ones — rats and cockroaches scrambling up the walls, customers hawking and spitting and chucking chicken bones, mold hanging off the ceiling, and kitchen areas that, given half a chance, a herd of health and safety advisors would have simply razed to the ground.

I'd been in so many Hà Nội shitholes that it seemed the proprietors almost went out of their way to make the place as repellent as possible. And yet, they were packed. Always.

So often did I witness this phenomenon that

my first and most important rule for dining in Hà Nội went as follows:

The moldier it looks, and the more crowded it is, the better the food is.

As a general rule, this served me well during my apprenticeship, although there were mishaps along the way, most notably at Lẩu 1 on Láng Hạ Street, just south of the U.S. embassy, in the west of Hà Nội, where I stopped by one evening with my old friend Nghĩa, he of the pig's-uterus adventure, for one of our regular dinners together.

This street was famous for goat meat offal and alcohol: grilled goat, goat hotpot, grilled goat's nipple, goat's blood, and goat's penis alcohol.

Lẩu 1, at 27 Láng Hạ, was a heaving warehouse, filled with men at low wooden tables, shouting, spitting, drinking, and grilling and boiling their own dinner on the tabletops. It was rough as bollocks, and I loved it.

That night, Nghĩa and I had been overimbibing on beer as he told me about life in Hà Nội pre–đổi mới, pre–rice surplus, pre–relative freedom.

"What I remember most is that I was always hungry," Nghĩa said. This was something I had never known in my nearly thirty years on the planet. "It was like North Korea back then. Not just because of the lack of food, but the lack of trust. Everyone spied on everyone else. We could never have talked like this. We could

196

never have even met."

Just as the mid-eighties policies of đổi mới and mở cửa ("renovation" and "open door") helped relax laws around private enterprise, they also marked the beginning of a more amenable attitude toward foreigners and the start of Việt Nam's opening of diplomatic missions in Western capitalist nations.

I was engrossed in our conversation, but urgently needed to step out to the toilet to relieve myself. I knew only too well the drill in a place like this. The toilet at 27 Láng Hạ would surely be more festering trough than powder room.

The filthy, reeking walls would certainly be coated with decades of piss. You could never redecorate a place like this. You could only tear it down, fumigate the entire area, leave it empty for a few years, as if it were infected with anthrax — and then and only then, think of rebuilding anything on the plot.

Yes, I'd been in many a toilet like this, and Lầu 1 did not disappoint. Only on this evening, when I turned the dilapidated corner into the rancid trough room, I found a Vietnamese man wrestling a live goat to the floor.

The animal was on its back, right in front of the piss trough. The goat wrestler beckoned me to step over the animal and continue my business. I wasn't quite sure what he had in mind for the goat, but it didn't look like the creature was going to enjoy it. As I unzipped to unload a liter or two of Bia Hà Nôi, I glanced back to see the man reach across the floor for a large knife before he slit the squealing animal's throat in one clean, deft cut.

The goat went quiet and limp as blood seeped across the floor. The goat killer gave me a smile and a wink, wiped his brow, and dragged the dead beast back into the restaurant, leaving a gory red trail in his wake. A trail that led to the kitchen, and eventually to the dining tables I'd just stepped away from.

Nearer home, there were shitpits aplenty. Close by Lê Văn Hưu Street, at number 13 Lò Đúc Street, there was one dish at one street shack, long one of my favorite Hà Nội finds, that I just couldn't convince Sophie to like. It was at a place called Phở Thìn.

I'd first noticed this bleak den as I stumbled home late one night from an evening at the abysmal whore-booze-and-drug-filled sinkhole that was the Apocalypse Now! nightclub on Hòa Mã Street. Expats shortened the name and simply referred to it as the Lypse, which seemed to add to its sleazy allure.

I had very quickly grown bored of Hà Nội's nightclub scene. Unlike pubs and clubs I had known in the UK, it didn't offer an escape from anything, but rather served as a reminder that my fellow expats were almost exclusively los-

ers, psychotics, deadbeats, junkies, and alcoholics.

However, one of the fringe benefits of going
out anywhere in Hà Nội even moderately late
was the trip home, either pedaled sleepily across
town in a cyclo, or on foot through the dark city
streets.

The boulevards were almost barren, but life
lurked under the few dim lampposts if you
looked or listened for it.

Most obvious were the women street cleaners.
Using stiff brush brooms and working throughout the night, they swished and swashed the gutters of coconut shells, noodles, rubbish bags,
and kitchen scraps. These hardworking women
would then gather large bundles of waste, sling
them into their pushcarts, and wheel them across
town to a collection point.

On two or three street corners you could find
flower and fruit sellers laying out their wares in
the 2 A.M. gloom, waiting to divvy the goods
between the many haggling traders who'd sell
the stuff at a markup in markets all over the city.

There were bicycle-riding hookers, half hidden
by shadows, who would whisper sweet nothings
from between the trees as they tracked potential
customers exiting the Lypse and the few other
late-night bars that existed.

And there were men crouching here and there,
dressed in shorts, bare-chested or with a T-shirt

rolled up to cool a belly. I was largely oblivious to them, until I'd catch the occasional clandestine glow of a cigarette in a hidden doorway.

It was Hà Nội at its most blissful. So quiet. I could hear everything from the creak and burr of the cyclo driver's pedals to his breath as he sucked and exhaled on a Vinataba. I'd wait for the inevitable release of those rough tobacco fumes over my head, and the equally inevitable plea in my ear as he'd lean forward and, with a conspiratorial croak, try to sell me Hà Nội's heady nighttime concoction of marijuana and "Madame Boom-Boom."

The calmest, almost-opiated moments I ever spent in Hà Nội were on cyclo journeys like this late at night. I often fell asleep.

The night I discovered Phở Thìn, I'd exited the Lypse and staggered home alone at 2 A.M., on foot, heading north up Lò Đúc Street. It was January, about 6 degrees Celsius, about as bone-chilling cold as Hà Nội ever got.

Through the silhouettes, under the sparse halogen glow, I saw a group of three cyclos, motionless, obstructing the pavement in front of me.

All three drivers were fast asleep, open to the elements on this harsh winter's evening. I'd always assumed these guys had homes to go to somewhere. It appeared, for these old boys at least, that their cyclos were their homes.

It was only as I walked slowly around them

that I felt the heat. When I looked closer at the wall they were snuggled up against, I noticed a faint glow through the shop-front grill, coming from under a ginormous vat. I knew what it was instantly. I could smell the strident beef note of a vast phở bò stockpot. These drivers were holed up here in the dark for warmth, and possibly an early breakfast. Clever. Any restaurant that kept its fires burning 24/7 had to have something going for it. Not quite an Olympic flame, I thought, but better: *an eternal beef soup flame.*

As I found out the following day, Phở Thìn adhered to the shithole rule with grime-encrusted bells on. This place took the term "craphole," beat it around the ears, slammed it into the corner, and flattened it to a pulp. Phở Thìn was a shitpit of the highest order.

In the front of the shop, open to the pavement, were two enormous blackened vats, likely relics of the Industrial Revolution. The kitchen area was completely covered in soot, the stove was caked in grease, and beef bones hung from great, dirty hooks above the cauldrons.

The customer entrance was lined with loaded bowls, half filled with noodles and spring onion. A rack of fresh eggs sat to one side, and a butcher's knife lay on a chopping board. The grubby board itself had heard a rumor about something called dishwashing liquid sometime back in the early eighties, but had suffered amnesia ever since. Stacks of cooked meat and stacks of raw meat sat side by side next to the filthy chopping board.

There was only one dish — phở bò — and only the bare minimum of options: raw beef, cooked beef, or a mix of the two; raw egg or no raw egg. Take your pick, take it quickly, eat up, *and get out*. That was the long and short of it at Phở Thìn.

One of the three handlers at the entrance took my order — raw beef with an egg. I waded into the feculent swamp to find a place at one of four grease-smeared stainless steel tables. Three ceiling fans hovered above the carnage: toothpicks, scraps of tissue paper, dropped chopsticks, spoons, discarded gristle, saliva, stray noodles, strands of spring onion, and blobs of hot red chili sauce.

I'd long been used to the peculiarly Hanoian style of "service with a snarl." At Phở Thìn there simply was no service, just snarl.

On this first visit and all subsequent returns, the server stuck his thumb into my soup — and of course it was the thumb with the creepy long nail meant to denote the nobility that he so obviously lacked — as he threw breakfast in my general direction.

These guys simply did not give a damn if I, or anyone else, was there or not. What they did give a damn about, I thought, was their soup.

It was a punk attitude I came to respect. And if, as I imagined sometimes, the Hà Nội street food scene was run by a bunch of punks, the Phở Thìn boys were undoubtedly the Sex Pistols. Never mind the bollocks, here's the phở.

Phở has no place on the poncey tables of nouvelle cuisine restaurants that play chamber music, nor in the "ethnic" section of the Hilton breakfast buffet. It's the single-dish spots like Phở Thìn, not seven hundred yards' walk from the four-star Hilton Hà Nội Opera Hotel, that had that vibe nailed through the floor.

The beauty of single-dish specialization is a point worth laboring, so I will do so again, and not for the last time.

If the place you're thinking of eating at serves only one dish, looks like it hasn't seen a lick of paint since Hồ Chí Minh popped his clogs, and is still in business, then the likelihood is that people eat there in numbers.

Despite their being total crapheaps, there's something about these places that keeps pulling the punters in. And in Việt Nam — north or south — that draw is only ever the food.

I had tried and failed to convert Sophie to the pleasures of Phở Thìn's punk rock pigsty. I simply couldn't fathom her reluctance.

"Tune out the decor, the people, anything your eyes and ears are registering, and focus on that bowl of meaty, noodly goodness in front of you,"

I'd tell her. "It's a belter."

"The meat is scraggy, poor quality," she'd sigh, tired of me talking up this shack.

"Well, OK, I know, but some of it isn't. Well . . . if they're having a good day, it isn't," I'd reply.

An image of Chris's wife flashed into my head. Nhũ was a Vietnamese country girl, brought up on scraggy beef, when beef was available, which wasn't that often in the eighties. One night, he took her to an Argentine steakhouse. His favorite push-the-boat-out expat hogfest. She couldn't eat it. "It's disgusting," she said. The quality and texture of the tender, melting slabs of fine bovine protein from one of South America's finest beef farms were completely lost on her. "It's doesn't even taste like beef," she said. "Not real beef, anyway."

Meanwhile, Sophie poked at her scrag. She wasn't done with her demolition job.

"Then there's the soup itself," she would go on, methodically laying out her case. "It's just beef bone stock. There's nothing more to it. Zero imagination. Without that garlic vinegar, a couple of chilies, and pepper, this would taste of nothing. Zero. Zilch. Nada."

"What do you mean? *Nothing?* You need anything more than boiled beef bones for a decent soup? It's a simple, no-nonsense, unpretentious, hearty soup."

"This is not the way I was taught to make phở," she would reply, exasperated. "It's just that it's better, it's different, it's more sophisticated in . . ."

I gave her my *heard it all before* look.

"You're not going to yabber on about how Sài Gòn does it better again, are you?"

We'd been over this territory a million times. I stood up for the Hà Nội end of things and ridiculed the south.

"Yes, we all know the streets are paved with culinary gold a thousand miles south of here, but Hà Nội, as you well know, is the home of phở, and this craphole has the best there is."

Sophie stared me out over her bowl of scrag-end beef noodle soup.

"Exactly," she replied stonily. "That's my point. It's the best there is in this town. And it's not good enough. Go to Sài Gòn one day, you'll see."

And so ended the conversation, always on the same note. It didn't matter how hard I battled. We'd go at it again, the next time we stopped for phở anywhere in Hà Nội.

But, what was she on about?

Pho bò was not my favorite Vietnamese nibble, but it was the national dish. Poets had written odes to the thing. Everyone in Việt Nam ate the stuff. It was probably Việt Nam's largest, most well-known culinary export, and a world-renowned dish, one that everybody knew, especially the Việt Kiều. A dish that came from Hà Nội, and Hà Nội was the home of phở, whether in traditional beef fashion or the naughty chicken variety. Fact. Fact. *Fact.*

I had totally out-facted Sophie with my facts. How *could* she, a French Việt Kiều, possibly take issue? It was barmy, *utterly* barmy.

I stood my ground, firm in my resolution that Hà Nội phở was the best phở. Phở Thìn made the best phở in town. And those soft, southern upstarts could take their namby-pamby bowl of ponced-up nosh and shove it.

Sophie shook her head as if to say, "You poor, pathetic, ignorant little fool."

There was, of course, one fact that I always chose to omit whenever we resurrected this debate.

I'd never tried phở in Sài Gòn. Sophie had.

CHAPTER THIRTEEN:
THE TEN COMMANDMENTS
OF STREET FOOD

I'm lookin' and lookin' and lookin' for something I ain't had before.

> — The Cramps,
> "New Kind of Kick" (1991)

There is a lot of snobbery around street food.
There are those who won't go near it for fear of
death. And there are those who won't go near
anything else for fear of deviating off Avenue Authentic. Both are wrong.

The thing is, street food in Việt Nam has an awful lot going against it and, by rights, it *shouldn't*
really work.

It requires a certain tolerance for noise, humidity, cold, heat, wind, rain, street hassle of every
shade, questionable hygiene, exhaust fumes, low
seating, and public displays of nose picking and
zit squeezing.

You'll probably need to shout if you want to
hold a conversation. You may need to learn to

tune out the slurps, clicks, and chomps of your fellow diners. You will have to get used to mess, both on the table and under it.

At first, the logical conclusion you would reach looking up from the blue plastic table is that this won't work. *How can it?* That the food triumphs in such circumstances is a testament to the street chefs and their insistence on using only fresh ingredients. That the whole scene should be enjoyable and an experience to seek out on a daily basis is some kind of a certificate of validation to Việt Nam and the Vietnamese. There's life on those streets. And you get to ingest a little bit of it too, every time you eat at the blue plastic table. I met foreigners who had lived in Hà Nội for five years and who had never once eaten on the street. To me, by now, that seemed unimaginable. Like visiting Disneyland and never going on a cartoon-themed ride.

Street food is a bit like smoking. It can seem somewhat disgusting at first, it takes a little time to get into it, but before too long, you're addicted.

And, like any addict, you'll soon find yourself heading down any dodgy alley, no matter how soiled, if you know you can score good gear somewhere along its sodden trail.

So, how does the novice find a decent street stall in Việt Nam?

Beyond a Knorr stock cube or ten, a bag of

MSG, and a tub of tomato purée, there's nothing processed about these places. Regardless of location, the food is just as granny made it.

And, to clarify, we're talking a combination of *pure* street food stalls, street carts, and "half on street, half in the front room" restaurants.

The Ten Commandments for finding good Vietnamese street food are as follows:

1. **One Dish**

    I've said it before, and I'll say it again: the narrower the niche, the better the dish. Granny Uyên cooks bún riêu because that's what she does best, everyone knows she does it best, and she can eke out a decent living while doing it. She hasn't got the time or inclination to consider doing something different. It's as simple as the jack-of-all-trades, master-of-none theory. And, when you're eating street food in Việt Nam, you should really sit down with a master, because there's one on every street corner.

    One dish, done well, no menu. My favorite restaurants in the south of France give you zero choice. It's just like home cooking. "This is what we're cooking today, take it or leave it." In Việt Nam, less is more, especially on the street.

The richer the Vietnamese get, the more I think they forget this. Visit any of the higher-end Vietnamese restaurants, stuffed with jewelry and graceful bodies that are perhaps a little too familiar with the surgeon's knife, and you'll be insulted with a ridiculous, Magna Carta–length menu.

2. **A Crap Sign**

   Invariably, we're talking generic, red-stenciled letters with the name of the dish on a plastic board, or possibly just a slab of cardboard with the dish written in pen. My favorite of all of these signs simply reads "Cơm," which means "rice." Anyone who reads it understands that you won't just get rice, but there'll be other stuff along for the ride, too.

3. **Old People**

   If the younger generation has lost anything in the taste bud department, the older bunch has not. As older Vietnamese people will not stint on quality when it comes to food, neither will they frequent a stall that doesn't do things correctly. As blogger Steven Halcrow put it, upon arriving at a stall in Hà Nội: "I was happy to see that the proprietor of the stall was a woman in

211

her 50s or 60s. This filled me with confidence, based on my own prejudice that all old people are great at making soup."

4. **Grime Factor**

It's more than likely that you'll be looking at a fairly basic, definitely lived-in place to eat. The cookware will be blackened, dented, bruised, and wrinkled, having likely been passed from mother to daughter. There will be dirt, there may be rats, but the food will not sit on the floor. Much of it will hang from nails pounded into the nearest wall.

5. **Wash-Hand Basins**

They might be scuzzy, but there the dishes will get a wipe. Not only for the hygiene factor, but also for the turnover factor. If the place you're thinking of eating at has a dedicated washer upper, or two or three, the odds are that they do a roaring trade, and ipso facto, there be good food there.

6. **Stacks**

Stacks of stools, stacks of bowls: they're waiting for business the proprietors *know* is coming. Or, it's already jammed, in which case, the place is a choppy sea of bobbing heads. If they have a lot of bowls, they're expecting a lot of people to come and eat out of them.

7. **Bia Hơi (Fresh Beer) or Mía Đá (Freshly Squeezed Sugarcane Juice) Nearby**

If you're eating something on the street, the chances are you'll want something to drink along with it. In Hà Nội, the street stall owners who respect their customers either have their own supply of bia hơi, or one very close by. Survey the surroundings near your chosen eatery. Can you see a bia hơi sign? Or, if it's particularly hot, a vendor of mía đá would suffice.

8. **We're Sold Out**

If at first you don't eat, try again. If you're hunting down something for lunch and it's midday and they're sold out, make a mental note and come back the next day. All the good stalls I have ever eaten at sell out early. Many make one batch of whatever it is, and when it's gone, it's gone.

9. **Ongoing Deliveries**

Whether it be fresh vegetables, noodles, bones, or fruit, if your vendor is regularly yelling across the street to the market trader there, it's because she wants the freshest of the fresh for her clients and she needs to top up regularly. Good bún chả vendors, for example, will buy just enough to satisfy the first few rounds of clients before yelling to the noodle girl to go and fetch a fresh load from the noodle maker.

10. **Just in Case**
    Have a stash of Imodium, *just in case*. In almost ten years, I only ever got sick once from street food. It was little more than an unpleasant evening at the plumbing with a splash of the trots. It was nothing remotely close to the ten days off work and on antibiotics that followed a course of duck livers in a high-end French restaurant in Hà Nội.

You have to make an effort, and spend a lot of money, if you want to eat badly in Việt Nam. The good stuff wallops you in the face as soon as you step outside the front door. You have to wade through a jungle of good to find the nearest expensive nugget of shit. Only a foolish or blind person with no sense of smell could honestly put his hand up and say, "Really, I just did not realize, your honor. And, for that, I am truly, deeply, sorry."

Whichever way you cut it, if you follow these Ten Commandments, you'd have to be extremely unfortunate to go wrong when eating street food in Việt Nam. If for some reason you do strike up a dud, at worst you'll be down a dollar or two, and maybe lose a bit of weight along the way. Either way, it's not a hardship.

Tom, a new staff member at the British Council, and his wife, Min-Ju, who was Korean, had just arrived after a six-year stint in Seoul. He was going to be my immediate boss. And they were both looking forward to three years in Hà Nội.

It had come down to me to organize a "meet, greet, and get to know" drinks and dinner bit for them. I went street. Very street. Well, actually, I went pavement. I went Binh's pavement chicken.

I was focused on the food, not the event. I knew that Binh, on the corner of Lý Thường Kiệt and Quán Sứ Streets, blistered up a killer char-crusted barbecue chicken. As the sun started to go down, he'd set up with a tiny tin-tray barbecue and a bucket of sweet, hot, marinated chicken legs.

He grilled to order. The beer was dispensed from a barrel, hidden inside a large metal box at the front of a shop. This was no bia hơi. This was bia tươi, an upscale Hà Nội beer. It was fresh, came in tankards, and was more expensive.

As everybody began gathering — selected staff and respective partners — Binh pushed together the low-level seating and three plastic tables to accommodate us all.

Min-Ju and Tom were the last to arrive. They pulled up in an air-conditioned yellow Vina Taxi and looked out of the window. I could see them talking animatedly as they paid the driver and mulled the getting-out bit.

Tom was dressed in a suit and tie. Min-Ju had on a knee-length cocktail dress and a string of pearls, and was immaculately made up. Her tea-dyed hair was tied back into a tight bun, and she wore emerald earrings, Chanel shoes, and a Gucci watch.

They sidled along the line of motorbikes we'd all arrived on and looked down at the plastic table set exactly at Min-Ju's knee height. Her astonished pallor struggled to make itself apparent from under the layers of makeup, but her eyes broadcast the shock.

She took out a tissue from her Hermès tote bag and placed it onto the low stool in front of her. She sat down, her husband next to her, and held her dress tight to her knees. She had preened for the opera, but found herself slung into the gutter.

I scanned my colleagues, still in their work clothes, sweaty faced, some already beery red, others with chicken-juice-coated beards — "Great chicken, Graham, nice find" — and I looked back at Min-Ju. She dabbed her face with a tissue, tending to invisible perspiration as she monitored the floor for anything moving or unsanitary.

I kicked myself. I'd become so obsessed with eating good stuff, wherever it might be, that I'd completely disregarded the sensitivities and expectations of others. I'd lived in Seoul. I knew how Korean women operated and, in general, they're pretty demanding. Definitely not the sort to sit ten inches above a filthy pavement, a yard or two away from the blaring traffic, with food served out of a bucket and grilled alongside gutter-crawling rats and the occasional defecating child. This wasn't really a pearls-and-Hermès kind of dining area.

The food was, as ever, spectacular, but on that night I had a flash of how I had felt, once upon a distant time, about eating on the street for the first time. It's just not something you dive into, free of inhibition, shedding all cultural baggage like you'd wipe clean a table. You needed to ease yourself in. And I'd given poor Min-Ju and Tom a crash-course in sweat, mess, and grease on their first night in the capital.

Some years later, Sophie and I had just returned from the local market. We arrived home to find a woman sitting on our doorstep. This was not an unusual event. We were coming toward the end of our Hà Nội tenure, and by this time we had moved to number 4 Quán Sứ Street. Our balcony overlooked Hàng Bông Street, Hà Nội's busiest shopping and riding boulevard. The ground floor to our house was an empty room. We'd been asked several times to sublet it to passersby who wanted to open a shop. We used it to store our motorbikes.

Unless you knew better, you could be forgiven for thinking the house was empty. At least once per week I would have to kick the person who was asleep, drunk, smoking, drinking, or just, you know, hanging out on our front doorstep, so that I could get in and out of the house. They'd always look at me with utter surprise and bewilderment. "Where did you come from?" their look would say. "And you want me to move?" And I'd wheel the motorbike out, lock the door, and trundle off to get on with the rest of my day.

But on this day, we decided to take a seat outside our house. Not on the doorstep, mind you. That spot was already taken by a woman in her late fifties who was sleeping with her head resting on the handle of our front door, a small basket next to her. We stepped gingerly around her and pulled up a pew at the impromptu beer seller who conveniently set up shop right outside our house every Saturday and Sunday morning.

If she was running low on beer before we went to the market in the morning, she would promise to save us a few glasses to make sure we had a drink upon our return. She did this without fail for the entire two years we lived at this address.

We got into a habit of buying fruit, the Vietnamese candies called xí muội that Sophie loved, and a bagged-up lunch from the local market at Hàng Da. We'd get everything else we needed outside the front door while having a beer and a bowl of peanuts. Flower sellers, shoeshine boys, cigarette vendors, egg dispensers, and newspaper sellers would all pass by in the half hour, and we would sit talking with Mrs. Liên, the mobile bia hơi woman who repurposed the front of our house for her weekend beer business.

On a particularly thirsty day, I'd sometimes nip up the two flights of stairs to the kitchen to grab an empty drink bottle and have Mrs. Liên fill it with bia hơi for us to enjoy later on.

Out of a sense of gratitude, I think, for us never complaining about her running her business from our front door, Liên booted the sleeping woman and told her to move her lazy arse from our doorstep. The woman roused herself back to life. She picked up her basket, pulled up a seat next to us, and asked, "Would you like some trứng vịt lộn?"

She opened the basket to reveal a set of eggcups, teaspoons, some herbs, and a dozen or more large white duck eggs. Specifically, duck fetus eggs.

Trứng vịt lộn is one of the more feared dishes

in Việt Nam, because, well, it's disgusting — unless consuming the crunchy bones of a visibly half-grown fetus appeals to you. While it does, in fact, appeal to many, many Vietnamese, this dish turns the stomach of most visitors like a tumble dryer on turbo-spin mode.

Like the Philippine dish balut, a rising foodie-hipster favorite, it's a shell with a bit of egg, a bit of half-grown duck, some feathers, a beak, and veins. It's a gross-out on a par with tiết canh, raw duck's blood in a bowl with chopped peanuts, which I'd had once. It had been like eating a nosebleed. *A huge one.*

When we declined, the duck egg seller, whose name was Quyên, informed us that she was also a palm reader.

Liên said, "She's good. No Mickey Mouse business with her readings." Sophie, who was translating the conversation to me, suggested we give her a turn. All she wanted was a beer and some nuts in return. At that price, I didn't have the heart to turn her down.

"You're not going to be rich, but you won't be poor either." *I can live with that,* I thought. "You'll travel a lot." *Sounds good to me.* "And you'll change your job a few times until you're happy." *Even better, count me in.* "You two are only together because you missed the people you should have been with." *Oh, really?* I glanced at Sophie.

"You mean we're such a pair of losers we can't even pick the right partners? What happened to us?" I asked with a smile.

"Oh well, if it was that loser I was with before you, I'm glad I missed that boat," said Sophie. "I'll settle for you, I think."

"I'll second that. Fancy another?" I pointed at the polystyrene froth box. She nodded and Quyên went back to trying to sell her eggs to us.

"They're good," piped in Liên. "She only buys the good ones."

CHAPTER FOURTEEN:
I NEVER
REMEMBER YOU

The pit of oil fizzed at groin height, threatening to attack at any moment. As I wasn't in a fighting mood, I stepped a safe distance back from the fury, held my shoulder bag in front of my zipper, placed my order, and retreated into the tiny den at 52 Lý Quốc Sư Street.

A stack of blue plastic chairs towered to one side of the entrance, awaiting the inevitable influx at this popular stall next to Saint Joseph's Cathedral in the center of Hà Nội.

There were four deep-fried items on the smeared menu board, which was hung at head height. However, the hungry flood that would soon stampede their way here were coming for one thing and one thing only: bánh gối, a brittle fried parcel of pork, glass noodles, and mushrooms, shaped like a pillow. It's a greasy Hà Nội winter staple, but still popular year-round, especially in the early evening.

Inside number 52 were a paltry six tables. The

waitress, whose long black hair was held back in a head band, delivered my order: a couple of chopped-up bánh gối, a wodge of herbs, and a small, square bowl of fish sauce, strewn with chayote, known locally as su su, which grows profusely in the mountainous regions of the north.

Just behind the wall next to me, I could hear the rumble of the pastry-making machine used to concoct the rice-flour-based parcel covers.

As I crunched open the pork-filled pastry, under the low, glowing fluorescent tubes, I took stock of what had ended twenty minutes earlier. The culmination of three years of work. And of the decision I had come to during the five-minute ride to this legendary Hà Nội hole.

It was the New Millennium. We were well into 2001. I'd decided to leave my job. Sophie had been promoted. We were leaving Hà Nội. We were going to get married in the summer in Toulouse. I was ready for a change. It was time to exit the education system. I would, as Quyên had warned me, change my job a few times before I was happy. It was time.

Minutes before creasing my teeth into my order of bánh gối, I'd stood, in despair, in front of my students at their "graduation party."

"They're unteachable," my friend Jill concluded after a single one-hour session with my students, known collectively as B9. Her eyes were wide with disbelief. I nodded sagely, as if to say, "Now you understand, Grasshopper." I'd been with B9 for two trying and protracted years. Jill was covering for me while I marked exam papers.

Without B9, I might never have started writing, might never have started blogging about street food, and probably would never have become a journalist. Without B9, I could very well still be working as a teacher today. I'm not ashamed to admit it: *class B9 broke me*.

Hundreds of lawyers, judges, and various criminal court officials were being paid more than their monthly salaries to take English lessons twice per week under a program paid for by the United Nations and administered by Hà Nội University and the British Council. I was one of the teachers. Many of the students fared well, some very well. Then there was my group, B9.

B9 was my Room 101 of English teaching: the floor sweepings of the dustier crevices of Việt Nam's Ministry of Justice. Twice a week they'd gather together in a classroom in the furthest corner of Hà Nội University. I'd park my Minsk in the campus car park on the whore-filled Phạm Ngũ Lão Street, climb the steps of dread into the university building, plod my way down the corridor of failure, and greet B9 in the room I'd nicknamed Doom.

I'd tried trendy, newfangled learning, I'd tried

parrot fashion, I'd tried games, I'd tried get-up-and-mingle. I'd tried everything, new or old, that I could rummage from my teacher's bag of tricks. Nothing worked.

And the students didn't mind sitting it out, for hours, twice per week. They were getting paid well. I'd long concluded that they were unteachable, but by now I'd also concluded, by default, that I couldn't teach.

In the two years that I ground out the rent with B9, we went through three different textbooks, all of them at elementary level, that were merely different shades of awful. B9 came in with little knowledge of English, and two years later, left in the exact same state.

A breath of musty air greeted me each time I entered the high-ceilinged, white-chipboard-lined classroom, which was (of course) situated next to the toilets. The classroom had desks for some twenty-five students, arranged in a U formation, with the teacher's desk positioned at the gap.

The B9 students wore blue shirts or white shirts, which denoted their status in the office pecking order. The men wore ties, and some took them off, as if they really planned on getting down to the business of learning my lingo. All of them, bar two youngsters, were about fifty years of age, and there were six women in the class. They wore the exact same uniform, minus the tie.

The youngsters were in their mid-twenties, and had already donned the flop-over hairstyle beloved of their seniors. It was a look akin to a death warrant. I studied their lifeless young eyes and imagined a Vietnamese version of Orwell's Winston Smith, clerking his days away in a bureaucratic chicken coop, filling out meaningless forms and typing out thick, dull reports that would never be read.

It was as we dragged our way through the third and final elementary textbook that I stood and watched the last nail slam shut on the coffin containing my teaching career.

I'd instructed the group to read the short letter on page 16 of *The New Headway English Course*, then discuss it with a partner. Nothing too taxing. Even for B9.

The B9 students began the task, in their way. For some reason, they would always read aloud to themselves individually, and completely out of sync with each other. The effect was like listening to a family of dysfunctional bees. I walked around the room and did a double take when I came to Mr. Thịnh.

Mr. Thịnh was a judge, and the most academically challenged of an already piss-poor group. He was a tall man with a thin, graying mustache, a ready grin, a discolored set of teeth with a gap you could drive a cyclo through, and a solitary long, gray hair growing from a mole on his right cheek.

He appeared to have been muttering through the text, just like everyone else, but as I looked closer, I noticed he was holding his book upside down, tracing the inverted hieroglyphics with his forefinger.

At the farcical B9 graduation party, a student passed me a tangerine, offering, "Apple, Mr. Graham?"

Mr. Thịnh, emboldened by the warm Bia Hà Nội on offer, came up to me and uttered his most meaningful sentence in our entire two years together.

"I never remember you."

For the last time, I closed the door to Hà Nội University and cranked the Minsk into gear. Sophie never did pay for the motorbike, a bone of contention that remains to this day. I'd ended up buying another Minsk, the same color. Matching Minsks. How romantic. I sputtered out of the campus and bid farewell to education, composing my resignation letter in my mind as I went.

Some people hit the chocolate when they get depressed. Me, I'm all about the lard. Classic Hà Nội comfort food, with that all-important warm grease, was like an opiate washing cotton wool through my veins.

I finished my bánh gối, dredged the last of my beer, took a cheap piece of tissue paper from the

227

chopstick container, wiped it across my mouth, and pondered. I'd been back in Hà Nội from Seoul for almost three years. What had I actually achieved?

It was as if a ball bearing had been dropped into a large, empty, spherical drum. It rattled around aimlessly. I searched and searched, but the ball bearing just kept rolling around the sides of the large empty space. It didn't make a dent. It made no noticeable impact whatsoever.

It was time for me to move on.

CHAPTER FIFTEEN:
IT'S SHIT IN
THE SOUTH

ORIG SÀI GÒN VIỆT NAM

SENT: 13 JUL 2001

GRAHAM HOLLIDAY
HÀ NỘI VIỆT NAM
TRAFFIC TERRIBLE FOOD WORSE STOP
ONE BÚN CHẢ IN EXISTENCE REPEAT
ONE STOP IT IS SHIT STOP DO NOT LEAVE
HÀ NỘI STOP

LEN

"This place is a disaster," snorted Len down the crackly phone line from Sài Gòn. "There's no bia hơi, the phở is all crap, and the traffic's a fuckin' nightmare."

The key elements of the telephone conversation fed like a tickertape telegram into my consciousness. And my consciousness was not happy.

Len was a colleague I had worked with previ-

229

ously in Hà Nội who had been promoted to a higher position in the Sài Gòn bureau. He wasn't enjoying the move from Hà Nội to the south. After three years in the capital, Len was not adjusting well to the difference in climate, the population, the noise, or the food.

"I bloody hate it," he said.

Sài Gòn, the loser in the American war, has always prided itself on being the livelier of Việt Nam's two largest cities. Unlike Hà Nội, Sài Gòn never sleeps. Come 9 P.M., the more obedient Hanoians are tucked away at home, shutters padlocked, lights out, whereas the Saigonese are just getting started.

Hanoians often call Saigonese frivolous, indulgent, and decadent, and the Saigonese often call Hanoians frigid sticks in the mud. Len, though an expat, was a Hanoian. I'd seen this time and time again. Expats who moved to Việt Nam and lived in Hà Nội first could never fully adjust to Sài Gòn, and the reverse was equally true. City loyalties ran thick with both Vietnamese and expats. It was all based upon the people, the food, the ambience, the pace of life, and the climate.

This did not bode well. By now we knew we were leaving Hà Nội. Sophie had been given a promotion for a new position in Sài Gòn. I was about to quit teaching and magically transform myself into a writer. We were out of Hà Nội and I was looking into new prospects for our life down south.

Several of my students were less than complimentary about Sài Gòn. "Everything bad in Việt Nam comes from the south," I was told by a dowdy government official. "The food is terrible" was another oft-repeated line.

We had little choice. The job dictated the move. We were ready to go. It couldn't be that bad. *Could it?*

"There is one bún chả place," moped Len. "But it's shit. You can't even find a boiled chicken."

Ah, Hà Nội, with its inevitable lines of boiled chickens adorning the entrance of every other front-room restaurant south of the lake. Soon after I chatted with Len, I encountered another boiled chicken in a place where it's not often spotted in the wild — at least, not without something fancier going on: southern France, where Sophie and I were married.

It was a marriage made in fish sauce. Sophie wore an áo dài to respect her roots. I wore a kilt to respect mine. We recited our vows under the fresco ceiling of Le Capitole, the epicenter of Toulouse.

At some point during a lull in the champagne, foie gras, and vodka colonels served by Sophie's sister; the lizard, gecko, and sea horse rượu shots I had managed to get though French customs; and the umpteenth "Izz eet true, zee Scottish man duz not wear zee culotte under zee kilt?"

Sophie had a word in my ear.

"We have to go to my sister's house. My parents are waiting." I hadn't noticed, but earlier in the (admittedly long) post ceremony banter, drinks, eats, and dancing, they'd slipped away.

What had I done? Had they informed the local triads? "Bloody Scots, taking away our women." I was genuinely scared. What was waiting for me?

"It's a Vietnamese thing. Prepare yourself," Sophie said as we reached the door of the apartment in central Toulouse.

"For what?" I asked.

"Oh, it's nothing. Just a Vietnamese thing. You'll see."

I gulped. And we entered Sophie's sister's dining room. In the center of the room was a table, upon which was a mountain of food laid out ornately. Peering over the scene were the framed photographs of Sophie's ancestors. They were watching me. Checking me out. Was I up to snuff? In the center of the table, there was a boiled chicken, stalwart of the Hà Nội night.

I was greeted by Mẹ, Sophie's mother, followed by Ba, her father. Both were dressed in their áo dài. A video camera was attached, limpetlike, to Ba's right hand, tracking our movements as we entered the sanctum.

I eyed the boiled chicken. Its glossy, pimply coat took me right back to the streets of Hà Nội and I looked at Sophie.

"You never told me about this. You never told me this is what Vietnamese people do to their newly married daughters and sons-in-law."

"Just smile. Endure. We only have to do this once."

It was new for Sophie, too, but the key difference was she'd been expecting it.

We paid our respects to the ancestors with a bow and then Mẹ handed us a small cake, called a phu, made of rice flour, sugar, beans, and coconut. Later research informed me that these cakes were "said to represent the earth and the sky" and were "associated with loyalty, flexibility, and honesty." A quick munch on the cake and, in the eyes of the ancestors and my new in-laws, we were properly married. The Western stuff was all very nice and fun, but in their eyes, this was the real deal.

When I thought about it later, I realized that I shouldn't have been surprised. How could the Vietnamese perform anything as important as a marriage without a serious and symbolic food element? There was food in everything the Vietnamese did.

In retrospect, I got off lucky. I pondered what Lâm, my former student in Hà Nội, would have to endure. Endless gifts, dowrylike payments, tedious, long, drawn-out ceremonies, days of photos, and he could forget about a honeymoon.

He'd be paying off the wedding for a good few years after the big day.

It was all over in a matter of minutes. That vast table filled with uneaten food, the boiled chicken, the photos of the ancestors. I half joked with Ba after the ceremony that I was disappointed there wasn't a uterus on the table.

"Oh, if I'd have known I'd have gotten one for you," he said. "You have to make sure you get a young one. An old uterus is a tough uterus. No fun at all."

We exited the lair and headed back to the party, to refill on Veuve Clicquot at the more relaxed, somewhat more debauched, alcohol-fueled Western end of the proceedings.

CHAPTER SIXTEEN:
HOÀ HƯNG STREET,
DISTRICT 10, SÀI GÒN

By my conservative reckoning, there were, at the very least, fifty different dishes to eat within a three-minute walk from our new home in Sài Gòn, depending on the time of day. *Fifty*. Mirror that a thousandfold, across the entire city, and you begin to understand the enormous number of lean-to restaurants and the vast availability of street food in Việt Nam's largest metropolis.

This home was not even in the center of Sài Gòn. We were stuck out in the boondocks of District 10, down a side road called Hoà Hưng, just off Cách Mạng Tháng Tám Street, a large thoroughfare commonly referred to as CMT8.

We had a two-story, two-bedroom house. There was a garage, and three trees in the graveled garden: a longan, a starfruit, and a jasmine. For Sài Gòn, a garden was a luxury, especially for folk like us: the poorer, unexpensed end of the expat community, without a gym membership clause in the work contract, a chauffeur, or a first-class flight home three times a year. In the land of soulless three-, four-, and five-story houses, with one room on each floor, an "almost a bungalow" spread out across three spacious, well-lit rooms on the ground floor was a luxury, too.

Our house was located on a side road off Hoà Hưng itself, further insulating us from the sound of motorbikes buzzing and honking day and night. However, from seven in the morning on weekdays, the primary school opposite our front gate had a loud line of amplified communist marching music. There was no need to set the alarm during term time.

Once we'd moved in and unpacked the cardboard boxes we'd had shipped from Hà Nội, and once Sophie had worked out the office commute, it was time to explore the neighborhood.

However, it wasn't the scene outside our front door that gave me my first introduction to Saigonese Vietnamese food. That happened on the other side of town. And Sophie had planned it.

(And now, I will proceed to piss off the population of Hà Nội.)

"They have a menu?" I asked Sophie, incredulously, as we sat down.

I stared at the piece of paper glued to the tiled wall of Phở Hoa Pasteur at 260C Pasteur Street in Sài Gòn's District 3.

"It's a menu," I said. "Look, there's a menu. There. Every table has one. I mean . . . *menus*. This is a phở restaurant, yeah?"

"Oh yes," replied Sophie.

The waitress gave me a worried look and handed me a cold towel. You need cold towels in Sài Gòn. For much of the time I lived in Sài Gòn, I felt like a narwhal marooned in Namibia: hot, wet, and fat.

If the power went out at 6 A.M., and it often did, I knew we'd have no power until 6 P.M. That meant either (a) sweating like a sauna-bound blob all day or (b) going to a District 1 café with air-conditioning and sipping cà phê sữa đá (iced coffee) after cà phê sữa đá.

The drinks list at Phở Hoa Pasteur was extensive, the phở list less so: raw beef, cooked beef, a mixture of the two, tendons.

Sophie knew what she was doing. She had a plan. Years of punishment at the gnarled, greasy paws of Hà Nội's Phở Thìn boys had been building toward this moment. Before spying the menu, I should've known by the scent. It was like the star anise triffids had attacked the kitchen. There was a fab stink goin' on in here.

I've thought long and hard about what it is that is so different between the phở experience in Hà Nội and the one in Sài Gòn. The following may offend many and please others, but these are the facts as I see them. There are eight definitive differences:

1. After years of eating phở in Hà Nội, the very first thing I notice walking into a Sài Gòn phở shop is the quiet. It's not that it's deathly silent, filled with morbid, miserable eaters tossing over their slop, wondering whether or not to slit their wrists later on this morning or wait until the afternoon. No, it's a respectful quiet. People talk, but do so at a low decibel level. In Hà Nội, well, people prefer to shout at each other. I always wondered whether the hearing aid business was the one to get into in Hà Nội. Incidentally, the only member of our family with a hearing aid is Mẹ, the matriarch. She's from Hà Nội. Need I say more?

2. A Sài Gòn phở shop is clean. I mean, not just generally clean, but spotless. Compared to Phở Thìn, it's like walking into a hospital ward. There are two floors to Phở Hoa Pasteur in Sài Gòn, and I swear there is a girl on each floor who does nothing but clean. Constantly. Whereas, in Hà Nội, at the end of the day, or when the soup has run out, the owner kicks any stragglers

out, sticks the tables and chairs to one side, and hoses down the floor so that all the debris, spittle, bones, and lemon halves swim into the gutter and on toward the sewer. Close the shutter, padlock the door, and you're all set for tomorrow's business. The walls never got so much as a dermatologist's once over, let alone a full-blast bleach facial.

3. It's organized. A waitress comes to you, she doesn't get the order wrong, and she doesn't stick her thumb in the soup, 'cause here's the thing: she brings the phở to you on a tray. The news that the tray had been invented had yet to reach the phở restaurants of Hà Nội. (Well, some of them, anyway.)

4. Herbs. Yes, herbs. Lots and lots and lots of herbs. They sit at every table, are constantly replenished, and are dewy fresh whole stems, with leaves meant to be torn off by the eater. No herbs in Hà Nội phở. Not on the table. Not like this.

5. Quẩy, greasy bread sticks, sit at every table on a ten-sizes-too-small plate. In Hà Nội, they hang in a tattered, holey plastic bag stuck to a rusty nail on the dank wall behind the phở vat.

6. It's "Chí," not "Em." Chí is the more respectful term for females; Em is not respectful, and has an unpleasant under-meaning, as if the person using the term could do whatever he wanted to the "Em." Sophie was never ever addressed as "Em" in Sài Gòn, not once in all our six years. God forgive the poor Hanoian male who would ever call her "Em," which they did, constantly. Hanoian males address every young (or not so young, but reasonably attractive) female as "Em." Advice to Hanoian males: you want to piss off my missus, just carry on the way you are. The wrath will be swift, and straight to the nuts. I knew one expat who had recently relocated from Hà Nội to Sài Gòn and was told in no uncertain terms to clean up after he'd chucked his tissue and lemons on the floor. He was just following Hà Nội tradition, but the staff was not amused. The shouts of "Em ơi" — think of it like aggressively snapping your fingers at a waiter — didn't go down too well, either. While he wasn't ejected from the establishment, it was clear he wouldn't be welcomed back, either.

7. The heat: Hà Nội has seasons, but

it's humid year-round, whether it be hot or not. The only time the weather is bearable in Hà Nội is for a brief month, between late October and November. Sài Gòn has two seasons: wet and dry. It's always hot, and sometimes very hot. This changes the way you appreciate phở in the south. It's never a dish to simply warm you up. It's something to savor.

8. The soup. Sài Gòn soup has had dental work, implants, and a lift, wears a Versace dress, and sports a stylish haircut. She looks like a million dollars. Hà Nội's soup, by comparison, is the spotty kid with the runny nose who got an A in science but has no friends. She's harmless, but she has one fatal flaw: she's arrogant. The Sài Gòn seductress, on the other hand, preens herself like a prize bitch at a dog show. She knows she looks good. No way she would ever feel the need to shout about her looks. Everybody wants her.

The phở arrived. Raw beef for Sophie, cooked beef for me. The bowl was about twice the size of a Hà Nội bowl. The beef looked lean and well cut. It was almost as if the server had made an effort to present the thing in an appealing man-

241

ner. The beef strips were in a round pattern, each overlapping each other, like interlocking tiles on a Tuscan roof. The Phở Thìn boys liked to saw off the unappetizing end of a cow and sling it into the bowl.

I laughed at the sight of it. "It doesn't even look like phở. And the meat, it's not scraggy," I said, looking up at Sophie with a veil of confusion shrouding my face. "It actually looks like good meat." Puzzlement was now writ large across my visage. "Is this really phở?"

Sophie ordered me to rip up a bunch of herbs, throw in a pinch of boiled bean sprouts, a splodge of hoisin, and a squeeze of lemon. This phở was a meal, not a snack. It was also about twice the price of the ones I was used to in Hà Nội.

I'd never put herbs in a phở before in my life. Sophie had never *not* put herbs in a phở in her life, until she moved to Hà Nội. She had a smug, "After all these years of you inflicting that Hà Nội crap on me, I'm gonna show you what's what" look on her face.

I knew I was beaten before I took my first taste. I wasn't beaten by the surroundings. I never took to them. I like my grubby wee back alley joints. However, I was realist enough to know it all comes down to the food, and Phở Hoa Pasteur, on that day, in September 2001, blew every bowl of phở I'd ever had previously clean out of the soup vat.

Sorry, Hà Nội. I know you won't like this passage of my book. We had some great times together, but on that day I dumped you for that prize-winning bitch down south.

I was almost shocked at my own lack of feeling as I ditched the Hanoian bowl so unceremoniously and suddenly. Could I really be that heartless? Clearly I could.

CHAPTER SEVENTEEN: PAPERBACK WRITER

I sat down at my desk in our house in Sài Gòn, intending to write an article on war tourism in Việt Nam, due the next day. Four hours later I looked at the screen. It was still blank.

Six months earlier, it had all seemed so straightforward. I was in a newly opened bar on Hàng Hành Street in Hà Nội, meeting with Tamsin.

She was something called a freelance writer, by her own account a successful one, and I had decided I wanted to be one, too. Writing would be my ticket out of the office and onto the success train. I would have these big thoughts. I'd go see things. I'd talk to people who *knew* things about *stuff*. And I'd write about these things, and that stuff. And editors would buy what I wrote.

Tamsin was five, possibly ten years younger than me. This was the first time in my life I found myself asking someone much younger than me for advice. As we talked, she looked me up and down, sipped her Halida, and wobbled her head from side to side to the deep house lounge beats, all while eyeing everyone who entered the bar.

"I only need to file one more feature and I'm set for the rest of the year," she said, her New York confidence further fueled by the power of positive thinking and weekends of tantra yoga.

Within five minutes of our meeting, she'd rattled off the articles she'd written that year ("The one-legged prostitute story was tough, but it's important that it's out there. The public needs to know"); the publications she'd written for ("I had to turn the *New York Times* down this week. I'm just, like, so busy. I mean, don't they understand?"); and the names of the editors ("Tina is such a sweetie, but what a pain. Constantly hassling me. And Graydon rings me, like, every day. I mean, *durgh*, like I need that kind of nannying?").

Tamsin bled confidence. She was doing what I wanted to do — writing words and selling them for hard cash. I mean, how difficult could it be? I'd always been good at English at school. Tamsin made it sound like I just needed a couple of e-mail addresses and a few wacky ideas. I could do wacky. I could get e-mail addresses.

"No way I'm accepting less than two dollars per word," she said breezily, referring to a commission she'd turned down that very day. "C'mon . . . do I look like I'd work for that?"

Back in Sài Gòn, the screen glared at me. For the umpteenth time that day, I pored over the editor's e-mail. I was missing something, surely.

"If you could send 1,000 words to me by next Wednesday, that would be great. We don't have a budget for text, but it's fantastic exposure for you. Oh, and if you could throw in some pix too, it would be much appreciated. We can't pay for them either, but like I said, think about the exposure. Really excited to see the finished piece."

This couldn't go on.

CHAPTER EIGHTEEN:
SÀI GÒN

For five years, every weekday morning, the coffee dripped through the flimsy metal filter into the glass at the café on my street. Inside the Dilmah-and-Lipton-tea-stocked café, warm La Vie water bottles snuggled next to Kent, Thành Long, Vinataba, and Marlboro cigarette packets. Plastic jars with blue lids were half filled with lemons and lychees and sweetened with sugary water. Cà phê sữa đá was always served with a small glass of room-temperature jasmine tea. A dollop of sweetened condensed milk lay in wait at the bottom of a tall glass for the slow, hot drip of caffeine. It was a simple brew. Hot water over ground coffee. I'd add ice and stir it up with a long, thin spoon.

Hoà Hưng was an unexceptional street. At one end there was a prison. Police vans with "CẢNH SÁT" written on their sides would scream down the street, ferrying prisoners from the court to their new temporary, or sometimes permanent, home.

Alleys exited the eight-hundred-yard-long road at ten, twenty, thirty, or more points, like rivulets joining a tributary that fed the beast that was Cách Mạng Tháng Tám — CMT8 — at the other end of Hoà Hưng.

Sophie would have already arrived at the office, where she worked on a development program for teachers in Vietnamese universities. At the same time as I was trying to be a journalist, I worked as an examiner, testing the English skills of students who wanted to study overseas, which took up roughly two weeks every month.

One of the most striking differences we'd noticed as a mixed-race couple in Sài Gòn compared to Hà Nội was the daily lack of stares and pointing. We weren't so odd after all. We were almost normal. People ignored us. I recalled how we'd previously dealt with the situation in Hà Nội.

"She's beautiful," said one of a group of young men in a watch shop talking about Sophie. "Yeah, she's Korean," said another. "She can't be Vietnamese," said the third.

This is the thing when you're a foreigner — or not really a foreigner, but a Việt Kiều, and you understand the lingo, but people think you don't. The Vietnamese, and Hanoians in particular, have no shame in talking about you right in front of your face as if you don't exist.

It was clear that Sophie and I needed a different kind of coping mechanism. The Korean allusion in the Swatch shop had given us an idea.

Occasionally when we went out to a street restaurant, or a choked Vietnamese hangar-style number with not a foreigner in sight, and the stares began to bite, Sophie would pretend to be Korean or Japanese. Anything but Vina. I could get by well enough in Vietnamese to explain that she was not of these parts and that I'd be ordering the nosh.

We would instantly get far better service. If the staff thought that we were a Korean-European couple, we figured, they also thought that we had more money and would leave a bigger tip.

It also put people off the scent. Sophie would always get the same questions: "Where are you from? What's your name? No, your *real* name, your Vietnamese name? How come you grew up abroad?" The implication being, her parents were traitors to the glorious communist revolution, and that she was stained with the same curse.

There were the constant questions, pointing, and laughing. After a few months of it in Hà Nội, we grew tired of it.

Of course, the Korean pretense didn't always work out well. One weekend we took off for the mountain "resort" of Tam Đảo. I knew Tam Đảo well and had stayed there many times, but this was the first time I was introducing Sophie to the place. We'd powered up in the morning on the Minsk and were looking for a hotel to stay in.

The usual form is, a guy on a motorbike either finds you halfway up the eleven-mile hill to the summit of Tam Đảo and hassles you the rest of the way, until you agree to go to his "friend's" hotel. Or, soon after you arrive in the small hilltop village, someone else tails you and performs the same routine.

I knew the score, and I also knew where I wanted to stay. But our follower had other ideas. He followed us across town as I looped back, round, up, over in as confusing a fashion as I could to make him think I wasn't quite right. This guy was relentless, peppering his attack with broken English. Just before he gave up, he turned and shouted, in Vietnamese, "Cheap Korean bitch!" It was the first and only time Sophie has ever earned that accolade.

Relatively speaking, life in Sài Gòn for Sophie and me was not that big a culture shock. Compared to Hà Nội, it was almost relaxing. Back on Hoà Hưng Street, at the corner café, I'd sip and stir and stir and sip and take in life on the street, day by day.

A motorbike driver, his legs akimbo, drove past. A cardboard box filled with cooking oil rested

251

on the foot plate. The two additional boxes, balanced behind him, were not strapped on. With a deft hand, he would reach back and hold them, hopefully, as he rode over Hoà Hưng's bumps and ditches.

A kid learned to ride a bicycle. His mother pushed him gently as, all around him, the Highway Code violations mounted.

Three old boys sat next to me. The two facing the street had gray hair and the one with his back to the road had dyed black hair. His gray roots were just beginning to show. He'd need an appointment at the Cắt Tóc later on to remedy that.

Each of them had a glass of trà đá, and one had a pack of Craven A cigarettes. All wore plastic flip-flops. In a bamboo dish lay a box of matches with a bright yellow flower and the words "Sài Gòn" emblazoned upon it. They had arrived on Honda Super Cub 50 motorbikes. Each held a plastic folder filled with official-looking documents dotted with blue and red stamps.

The electrical and telecommunications system for the district sagged from the trees that lined the street. Hundreds of black-plastic-covered cables hung like rolled-up curtains, waiting to fall.

Farther down the street, a man with a naked paunch, hands on hips above his dark, belted trousers and faded red flip-flops, stood staring at the street. A line of men were hunched behind him over low tables, drinking tea, smoking, smiling, and chatting. Two young women in cheap, bright nylon clothes linked arms and giggled their way down the street, their feet pointed outward, their hair tied up with elastic bands.

A woman with a single three-tier glass cabinet and gurgling pot sat on a stool outside the café. She had no sign to tell people what she was selling, but somehow her customers knew. Two girls on a motorbike stopped to buy take-away bags of her soup and noodles.

Every once in a while, these scenes would take an unexpected turn, with an impromptu performance by the street's resident "family mad," as Toàn, who had quickly become my regular xe ôm, called them.

They would put on the street performance-play approximately three times per year. There were various iterations, but the most popular one was "the running of the wife."

You'd hear the screams first. That was the wife. She'd enter stage right, from the CMT8 end of the street, plastic flip-flops flapping down the street as she bobbled along, clearly perplexed and breathless, in an áo bà ba, her long black hair flailing behind her.

She was closely followed by the husband, the lead male and villain of the piece. He had on a pair of shorts and equally flappy flip-flops. He was a skinny fellow with mad eyes and a bare chest covered in cheap tattoos. He carried a butcher's knife in his right hand, while shouting obscenities — lots of them. In retrospect, it was he who taught me an abundance of highly colorful Vietnamese vocabulary.

The neighbors would pour out of their houses. This was a time before the ubiquitous use of mobile phones, but the bush telegraph worked impressively quickly along the street. By the time the wife had taken to the stage and run all of twenty yards, the whole neighborhood would be out to watch the running of the wife, and they would all giggle and smile, as if approving of the street theater.

The leading pair put on an impressive, if brief, performance. It would generally last around five minutes in total. The key chase scenes were punctuated by one or two seemingly ad-libbed set pieces that involved full-on face-to-face arguing, bitching, name-calling, and gesticulating with fingers and the blunt end of the butcher's blade.

A crescendo never really came. The end, such as it was, would invariably be another chase scene, down an alley and off the stage. I'd still be able to pick up the screaming of the running wife echoing up the walls, but I could no longer see the action from my café vantage point.

As they disappeared from view off the main street, I always half expected the neighbors to applaud, or maybe request an encore as the "family mad" went back to their lives, only to repeat the spectacle at random points throughout the year.

No one ever thought to contact the police. It reminded me of whenever Sophie and I saw the aftermath of road accidents: the Vietnamese refrain most commonly heard was "Is there any blood? Is there blood?" I'd never seen a motorbike road accident before moving east. At least not a messy one. It struck me as morbid, but an oddly *human* thing to ask. And not something specific to Việt Nam.

About the cast of our own local drama, Toàn would say in his sparse English, "Oh, it's just them, at it again," then he'd twist his hand at the side of his head and squint knowingly at me and the other xe ôm drivers who had season tickets at the café.

"At it again." With a butcher's knife. The running of the wife.

I got the impression that no one on the street took the quarrel seriously. It was understood that the violence was predominantly verbal. I couldn't understand everything that was being said, but I observed the lack of worry on the faces of everyone on the street. This family clearly had a history, and there were no family dispute intervention officers in Sài Gòn to step in and take control.

It was an ordinary street in Sài Gòn, with fifty or so restaurant options, at least ten cafés, twenty-plus regular street sellers, a small market, and some world-class street performers.

Just a normal street in Sài Gòn. And this was our home. I had never before lived in a street with such enormous homespun variety.

CHAPTER NINETEEN: ENTER HẺM HOÀ HƯNG MARKET

Regardless of their relatively low income, these street sellers, much like me, a wannabe freelance journalist, were their own bosses. That was, as far as I could tell, the only point of commonality in the way we lived and worked.

Economic necessity meant they would be out on the street every day of the week, but "independence" meant they could, in theory, bunk off, too, whenever they wanted. The big thing with these guys was that there was no one to report to. No quartermaster whipping them, no clock-watching boss or obnoxious colleagues to cope with.

The Hẻm Hoà Hưng market scythed a path down one concrete alleyway, midway along Hoà Hưng. In all, the market was little more than one hundred yards long. At the entry point were fruit sellers, vegetable stands, and butchers spread out to the main street, because there wasn't enough space along the alley itself, especially at the weekend when the chợ (market) would double in size.

If you want to really discover Việt Nam, it's here in the dungeons, crannies, and sewer pipes of alleyway markets, like that on Hẻm Hoà Hưng, that you'll find it. Not in the big brash markets of Sài Gòn, like Bến Thành. Nor in backpacker-land around Phạm Ngũ Lão Street, filled with dreadlocked travelers eating banana pancakes, trying hard to find themselves in budget accommodations. Nor will you find it on the slick and snazzy Đồng Khoi Street, nor on any number of central Sài Gòn thoroughfares.

If I could ever say I discovered Việt Nam, it was on the Hẻm, specifically Hẻm 83 Hoà Hưng, where I really got to know the food makers of Sài Gòn.

Hẻm 83 was a normal market, one of a slew in Sài Gòn, but it was *our* market, close to home. Where Sophie and I went together at the weekend to buy vegetables and have breakfast and buy lunch to take home. Where, during the week, I would come alone, while Sophie played the office drone. It's where our son, who was born in Sài Gòn in 2003, got his first taste of congealed pig's blood, steamed tapioca, frazzled bánh xèo pancakes, and the child-friendly porridge that is cháo trắng. *He what?* you ask. Yes, he ate street food. And he loved it.

For over five years I got to eat at every stall including one hidden down a warren, off the main Hẻm alleyway — call it a sub-Hẻm — where I found Miss Phạm Thị Ngọc Yến. There were no signs, just a set of ingredients laid out like a jigsaw puzzle. I had to put the pieces together in my head to figure out what she was serving.

It was hủ tiểu, a sweet noodle soup made with a few small prawns, kidney, slivers of pork and pork liver, Chinese celery, the chivelike hẹ, and bean sprouts. Often, as was the case at Miss Phạm's, you had three different noodles to choose from: the flat kind most often found in phở; clear tapioca noodles; or, my preferred option, the thin, round, yellow noodle called mì. Regardless of carbohydrate variants, the constant powder in the keg was the superb pork stock foundation.

This is possibly the most sugary pork broth in all of southern Việt Nam, which can be explained in part by its origins. The roots of this dish stretch across the border to Cambodia, where sugar-infused soups are ubiquitous on the boulevards of Phnom Penh. The Vietnamese often call the dish Hủ Tiếu Nam Vang (Nam Vang is what the Vietnamese call Phnom Penh, the Cambodian capital) to recognize the soup's source. Chinese Cambodians purportedly brought the dish to Việt Nam. And, as is ever the way, the Vietnamese got their boots on and made it their own. What was, once upon a time, a simple, slightly sweet Cambodian pork stock noodle soup, the Vinas pimped out with an outrageous number of options: congealed pig's blood, squid, pork, offal, prawns, caramelized shallots, lettuce. You can even have it without stock, or "dry." (I always went with "wet" myself.) As Vietnamese cookbook author Andrea Nguyễn says, "Hủ tiếu is the extreme have-it-your-way Vietnamese food experience."

There is also a rarer variant, hủ tiếu Mỹ Tho. Mỹ Tho is a hick town an hour or two south of Sài Gòn, in the Mekong Delta's Tiền Giang province. This version lacks the Cambodian namesake's sweetness, but it does boast a sizable added punch in the form of a whole pork knuckle, planted like an islet in a soup sea. I prefer the Vietnamese-Cambodian style of Miss Phạm's hủ tiếu.

As is traditional in these parts, Miss Phạm was clueless on the numbers side of things, but from her front-room serving hatch, she had a very sharp eye on the bottom line.

"I don't count how many bowls I serve. I just count the money," she said.

She guessed she sold between 100 and 150 bowls a day.

"It's difficult to make money. One hundred bowls is not enough to make a profit," she said.

Miss Phạm had been making and selling hủ tiếu for more than twenty years. She was single, and lived at this address with her parents and her aunt. Her three sisters were all married and lived elsewhere in Sài Gòn.

This one stall supported four people. She worked seven days a week. Her cousin, who lived in Tân Bình, came over to help out whenever she could. Miss Phạm tried to take ten days off every year for Tết, but she didn't take any anniversary days for deaths, birthdays, and the like. "I have to stay open to earn money," she said.

She started cooking at 3 A.M. and served from 6 A.M. until the pot gave its last, which was often well before 10 A.M.

On the table were a range of condiments: soy sauce, nước mắm, half lemons, vinegar, pepper, and sliced yellow chilies. Each table had a plastic plate with a roll of toilet paper on it, in lieu of napkins and, you know, just in case.

"A good hủ tiếu must have fresh ingredients," she said. "I buy the shrimp alive, and prepare and cook them myself. I don't have any big secrets. I just continue my family's recipe."

She bought the pieces for her jigsaw puzzle from Big C supermarket on Tô Hiến Thành Street, from Chợ Hòa Hưng at 539A Cách Mạng Tháng Tám, and from Ban Co wholesale market in District 4.

When I first started visiting Miss Phạm, I'd ask for "the works," but I soon learned to order

261

without the more unsavory parts of the pig, or the lòng, as they're called in Vietnamese — the intestines and crunchy bits. On the other hand, I had a weakness for the huyết (clotted pig's blood) that resembled rubbery lumps of coal in the middle of my breakfast. I supped her soup and commented upon its sweetness, and how Hanoians I'd known had ridiculed the southern sweet tooth.

"There is more sugar in the south, for sure," she said. "And, there's the influence of Laos and Cambodia. But, it's worse over there. If you go to Cambodia, they have big jars of sugar on every table," she said.

However, she wasn't about to roll over and take that jab at the midriff from her northern compatriots.

"Food in Hà Nội isn't as delicious as here in the south, though phở in Hà Nội *is* quite good," she said, making a sole concession to the north. "But the food up there is just not as diverse. There are more interesting things to eat in the south. And we have the herbs. We have a lot more herbs."

Under my red plastic dining table were pig bones and toothpicks. I'd kick them to one side as I took my seat and began dousing the soup with nước mắm and chili. Behind me was the corner wall of the main Hẻm alleyway, the side entrance to the chợ. Stenciled upon the wall's surface were the ever-present mobile phone numbers of the concrete cutters, like a secret code for locals. Few foreigners would know why the numbers were there or what they indicated, but you would see them all over Việt Nam. What other information could be passed on using stenciled numbers and letters in full sight of foreigners ignorant to the meaning? I wondered. Was this system used to relay information during the American war, or any war, for that matter? Covert messages left in plain public.

It turned out Miss Phạm's soup wasn't just popular with the inhabitants of the nearby passageways and cul-du-sacs.

"I don't just serve locals," Miss Phạm said. "People from overseas come here. There's this one man, a Việt Kiều, who told me he comes straight to my stall from the airport every time he arrives in Việt Nam. He missed the taste of my hủ tiếu. There are quite a lot of people like that, the Việt Kiều I mean. They miss this soup."

But why would that be? I asked her. I mean, American Việt Kiều had access to all manner of ingredients. How come it tasted so different at her stall down this grubby little alleyway?

"Hủ tiếu anywhere else, outside of Việt Nam, it's not the same. It can't be. The ingredients, the atmosphere. It just can't be the same," she said.

I knew what she meant. I'd tried Vietnamese food in restaurants in England and in France and always left disappointed. It was lazy and/or tasteless, always soulless, lacking any vital life signs. Vietnamese restaurants in Britain lacked a pulse. They were graveyards for a great cuisine. Even my mother-in-law, who used to run a Vietnamese restaurant in Andorra, would say the same. Sometimes, to my mind, with great irony.

"I can't cook Vietnamese food like I did in Việt Nam," she would say. "No one would eat it." She believed, and perhaps rightly so, that her sensitive Western customers might be put off by a challenging whiff of mắm tôm here, a splash of nước mắm there, and a chunk of congealed blood staring up at them from their soup.

Even within the family. *Our family.* They were all great cooks, making good food. But, it was just not the same. As Miss Phạm said, "It just can't be." And, even with her affluent Việt Kiều customers, an established hủ tiếu slot, and loyal locals, Miss Phạm found it hard to turn a profit.

"There's just no way to make money anymore, so they all stopped," she said, referring to her colleagues in the gradually dwindling market. "Local people go to the supermarkets these days. The small markets like this are dying out in Sài Gòn. The government wants to close down all the small markets like this. I feel sorry about that."

She went on to explain the plot being hatched by the powers that be.

"There's a plan the government has, across the

whole of Sài Gòn. The government wants more hygiene, and for the streets to be more peaceful. I'll keep going, even if I have fewer customers. What else will I do?" She continued, "I feel sad about it, but it makes sense. A lot of the street food places are not really hygienic. People get sick. The government doesn't really have a choice, so I think it's the right thing to do."

While on one level I agreed and empathized with her, on another I thought the Vietnamese might completely lose the plot on this one. I'm all for hygiene and reasonably safe food — I personally think a few microbes in your dinner are a good thing for the human race — but I could not imagine a scorched-earth policy as applied to street vendors. For what? So that you can look developed? So that your incredibly vibrant, varied, buzzy, crazy, fun city streets can look just like anywhere else? If that was the future the authorities had in mind, I was against it.

Alarming signs were already there in Sài Gòn. Just like I'd seen in Hà Nội, trucks full of cops pulling up to clear an area of vendors were a not-uncommon sight.

"That's why, now, you see the police coming and clearing the streets every now and then. All the street sellers have to run. Have you seen them?" another seller on the market asked me one day.

I had seen them. The police would arrive,

blitz through a street-stall-festooned area, and violently nab stools, panniers, and baskets from the traders who hadn't been quick enough to exit the firing zone.

It always seemed random. Always petty. The sellers had been playing a game of cat and mouse with the cops and their occasional bursts of law enforcement and vile extortion ever since. It was a barmy plot to cleanse the streets, and it had little long-lasting effect, but it seemed to annoy everyone involved.

Some vendors told me that street food sellers had been banned in parts of Sài Gòn as early as 1998. However, you'd have been hard-pressed to believe there were any laws against street vendors by looking at the streets in 2004, or even in the present day. Indeed, in 2004, any laws associated with street vendors were ambiguous at best and, such as they were, came under a "decree on traffic law." The street sellers adapted their tactics and kept an eye over their collective shoulder.

"Laws," "edicts," and "guidance" at the local level were arguably more prevalent. "Officially" speaking, the market where I ate my hủ tiếu on had ceased to exist before Sophie and I ever moved to Sài Gòn.

"The government closed the market around 2000," another trader, who'd sat down for a meal at the hủ tiếu stall, told Sophie and me one morning as we gobbled. "So, it's officially closed, but it's not closed, as you can see," she said, waving a hand across a scene of fruit, vegetables, fish, meat, soups, noodles, and stir-fry sellers. "If you have a house down this alleyway, you can still work here, but you can't sell fish, meat, fruit, or vegetables. Soups are OK. Things that are ready to eat are fine, if you live here," she added, as I surveyed what I now realized was the overwhelming illicit trade all around us.

The trader was called Thủy. She had a small phở stall around the corner on the main alleyway that formed the market.

"Before the market closed, you could find everything being sold down here," she added. "Phở was a good business to be in. There were no competitors and shoppers needed to eat."

We became regulars at Thủy's stall, not because it was fantastic phở — I always found it a little bit too sweet — but because she could always be relied upon to have the biggest batch on the market. If I was late, as I often was, she'd still always have a bowl for me.

"The government asked me to put my business back inside the house, but you can see it's too small." She pointed to a postage-stamp-sized front room. "It's too hard to sell from in there. I keep an eye out for the police. I've not had to pay any fines up until now, but it's clear the government wants us off the street."

This sense of not being wanted on the streets seemed to haunt everyone I spoke to. Back at Miss Phạm's, as I took a break from bending forward to ingest her tantalizing soup, I asked her, just like I asked Nga in Hà Nội, and everyone else I met: What about the soul? These markets are the heartbeat of Việt Nam, not just Sài Gòn and Hà Nội, but the entire nation.

"Sure, with all of these changes, the city is losing its soul," she said. "It's natural, if there's no market here and no people. It slowly dies."

The romantic foreigner side of me felt attached to street food. It wasn't about a hard economic reality for me. I made the choice to eat it, initially out of curiosity and subsequently because of the superior taste. However, the less commonly accessed, logical, pragmatic side of me realized that despite Nga's protestations at her bún chả stall in Hà Nội, a change — not all for the good — was inevitable.

Miss Phạm pointed down the Hẻm Hoà Hưng alleyway and shook her head as if to say, "All this will be gone one day."

At the corner, two yards from where I sat hunched on plastic as usual, a woman sold súp cua, a crab soup, from a shiny stainless steel vat strapped to the backseat of a motorbike. On the handlebars hung white and blue plastic bags filled with plastic cups, bowls, and spoons.

Opposite, a sole parasol covered a nước mắm seller. She had a cardboard sign hanging off the front of her mobile stall.

How many cardboard signs were there in this city? In this country? How many mobile traders? Thousands, certainly, tens of thousands probably, hundreds of thousands even. Vital cogs in the gastronomical and economical turbine that turned Việt Nam, from north to south.

I asked Miss Phạm a question I made a point of asking everyone in the market.

"So, apart from you, who makes the best food in this market?"

I thought she'd at least take a moment to think about it, to brood and recollect tastes over the years. Surely numerous soups had held residency on the Hẻm, and more had arrived on the back of a bicycle, a cart, or a motorbike only to disappear again when sold out. But no, Miss Phạm didn't hesitate.

"Bà Sáu," she said. "There's only Bà Sáu bún mắm."

Bà Sáu? Bà Sáu bún mắm? What was this bún mắm she spoke of? It was a new one on me. A clue. A tip. A ticket to meet a soup star. Only I didn't know it yet. Bà Sáu's time would come.

CHAPTER TWENTY:
NOODLEPIE

I hadn't chosen the easy path into the world of blogs. The cobra-heart-popping, half-grown-duck-egg-eating, larvae-munching, freak-readers-out food blog would, on balance, have been just the ticket for a large online following.

That direction would have been all too easy. Entertaining too, but representative of Vietnamese food? No.

Blogs were hot. Mainstream media was trembling in its tattered boots. Citizen journalists were the new Walter Cronkites. A digital fog was sweeping in. The media, as we had known it since Gutenberg's press, was about to go the way of the dinosaurs.

I wanted to be a part of this new wave. And from the get-go I realized I had to find a tight focus. I'd need to write about something I was passionate about. In the end, it was an easy choice to make. Street food in Sài Gòn suggested itself at every corner. Even better, there were, as far as I could tell, very few people blogging from Việt Nam. And no one anywhere in the world was blogging about street food, and I was living in the street food capital of the known world. It was, as they say, a no-brainer.

I first became interested in blogs in 2002. The earliest blog output of this era resembled the homespun, typewriter-written, photocopied, and hand-stapled indie music fanzines I had put together with friends in the mid-eighties. It was punk. And blogging felt punk. I liked punk. And, just as important, it didn't sound that difficult to do.

Blogging was the opposite of old-school journalism, in which information is gathered, jealously guarded, and hidden away before publication. My first instinct was to share, not to hold back. And it wasn't that I was in the scoop business while writing about street food, anyway. In retrospect, I like to think it was a pure form of foreign correspondence: a letter from somewhere foreign, translating something foreign for the benefit of mostly foreigners. My only desire was to make sure that fish sauce dripped through the screen to every reader.

But what caught me off guard was how quickly one can become an authority on the subject. In 2004, blogging really was like putting your head above the parapet. You were very quickly visible. And, to some, I was suddenly an expert on

271

street food. A translator or medium for Vietnamese culture, and a point of contact for each and every foreign journalist, food explorer, blogger, weirdo, misfit, and dropout who happened to come across me on the Internet.

On the surface it seemed as if any dimwit with access to the Internet and the ability to type one key after another and form a legible sentence now and then was immediately deemed an authority, because . . . *well, you were on the Internet, maaan*. The reality wasn't far from that.

I was there, on the ground, somewhere other people were not, and I was doing things other people were not — or, at least, digitally recording them. As a blogger, you became a source. A contact. And contactable. As expert qualifications went, that seemed to be about it. And, by virtue of having a blog, I was fully qualified.

Suffice it to say, I gave myself three goals when I started blogging:

To explain the what, where, who, why, when, and how of street food in Sài Gòn.

To file away an archive of memories for when we left Việt Nam. You know, to salivate over.

To learn the technology.

The only blogs I read at the time were *SliceNY,* a

pizza blog in New York, a city I'd never visited, and *Eggsbaconchipsandbeans,* which blogged nothing but plates of eggs, bacon, chips, and beans found in eateries across London, a city I knew well. And then there was *FatManSeoul,* on which an anonymous (and presumably over-weight) Malaysian man who was working in Seoul blogged his lunch so that his family back home could see what he was eating on his many extended business trips. It was that simple. And *FatManSeoul* was my template. The appeal of these blogs, for me at least, was the people be-hind them, their voices and personalities.

I needed a name. I chose *noodlepie*. "East meets West in Sài Gòn" (or West meets East, to be more precise) seemed too obvious and sim-ple, whereas *noodlepie* seemed to encapsulate the "bún chả meets bangers and mash" concept succinctly, accurately, and, to my mind, styl-ishly.

Only later did I discover that noodle pie was an actual thing. A Russian thing. A delicacy, appar-ently, though one I've never tried. Subsequently, a prospective restaurateur in London approached me to use the name. "It's so original. We'd like to use it for our restaurant." An unimaginative children's book author did the same.

Street food is a gargantuan topic. Choosing to blog and write about it was my own personal

273

Mount Everest.

Zoom out from this sprawling octopus of a city, eaten in and slept in on a daily basis by around eight million people, all of whom call Sài Gòn home. A population approaching the size of New York. Too many people. Too big.

By focusing on street food generally, I knew I would have an endless supply of edibles to write about and photograph. However, I also knew I would never, ever, no matter how hard I tried, ever reach "the end," as in a comprehensive log of street food, in all of its forms, across the whole of Sài Gòn. I knew I had no chance of accomplishing this. But I would begin the journey all the same.

I never believed the classification of "expert" applied to myself. I could barely string together a Vietnamese sentence, and often had some difficulty dissecting the key components of my dinner. Yet, at the time, my blog was one of the only sources of information about Vietnamese street food online.

Of one thing I was always certain: Sài Gòn street food was far too big a topic for anyone, especially a non-Vietnamese foreigner, to ever become fully versed in. Like a chess player attempting to know all the possible moves in any given game, *it just wasn't gonna happen*. I knew I would never be able to say that I truly understood Vietnamese food and culture, but I was having fun cleaving my own path through the delectable morass.

As for my facility with the native language, I nearly always traveled with some form of translator. I could do numbers, ingredients and dishes, directions, names, and some other basic phrases, but if not for the help of Sophie, Vietnamese friends, and expats with far greater linguistic skills over the years, I'd have only ever gotten the bare-bones information from each of the vendors I frequented and wrote about.

In large part because I blogged about street food in Sài Gòn, my attempt at professional journalism took off enough to call it more than an experiment. Foreign correspondents were officially banned from using Sài Gòn as a home base. As a result, I'd had to become slightly creative in the way I worked and wrote.

I called it "location-nonspecific journalism." I'd scoured every newspaper and magazine Web site I could find and built a database of editors. It took weeks. And then I pitched them regularly. While I did "worthy" stories for the more obscure ends of the BBC, the *Guardian,* CNN, and others, my bread and butter was far more curious.

Based out of the spare bedroom upstairs at our house in District 10, I worked as the wildlife columnist for the UK-based *Scotland Maga-*

zine. I was the ecotourism travel columnist for the Scottish *Sunday Herald* newspaper. I was a regular contributor to the Fleet Street–based *Press Gazette* in the UK, and to the Asia edition of *Time* magazine and the *South China Morning Post,* both based in Hong Kong.

Most of what I wrote and sold had nothing at all to do with Việt Nam, while many of my editors had no idea I was based on the other side of the world. But it didn't matter where I was based. For all intents and purposes, I could have been located anywhere. I realized quickly that this was the way I wanted to earn my living. From a laptop. Anywhere in the world.

I never did manage to find the financial goldmine that Tamsin, the successful freelance journalist based in Hà Nội, had dangled in front of me a few years earlier. Over time, I learned to turn down the cheapskates who came calling with offers of "great exposure."

I continued to work regularly as an examiner for the International English Language Testing System (IELTS). And to exploit it for street food insider knowledge whenever an opportunity presented itself.

The test was divided into four parts. The oral exam followed a script. It was eleven to fourteen minutes long. It was recorded on audio cassette. I did hundreds of them.

Discussion questions followed topics. Often there was a food topic, with questions like "Would you please describe a restaurant you enjoyed going to?" and "What are some of your favorite foods?"

There was some room in the script for the examiner to wiggle. To linger on a topic for more than thirty seconds. So, whenever the food topic surfaced, I lingered.

"Please, tell me, what are some of your favorite foods?"

"I like traditional Vietnamese foods, like bánh xèo."

"And why do you like it?"

"It's so fresh. Everything is cooked in front of you. It sizzles in a hot frying pan on a wood fire. It has to be cooked and eaten quickly, with a lot of different herbs."

"That's interesting. And where do you like to eat this dish?"

"I can make a good one at home. My friends say I do it very well."

"Yes, yes, but where do you go out to eat it?"

"In Bến Thành market, there is one. It's quite good."

"OK, but look, we're in an exam here, and if you don't tell me exactly where you really go to eat this dish, you can kiss good-bye to a pass, got it?"*

---

* The last bit of that conversation only ever happened

"Bánh Xèo on Đinh Công Tráng Street. It's the famous one. At number 46A. Not the one opposite. That one's total crap. 46A's is delicious. I'll take you. I'll pay."

"Well done. You've passed."

Before I entered the examination room and gleaned that morsel of information, I'd received two e-mailed bánh xèo hints, both with a location. Great, you're thinking, I now had three different bánh xèo spots to check out. Wrong. All three had independently suggested the same joint. 46A. By accident rather than design, I had managed to triangulate this city's bánh xèo sweet spot.

I'd eaten bánh xèo a few times before, but I'd always come away feeling a bit "Hmm, yeah. *Hmm, so what?*" Which was a shame, because (a) it had a cool name; (b) like the exam taker said, it was an "action food," sizzling in oil like it was looking to leap out of the pan; and (c) I really liked "action food."

Saigonites, it turns out, flock to this fifty-seat outdoor alleyway eatery. Bean sprouts, shrimp, and fatty pork nubs are hurled into a thin, watery batter. It's fried to magma-hot, flipped over, and served in seconds. 46A first opened in the late 1950s. It was, the owner told me, the first of

---

inside my head. But I always made sure I got my tip.

its kind, and it remained the most popular in the whole of Sài Gòn.

On one visit, I got talking to one of the five cooks seated at floor level, juggling frying pans over hot charcoal. She charmed me by saying that she had a favorite frying pan, like it was her pet. Her bent pan looked as though it had been driven over, or been used to beat rude customers, or maybe it had shored up a truck axle. But this, she insisted, was her favorite, pointing at it, one of six she simultaneously juggled in her bánh xèo circus. She told me it was fifty years old, the same age as the restaurant. I wasn't sure whether to believe her or not, but I couldn't argue with the knackered state of the kitchen utensil she stroked and bashed in front me.

Across the street at 49A there was a much larger, more modern copycat bánh xèo restaurant. Tellingly, it was entirely devoid of customers every time I dropped into 46A.

What I loved about many of these "famous" places in Việt Nam, like Phở Thìn in Hà Nội and countless thousands of other places, was that despite heaps of loyal customers and sacks of cash coming in, they never lifted a finger to improve the aesthetics of their restaurant.

Bánh xèo needed to be devoured as soon as it hit the plate. There was never any waiting for late dinner arrivals, prayers, or the shuffling of chairs. You needed to leave the civilities at home. None of the "Oh no, please, you start," or "Oh no, please, you should try it first." Stop it right there. *Dive in*. A bánh xèo pancake should be crispy on the outside and ever so slightly moist on the inside. Leave it hanging around too long and you've got a soggy crepe on your hands. And you don't want that, believe me. Fortunately, as I'd learned in Hà Nội, there's no faffing about at the Vietnamese dining table.

Bánh xèo came with a plate of nine different leaves and herbs. The most important to my mind was cải bẹ xanh, or mustard leaf. I'd use it to wrap my custom filling of bánh xèo and selected herbs before giving it a quick dunk in the nước mắm and shoveling the entire parcel inside. Crunch, chew, and swallow. It was a devastatingly good mouthful.

It wasn't so much the bánh xèo itself as the herb bomb, wrapped in its mustard leaf casing.

Some months after I first started blogging, I found myself showing yet another journalist around Sài Gòn.

"What you're really doing when you're blogging about food, writing about food, broadcasting about food, is enthusing about life. At least you are if you're doing it well," I said with an air of *oh, that sounds rather good*.

I was seated sideways, sunk in the back of a taxi facing journalist Brett Martin, who was

in town on assignment with *Bon Appétit* magazine, as we honked our way across Sài Gòn's
motorbike carpet to Nguyễn Đình Chiểu Street
in District 3. I was about to introduce him to
something spectacular.

My oh-so-smart remark was really a rehash
of a remark made in 1985 by Alan Vega of the
immeasurably unsuccessful, yet hugely influ-
ential and uncategorizable band called Suicide.
He'd said, "Suicide was always about life. But
we couldn't call it Life. So we called it Suicide
because we wanted to recognize life."

In its own way, my blog was about life. Sài
Gòn was drowning in life. The best subjects
were the ones right in front of me, and in Sài
Gòn, my subject, any subject, was not under my
snout, but in my face, CinemaScope, 24/7.

Brett was the latest in a line of print, photo,
radio, and TV journalists who'd been in touch
with me to talk about Việt Nam and eat street
food. I met with them all. My blog had become
a magnet for every weirdo, geek, nerd, loser,
freak, journalist, blogger, misfit, oddball, wast-
rel, bum, has-been, and lost soul who in some
way saw street food as a Band-Aid for whatever
ailment it was they had. Or feature they had to
write.

I enjoyed showing them around the country in
2004. I had pushed open the portal to my street
food world. I could still remember how impen-

etrable it had seemed to me all those years ago in Hà Nội. Only I didn't realize at the time quite how many people would want me to guide them into this unknown world. Neither did I realize, at this time, the entrepreneurial opportunity that lay out there for people like me with the detritus on the street.

Along with that freak's brew of fun-to-be-with contacts, many of whom I correspond with to this day, there were the ones I didn't quite click with. "The brigade of dread," as I started calling them. They'd show up in their Ralph Lauren polo shirts, sometimes a Panama hat, often in linen, and they would opine.

I took Brett, one of the good guys, to a bánh tráng phơi sương restaurant where I'd taken many others.

The restaurant, Quán Cô Tấm, was conveniently located opposite Sophie's office, on Nguyễn Đình Chiểu Street in District 1.

I ordered. Brett and I talked.

Bánh tráng phơi sương seemed to descend from some celestial garden in the Sài Gòn ether and thud onto the table in a green cloud. Center stage we had thin slices of boiled pork. Nothing fancy going on there, just pork. The accompanying bowls and plates held the building blocks to transform the meat into the dish. A stack of soft rice papers sat on one plate, while a sweet nước mắm, pickled carrots, small leeks, raw bean sprouts, and cucumber sliced lengthways occupied a series of small bowls. And then came the mighty herb trough.

It was while I was sitting here nibbling that I decided this dish needed a deeper dissection than I'd previously given it. It needed the full Vina-autopsy. I didn't know it at the time, but this one simple dish, more than any other in Việt Nam, would for me come to represent Vietnamese food in its most pure form.

The herbs were at the heart of this dish. Nearly ten different varieties. I didn't know what most of them were called. But someone, somewhere in this town, I thought, must have some mightily impressive semilegal herb garden hidden away, and the owner of this restaurant knew who that was. And I wanted to meet that person.

The only thing of any note I ever said to any of the visiting journalists, and the only thing I stand by to this day, was what I said to Brett as we peered at each other over that verdant herb mountain on Nguyễn Đình Chiểu Street.

"What worries me with all this progress is what happens to all the food, the street food," I said, pointing at the increased number of cars, the flashier motorbikes, the Gucci-sunglass-wearing kids who never existed when I first arrived in the country. "What happens when everyone's got enough money? A motorbike, a car, a house? Where does the street food go? Will there still be a place for it? Will these great dishes disappear behind closed doors?"

CHAPTER TWENTY-ONE:
THE TAPE

I'd noticed the same thing the whole length of Việt Nam. Between the tip of the Mekong Delta and the border with China there were, on the main roads, almost no breaks in the bricks and concrete. To drive the length of Việt Nam's main artery was to drive between walls of houses, shops, restaurants, factories, bus stations, schools, hospitals, police stations, Communist Party offices, markets, soup sheds: there was not one significant area of open, undeveloped space between Sài Gòn and Hà Nội.

From Sài Gòn, in a car heading west, the monotone concrete blocks comprising two-, three-, four-, five-, and six-story buildings effectively walled in the road. Each building offered something to the passerby, some form of financial transaction. None of the buildings offered me what I was looking for, however.

I'd long since given up riding the Minsk. If driving in Hà Nội required a death wish, doing the same in Sài Gòn came with the undertaker's invoice. I'd done my time on two wheels. Early on during my southern stay, I'd decided to quit while I still could. For any trip involving half a day, like this one, I hired a driver.

While the trip was, in essence, a pilgrimage to a recommended lunch spot, I was hoping to find out more about the herbs. See where they grow. A small detour, I figured.

I'd spoken with Mrs. Tấm, the owner of Quán Cô Tấm, that fabulous restaurant serving bánh tráng phơi sương opposite Sophie's office in District 1. I'd been looking for a way in on the herb front.

And I found one. But it was vague.

"We buy the herbs from Tây Ninh," Mrs. Tấm told me.

"Where? Who grows them?" I asked.

"A farmer. I don't know who. Someone delivers them each morning, but he's not the farmer. He's just a middleman," came the reply.

"Well, do you know the name of the farmer?"

"No. Look, we just buy the herbs from a supplier, it's not rocket science. He supplies herbs. We buy them. It really is that simple," came the translated response of her next reply inside my head, but what she actually said was, "The herbs grow everywhere in Tây Ninh."

"Everywhere"? Hmm . . . If I was to take Mrs. Tấm's word for it, I'd find myself tripping over the greenery. I just needed to get up the road to Tây Ninh. It would take an hour, more or less, depending on traffic.

Inside the car, the driver had inserted THE TAPE. I knew THE TAPE. I knew THE TAPE well. My translator, a student called Huyền who sat in the back of the car, knew THE TAPE, too.

In cafés. In bars. If it weren't for whiskey, beer, and devilish homemade spirits, when THE TAPE came on you could be forgiven for thinking you'd arrived in a waiting room halfway to purgatory.

The advice I have for you, if you ever find yourself in the presence of THE TAPE, is firstly to leave. Don't let that musical thumbprint plant itself inside your brain. You will never be rid of it. I speak as one who suffers.

If, for whatever reason, you cannot leave, locate the speakers and position yourself as far away from them as possible. And if there's a little bit of the terrorist in you, carry scissors at all times and find wires to snip. Any wires. Just make it stop.

And it doesn't matter where you are in Việt Nam, THE TAPE has legs. It will follow you.

THE TAPE is a well-known commodity within the expat community. One blogger, Michael Sieburg, wrote about it. He even considered setting up a charity to aid the listening public, writing:

My co-worker has decided to yet again play THE TAPE. Anyone living in Sài Gòn knows what I'm talking about. Go to a pool hall, a coffee shop, ride a bus to Mũi Né, walk into a bookstore, anywhere you go, you hear it. It's the one tape with Western music that everyone has. Everyone. The Eagles. The Carpenters. Richard Marx. "Unbreak My Heart" ... People here really love this tape. I've heard "Hotel California" more times in Sài Gòn than on VH1 ... I am not exaggerating saying I hear this tape at least four times a week ... with the widespread overplaying of THE TAPE in mind, I have begun thinking of starting a charity, '(New) Music for Việt Nam.' The idea is to carry around tapes (CD) with your favorite Western mix. Anytime you hear THE TAPE, give whoever is playing it a copy of your mix. Or just remind them that Trịnh Công Sơn or The Bells are far preferable to Richard Marx.

I'm not sure if his idea ever took off, but I'd wager very good money THE TAPE is still broadcasting pain, loud and clear across Việt Nam to this very day.

The only way I could intellectualize it, after many years pondering the subject and little else, was that the Vietnamese simply didn't listen to music in the sense that I would. To them, music is just another noise in the sonic bouquet. OK, it can be a more melodious noise, although admittedly it's a bit of a stretch when "Please Forgive Me" by Bryan Adams comes on for the *millionth* time and you just want to scream, "NO, I WILL NOT FUCKING FORGIVE YOU! EVER!" But, to the Vietnamese, it's essentially just background noise. THE TAPE should not be something to concentrate on, consider, or use to provide the soundtrack for your mental breakdown.

Why else would the staff of a hotel restaurant click Play on THE TAPE *every single day,* breakfast, lunch, and dinner, without ever getting bored of it or thinking to change it?

After long and hard thought I came to the conclusion that they were simply not listening to it. No one was. But I was. And I could not avoid listening to it. It resides in me to this day.

I looked at the driver and smiled. "Oh. You have THE TAPE?"

He smiled back as he crooned along to the playback, "Please forgive me, I know not what I do."

"So, how long did you say it was to Tây Ninh?" I asked Huyền. She was twenty-three years old, had recently graduated in languages, was keen to study abroad, and had excellent English. Frighteningly for me, I seemed to know more about

Vietnamese food than she did. Was the younger generation losing its skills that rapidly? Or, had I really learned that much since the days of the pig's uterus in Hà Nội? Huyền didn't cook. Her friends didn't cook. Whereas all the Vietnamese I knew of my own age did know how to cook. While Huyền and her friends were hardly a representative straw poll sample of the Vietnamese youth, this was alarming news.

If you don't have any solid contacts, and you don't know exactly what it is you're looking for (and neither does your translator), finding herbs in Tây Ninh takes a little bit longer than you might think, especially in the middle of the rainy season, when the rice paddies are green, the banana trees too, the buffalo are grazing, and the streets are lined with concrete. To the untrained eye, everything green could indeed be herbal. I had little idea what I was looking for: bush? tree? shrub? wallflower? I was as clueless as the first time I came face-to-face with those slices of cooked uterus almost ten years earlier.

I'd been on a similar quest years earlier, farther north, in Hội An, in central Việt Nam. I'd been assured there was a kind of cress grown in and around the ancient town that could be found nowhere else in Việt Nam, or indeed the world. And, like the lady at Quán Cô Tấm had told me, I had eventually found it growing "everywhere," on patches of dirt and in fields.

About sixty miles northwest of Sài Gòn, we arrived in the suburbs of Tây Ninh. There had to be herbs here somewhere. Putting my Hôi An head back on, I suggested to the driver that we turn down a dirt road. We did, and three minutes later it ended in a cul-de-sac next to a Catholic church, almost a mile from the main Tây Ninh–to–Cambodia road.

We got out and walked. It was green. This was farmland, dotted with detached houses, most of which had two rooms on the ground floor, two rooms above. Outside a smaller house, we found a woman called Hương.

She grew herbs. I could see that. At least I thought I could see that. Between me on the road and her at her front door was a small plot. The whole area was sheltered from the traffic noise by the distance and banana and coconut trees.

Alas, she could not escape the sound of her neighbor, some two hundred yards away, who had the window wide open as his karaoke machine strafed the neighborhood with Vietnamese folk standards. Maybe the herbs liked it, but surely no human could.

"I've grown herbs here for many, many years," Hương told me over the din. She was nearly fifty years old, had her hair in a ponytail, and boasted the healthy glow of someone who spent a lot of time outdoors.

There was a big white number 47 stamped across the door of her one-room house. A pomelo tree sheltered two barking dogs that were chained to the front step railings. Two shutters shielded the room from the sun. The slapdash mess of corrugated sheeting that attempted to form a roof looked like a slew of crinkled papers on an untidy desk.

Hương was dressed in a powder blue áo bà ba, with her wrinkled feet jammed inside a pair of those omnipresent yellow plastic flip-flops. She talked to me about how she farmed.

"I used to grow lots of herbs before, but it's easier just to concentrate on one kind," she said, pointing to an immaculately laid-out garden with nine rows growing nothing but the herb tía tô. Hương grew and harvested the crop and a supplier came to buy it. It ended up on the local markets, in Sài Gòn, and beyond.

"Tía tô is so easy. It survives the rain with no protection from nets or glass. And there's always a market for it."

Tía tô (known in the west as red perilla) is commonly found on side plates at bún chả and bún ốc stalls. It's purple and green and has a big, earthy flavor. It sparkles when dunked in fish sauce and munched with spades of noodles. If I had a top-five list of favorite Vietnamese herbs, tía tô would be on it, probably at number three, I reckoned. I had no idea why it was so little used in the West. It would be so easy for an enterprising chef to create some kind of Oriental garden salad thing, chuck in some papaya, a glug of vinegar, a splurge of mustard, and call it Vietnamese drizzled leaf salad, Asian herb fantasia, or some such.

Hương told me that her children were grown up, had moved not far away, and worked in offices elsewhere in Tây Ninh province. She cultivated the field alone, while her husband toiled at a local footwear factory.

"You cannot live only by farming. Not on land this size," she said, indicating the thirty-by-twenty-yard plot. "The families you see with bigger plots, with nets covering their herbs, they can make a living from herb growing, but we can't."

All around this area of Tây Ninh, off the main road, hidden behind the concrete perimeter, were netted farms, some covered in plastic. Mustard leaves, lettuce, cabbages, and herbs all grew well with the artificial temperature boost provided by the cover. However, Hương's patch was a sideline for the family, not their main source of income.

In a larger, more modern dwelling next door, I sat down with the extended family, who had been busy sorting leaves in the front yard when we arrived. The living room was sparsely decorated. Those decorations that existed were mostly Catholic in nature: a painting of the Last Supper, a statue of the Virgin Mary, and a crucifix.

Hương lived here with her husband, Trần, two young nieces who studied nearby, and Hương's mother, Mrs. Phụng, a tiny, gray-haired, seventy-five-year-old lady with a bare-bones command of English. She was not more than four feet tall, had on a pair of black silk trousers and a similarly colored áo bà ba. She wore glasses and stroked a string of dark brown worry beads.

To one side of the television, placed in the center of a large wooden cupboard, was the family altar. There were four framed photos of dead family members and a packet of cigarettes as the offering of the day. Offerings to the ancestors were always of items they had enjoyed during their time on earth. The idea was, these things would help them on their journey to the next life. To the other side of the TV was a remote control, encased in a polythene cover to protect it from dust. A hammock hung from the ceiling in the center of the room, right in front of the TV.

I sat on a wooden bench on one side of the room. In front of me was a glass-covered coffee table, with family photos captured under the glass. Under the coffee table lay a feather duster and a straw broom. Vietnamese women were always cleaning, sweeping, dusting, and gathering. One of the teenage nieces picked the duster up and fluttered across the few surfaces in the room as we spoke.

A blackened San Miguel ashtray with six cigarette butts inside sat on the ledge under the coffee table. The ceiling fan wafted the ash over the brim in short bursts.

"In this area, we mostly all farm tía tô, lettuce, húng quế [basil] and rau răm [Vietnamese coriander], Hương's bare-chested husband, Trần, told me.

"The best price we get is for húng lủi [mint]," which they sold for about 30,000 đồng for one kilogram. It has a "curly leaf and a curly body. We manage to get a crop every single month, twelve months of the year."

"The best thing about this work is that it's very flexible," Hương explained. "It's best to plant in the morning and water in the evening. But you can add fertilizer whenever you want. We use the waste from the chickens. We spray chemicals every now and then, to prevent the pests."

I was curious about the herbs, whether their use was of medicinal value, or was it just for the taste.

"The herbs we grow are all about the taste," said the husband. "There are few medicinal benefits."

Having said that, Mrs. Phụng insisted one herb, tía tô, could be used for medicine, although she had no idea what condition it could be used to help.

"If you dry it under the sun, you can use it to

help cure sickness."

"What sickness?"

"I don't know exactly, but some people say it helps you if you are sick."

"Do you use it?"

"No, I've never used it."

Much like the "famous" restaurants of Hà Nội, it sounded to me as if Mrs. Phung had heard someone say something about the medicinal benefits of these herbs. And, that something just had to be true. After all, she'd heard it. Even if her husband had not.

Tây Ninh, Trần told me, had been the home to herb growing in Việt Nam for dozens of years.

"I have no idea why, but lots of big suppliers come here. It's important to have good soil and we have that here, but more important is how the farmers grow their herbs. What techniques they use," he said.

The family had been based on this land for four generations, since 1954, when the Vietnamese booted the French out and the country divided into two, North and South; it remained divided until 1975, when the Americans in turn got the boot.

"We came from Hai Đường, where we lived in the north," explained Trần. "We took a boat from our home to Vũng Tàu, and from there we got a lift in a car to Tây Ninh. Lots of displaced northerners live in this area."

Trần continued, while his wife nodded along, "The rice fields where we worked during the war were ten miles away. We'd walk there at the beginning of each week and stay there until the following Saturday. Then we'd walk back home again for one night and to go to church on Sunday. It was a very hard life back then. We only had a little bit of rice to eat. Mostly, we ate cassava roots. Quite a bit different from today."

The war. The American War. Long discussed, debated, lamented, and regretted in the United States. However, I can count the number of conversations I had about the war with Vietnamese people in Việt Nam on the fingers of one hand. The Vietnamese had long since moved on. There was no bitterness. The past was the past. The present and the future was the focus now. And, in a country where the average age is under thirty, most Vietnamese in Việt Nam had never known war.

Trần's family started to grow herbs in 1982. Today, the patio at the front of their house was filled with herbs, half sorted. "The buyer will come by later today."

What about those herbs, and the plates they would wind up on? Where, I wondered, did the family go if they ever wanted to eat bánh tráng phơi sương?

"Oh, we might do that at home, but we wouldn't go out for it," said Trần. "Some people say the

297

restaurants on Highway 22, the Trảng Bàng Road, are famous."

Another "famous" recommendation. I'd seen a number of bánh tráng restaurants on the way to Tây Ninh. Indeed, Highway 22 was the road where I'd planned on stopping for lunch on the way back to Sài Gòn. But with bánh tráng phơi sương, I didn't care if I was about to go somewhere "famous" or not. It was boiled pork and a bag of herbs. It was harder to muck it up than to do it right.

CHAPTER TWENTY-TWO: "VIETNAMESE FOOD IS NOTHING WITHOUT HERBS"

Under the angelic airbrushed gaze of her own portrait, the bespectacled Cô Ba barked orders at her waiting staff. She shook keys at inattentive cooks and marched to and from the cash desk with a gait that Himmler would have envied.

The peace lilies lined up in terracotta pots at the entrance shuddered, betraying the force of nature inside this warehouse-sized restaurant called Bánh Canh Trảng Bàng Cô Ba, some thirty miles northwest of downtown Sài Gòn.

In no other restaurant anywhere in Việt Nam had I ever seen an owner's likeness so prominently on display. From the large road signs, the many restaurant signs, and her business cards, Cô Ba's caring face radiated. These were ominous portents, suggesting a Trảng Bàng–sized ego lurked within.

Cô Ba's bánh tráng phơi sương restaurant was located on the main Tây Ninh–to–Sài Gòn road, aka Highway 22. Her family had been in the

299

food business for five generations. Cô Ba took over the day-to-day running of things "when the Americans came," as she told me. For more than one hundred years, someone in her family has served food from the same location.

Ten frightened-looking staffers cooked, served, cleaned, washed herbs, administered soup servings, made drinks, and set tables, all in a flash. As was customary at places like this, they also scrubbed and waxed customers' cars, vans, and buses. In seconds, my stainless steel table was filled with meat, noodles, cucumbers, nuts, rice paper, iced tea, cold towels, and a big, varied, green bush of herbs, which was what I'd come all this way for.

Cô Ba had helped out since she was eight years old, when she started serving her parents' customers. At that time, her family only made the noodle soup bánh canh, which is a clear pork broth served with udon-style noodles that possesses a purity of flavor lacking in other Vietnamese soups, with their abundance of ingredients. And it was at that young age that Cô Ba first learned to make noodles.

At thirteen years old, she graduated to other duties. She would go to the market to buy the supplies for the coming day: the pork knuckles, the trotters, and, yes, the herbs.

Then, at sixteen, Cô Ba began to run the business proper.

Cô Ba's sons and daughters all worked in the business now. Her own grandmother had only officially retired when she turned one hundred years old.

"I'm here to ask you about the herbs," I said, through Huyền, after an incredible lunch spent munching what seemed to be half the region's herb supply, succulent fatty boiled pork, soft rice paper, and pickled leeks. It was an herbal hit, but I knew it would be. Like I said, it's almost impossible to ruin, as long as you have the right ingredients.

"No, no, no. Noodles. That's what you need to know about. I'm famous for them. My bánh canh is very famous," said she, arms folded, looking me right in the eye.

Bánh canh relies on a few basic elements, perfectly done. First, there's the tenderness of the pork. Then, the quality of the broth, which is both meaty and ever so slightly aromatic. And last, there's the freshness of the noodles. Put the lot together and you have one of the simplest Vietnamese soups out there, yet one of the best and probably one of the hardest to replicate on the stove back home.

A park bench was situated to one side of the restaurant, which was filled with numbered tables. The joint was clearly successful, and quite an upgrade from the shed of one hundred years ago. However, it was awash with the functional, but ugly, decor of almost all Vietnamese restaurants. In other words, they were doing well, but they were stuck out in Hicksville, which necessitated only the barest nod to aesthetics.

Behind Cô Ba's cash desk, a TV awaited the click of the remote control. Fixed to the wall next to the altar, at the other end of the restaurant, a different TV played a soap opera. A midlevel Vietnamese restaurant with a TV that is not turned on is like air without oxygen. Cô Ba, and *only* Cô Ba, controlled access to both the đồng and the remote.

Cô Ba wore a jade bracelet on her left wrist. On the ring finger of her right hand was a good-sized diamond ring, and on the middle finger of her left hand was a gleaming, green rock.

She was a success, all right, and she possessed the Holy Trinity of Vietnamese trappings to prove it: multiple TVs, rocks, and, by the looks of it, the shiny Honda Spacy parked out front.

We took a seat at table number 8 to discuss her food business, though it was really more of a lecture than a discussion.

"Bánh canh and bánh tráng phơi sương are always served together. It's a marriage," she said. "You always have bánh tráng phơi sương first, followed by the soup. That's the rule. That's the way I do things here."

I noticed that Cô Ba's face only lit up when she talked about the very old days, not the recent

302

past. The old days were about struggle. Looking around the place now, struggle seemed to be the last thing on her mind.

Her ancestors' original stall, and the one she first worked at, was a double-pannier, over-the-shoulder number. This was the case with so many of the food sellers I'd met all over Việt Nam.

"It was when the French were here. At that time, this area was a small bamboo forest," she said. "We had a little stall in that forest. After that, we bought a mobile stall."

They finally moved the business into a rudimentary shop in 1977, two years after the Americans left.

"We chose this place so that the buses and cars could stop easily," she said. "Nowadays, the road is double the size it was during the war."

The roads around Trảng Bàng became famous during the American War. Associated Press photographer Nick Ut photographed a young girl called Phan Thị Kim Phúc fleeing naked from the nearby Cao Đài temple. A napalm bomb dropped by the South Vietnamese had severely burned the girl's back and killed four others. The photo won Ut a Pulitzer. Phúc recovered from her wounds; she later became a Canadian citizen and set up a foundation to aid children affected by war.

Cô Ba turned to me with a direct, insistent look on her face.

"But it's the noodles you need to know about. This isn't a history lesson."

"Actually, not really," I replied. "I'm all about the herbs. Bánh tráng phơi sương absolutely fascinates me because —"

"No, no, no. My noodles are famous, you know. Famous," she repeated, sounding like Cleopatra dispensing an asp on a mission to kill my line of questioning. "It's all about the noodles here, my boy."

I'll admit that the noodles did interest me a bit. However, I had a feeling that if I allowed her to, Cô Ba would talk noodles into my dotage and into her grave. I looked at my watch. Looked at her. And prepared myself.

"To make bánh canh," she explained, "is a complicated process."

At one point during her diatribe, my thoughts turned to "Mandarin nail clippings." It was a term I used to describe the effect of both the overly flowery descriptions some Vietnamese tended to use, and which their language was prone to, and to illustrate the near-mystical impression that Asia made on the buffoonish end of the tourist fraternity. So many easily led types seemed to regard this part of the world as deeply mystical, "zen," on a higher plane — hence, my equally buffoonish "Mandarin nail clippings," which I'd pull out to describe and dispel bullshit whenever and wherever I felt I could hear it. Cô Ba got her box of toenails out and continued.

"You take the rice and you make it into a powder. You put it into a bag and place it under a rock. Are you following?" she asked, not really expecting or even wanting an answer. Her glasses slipped a notch down the bridge of her nose as she peered across at me. "Leave it like that for one day so that it forms into a dough. You boil this for one hour, or until one incense stick has burned to the stump."

"At that time, and only at that time, turn off the gas and take it out. You have to leave it to go cold. It will begin to go elastic," she said, miming something long and elastic with her hands. "Then you throw it into a round basket and boil it again. Pour cold water over it, and then boil again. You need to repeat this ten times, until it's clean, cold, and solid. When the water stops going cloudy. When the starch has almost all been released."

Then, and only then, I heard her say inside my mind, if the Mandarin said so, the incense had burned, the moon was in the right quarter and the family's two-hundred-year-old lucky golden anchovy had turned ninety degrees to the west inside the family fish sauce vat . . .

"Then," she said, "you are ready to form the dough and make the noodles. They need to be used when they're fresh."

Finally. In truth, it took almost one hour for Huyền to drag the conversation this far. I was beginning to fade.

"Now, the rice paper," she said. "To make bánh tráng, you need to choose very, very white rice, which you make into a fine rice powder. Once you've made the rice paper, you can grill it as a snack. It's called bánh tráng nướng. It fluffs up."

Cô Ba shouted at a nearby serf, who ran to the back of the restaurant and returned with a plastic bag filled with examples of fluffed-up bánh tráng nướng.

"You see. You see?"

"Yes, yes, I see."

Unlike the noodles, the rice paper did interest me. The name of the dish, bánh tráng phơi sương, was built around the alleged production method of these papers, the bánh tráng. Generally, in Vietnamese cooking, rice papers are stiff. They are dipped quickly into hot water to loosen them up and then used to wrap meat, fish, herbs, vegetables, and noodles, depending on the dish. But bánh tráng were different.

First, bánh tráng only came from this area. The papers were soft, not stiff, and the alleged process behind making them soft was all a little bit too romantic for me. I didn't believe a word of it.

The rice papers were said to be softened by the morning dew. To my mind, we were back in the Mandarin nail salon, chewing licorice sticks and wafting frankincense. I turned to Cô Ba, and to paraphrase, in my best British conversational English, I challenged her.

"This thing with the early morning dew on rice paper? It's all a bit 'temples decorated with rice paper, girls flitting about looking at lotus flowers, plaintive smiles on their faces, children on the knees of elders receiving wisdom while the dew melds into the day's fresh rice paper.' I mean, *come on,* Cô Ba. It's all a bit bollocks, innit?"

She looked at me, her face telegraphing hurt, perturbance, and suspicion. "How dare you — YOU — question our centuries-old customs?" her eyes seemed to say.

"Absolutely not," she replied sternly. "It's all true. In the late evening, we line out the rice papers to catch the dew. I have a space at my sister's house where we do this. It's very easy. You put them outside on a table. It takes two or three minutes, depending on the weather."

And for a moment, I swear I saw a gossamer-light Vietnamese maiden floating outside the window, trailing flower petals and a microphone attached to a karaoke machine.

So, the dew thing. It was true? I was astonished. Sure enough, I would discover on a back road on the route back to Sài Gòn, you can see bamboo frames in backyards and gardens laden

307

with hundreds of rice papers awaiting the morning dew.

The herb list for bánh tráng phơi sương is long. You may never find all of the herbs included in your serving. You may never even find the real names, either in Vietnamese or English, of several of the leaves.

If you put the Vietnamese Wikipedia rendition of the herbs associated with the dish into the Google Translate blender, you get something very, very odd indeed:

"The upper part consists of lettuce, perilla, chives leaves, leaf frogs, as bright crest, talismans, Melaleuca guava leaves, basil, thyme slip, need water, the moon, as bright chestnut, the cinnamon, coriander ship . . . in addition to a long slicing cucumbers, pickles and sprouts. The leaves are included only in the South, including leaf frog, ready to, Melaleuca guava, talismans."

Yum. Delicious. Gimme.

It took many attempts, over several years, for me to identify the names of all the possible leaves that you could find in an order of bánh tráng phơi sương. And even then, I'm not sure I got it 100 percent correct.

Varying quantities of the following might appear on your plate. There are normally between eight and ten different leaves per order. Some of the herbs were quite rare in Tây Ninh province, and uncommon or nonexistent elsewhere in Việt

Nam. Even in Tây Ninh, there was no guarantee that you'd find all of these herbs in your serving of bánh tráng phơi sương. Outside of Việt Nam, well, you can forget about it.

And, to give you an idea, there are *twelve* distinct herbs used for bánh tráng phơi sương:

Quế vị — sweet and sour taste.

Cóc non — sour, often used in canh chua, a kind of fish soup.

Rau nhái — has a yellow flower. According to one translated Web page, this means "wild cosmos," which I like. A lot.

Rau sống — general term for green leaves found along the riverbed. Cô Ba cuts the young leaves from the whole bushes that are delivered to her.

Rau cần — Chinese celery.

Diếp cá — fish mint.

Tía tô — perilla. Strong aromatic flavor.

Rau om — rice paddy herb, with a lemony citrus tang.

Hẹ — Chinese chives filled with oniony, garlicky, leeky flavor.

Rau chùa — sorrel. Sour and tart, biggest,

glossiest leaf of the lot.

Lộc vừng — sesame leaves.

Tràm ổi — guava leaves.

It's quite a hedgerow. Cô Ba painstakingly went through each and every herb with me. When she found two missing from our bundle, she dispatched a lackey to find them while she continued to talk.

"Oh, the deputy prime minister comes here, even the prime minister. My restaurant is very famous. Look here." She peered through her glasses to retrieve a phone number on a battered Nokia cell phone. "Look, Hun Sen's number," she said, jabbing at the Cambodian prime minister's phone number. "Oh yes, they all come here to my restaurant. It's on the way to Cambodia, after all."

True enough. The border was less than forty miles away. Phnom Penh, the Cambodian capital, was 123 miles to the west. Plenty of speeding black government Mercedeses and BMWs would have found a welcome respite at Cô Ba over the years.

"I serve this food the traditional way. Nothing has changed. It's very different from the way everybody else does it around here," she said, referring to the score of restaurants selling the same dishes on this stretch of road. "I am very successful. This is the right way to serve it and I have every intention of keeping it that way. This is the original taste. That's why it's so special. It's a dish that stands out because of the herbs. It's like a medical garden when you examine it. These herbs can cure many things."

But just like Hương, the herb farmer I met earlier in the day, Cô Ba, when pressed, had no idea exactly what it was that the herbs could cure. Anyway, at the end of the day, when it's twelve Mandarin nail clippings past a waifish Vietnamese maiden, to my mind at least, it's not about hippie-dippie cure-alls; it's all about the *glow,* the buzz, the primal allure of nature's green stuff on the human tongue.

"The herbs make things tastier, and it's healthier for you."

Cô Ba's insistence on talking about her noodles and her bánh canh made perfect sense. That's the dish that required some thought and some cooking, and there was a history there. This was the dish she had first learned to make, and it was the same dish she served today.

All the same, I was glad she relented and agreed to talk to me about bánh tráng phơi sương. I wondered: Could she, the most famous cook of Tây Ninh, possibly of all Việt Nam, ever envisage Vietnamese food without herbs?

I persisted. I wanted — *needed* — an answer. Cô Ba considered.

"No. No way. Take away the herbs and it's not Vietnamese food anymore. Everything that goes with this dish *makes* the dish. The meat is secondary. It's all about the herbs. Vietnamese food is nothing without the herbs."

Green smoke, brimstone, floating Buddhas, swiveling swords, long white wispy beards, warm Bia Hà Nội, pumpkin seeds, and nước mắm all collided inside my brain.

Cô Ba had spoken. And, I agreed. One hundred and ten percent.

Vietnamese food is nothing without herbs.

Yes, there are intestines, wombs, half-grown duck eggs, bear-bile-injected drinks, chicken feet, scorpions, "countryside" rats, crocodiles, sparrows, squirrels, and snakes, but shock value, freakishness, and the offcuts end of the Vietnamese culinary canon all sit squarely at the fringes; they're not the main course in this magnificent country.

At the heart of Vietnamese food are herbs, not fish sauce, not offal, not the freak show menu items. The single thing that alters, distinguishes, and sets Vietnamese apart from Thai, Cambodian, Lao, or any other Southeast Asian cuisine is the presence and abundance of herbs. Simple, beautiful, freshly cut herbs, from the swamps, hedgerows, gardens, bushes, woods, and jungles of this incredible, food-filled country.

And the garden-clippings basket adorning a

plate of bánh tráng phơi sương became, to me, the epitome of everything good about Vietnamese cuisine. From the pig's uterus to its ears, trotters, tail, and crispy barbecued belly, there were always herbs at the core of the taste.

Farmed, nurtured, and plucked from the fields and mangrove swamps of Tây Ninh province, this green ambrosia electrified an otherwise fairly mournful set of ingredients.

That herb power jolt took a simple pork dish and sent it to a taste galaxy far away. As the chef said, *Vietnamese food is nothing without herbs.*

CHAPTER TWENTY-THREE:
NO MAGIC INGREDIENTS

Everyone in Sài Gòn had an opinion on food, and by now I'd gotten better at uncovering those little tips for this soup and that noodle. Better at asking where was the best this and best that. And I got better, quicker replies.

This was probably because I became more discriminating about who I asked for advice. I knew I could rely on the neighbors, by whom I mean the *hundreds* who lived on our street. The legions that saw me, a white guy, walking the streets every day, stopping off for a bowl of noodles here, a bánh mì there. They knew they didn't have to churn out some tired hotel buffet tip for me.

It was the recommendation of my regular xe ôm driver, Mr. Toàn, that first led me to a restaurant called Mì Hoành Thánh, at 276A Cách Mạng Tháng Tám Street in District 10. Hoành thánh are wontons and mì are thin, al-dente, yellow noodles. Mì hoành thánh is a wonton and pork noodle soup.

Toàn had more fingers than he had teeth, could speak some English, and was a fixture at the local café, where I was guaranteed to be able to find him if I needed a ride. He taught me all the local shortcuts, down alleyways I didn't even know were alleyways, right there in my own neighborhood. Once, as we wended our way down a particularly narrow and convoluted set of spaghetti junctions, a thought occurred to me about the Americans, and that war.

How could the Americans have ever won? How could you ever understand and then break a people capable of creating such a random, chaotic system of alleyways, bunkers, dead ends, gullies, paths, and walkways? Sài Gòn's may have been more numerous, the kind of thing a cartographer wakes up in a sweat over, but they were not that dissimilar to Hà Nội's own tangled walkways.

There are many reasons why the Vietnamese have defeated every foe who would try to make war with them. One of the clues to those victories, I was convinced, was in the buildings and alleyways that made up their gloriously chaotic cities, and the hive mind that designed and built them. How could you ever formulate a battle plan to defeat an enemy capable of that?

At the end of one of Toàn's elaborate, circuitous trips, up, down, and around innumerable

District 10 back passages, we arrived at Mì Hoành Thánh.

Vietnamese restaurant names are unimaginative as a whole, but, at the risk of repeating myself, finding an establishment named after one dish is always a good start. Finding it packed is even better.

The checklist of all the other signs to look out for had been ticked. I paid Toàn, and in I went.

Mì Hoành Thánh was a textbook example. They did one thing. They did it well. In the end, I often came here for a "mang đi về" (takeaway). "Đi" = go. "Về" = home. (I never did learn what "mang" meant.) In that respect, our lives in Sài Gòn were quite different than in Hà Nội, in that we ate at home far more, cooked at least once per week, and relied upon mang đi về discoveries close to home. The change in our jobs, the vast size of the city, the clogged streets, and, mostly, the arrival of a child, all conspired to make us relatively more homebound.

But, on this evening — my first visit to Mì Hoành Thánh — I was doing the full dine-in experience: candlesticks, napkins, dinner jacket, and bow tie (metaphorically speaking, of course). I took a seat alongside a group of pajama-clad women and a man in a T-shirt and jeans.

If you've ever seen a team of Formula One or NASCAR mechanics at a pit stop, you'll have a pretty good idea how a place like Mì Hoành

Thánh works. The super-fast, lightweight car rolls into the pits. Two guys jack it up — one at the rear, one at the front. Twelve men unscrew the four wheels and put new ones on. Maybe a couple of folks replace a nosecone, a rear wing, or a spoiler. Someone wipes the driver's visor. It's over in seconds. The car screams out of the pit lane, back onto the track.

It was the same process at Mì Hoành Thánh.

This joint had a steamy and highly efficient production line. There were two guys in charge. The younger, with belly out, was on wontons, leaves, greasy fried crackers, and thin, fat-free pork slivers. The elder was streetside, with belly covered, handling the soup and noodle end of the proceedings.

The bench-style seating at the wooden counter had room enough for three or four punters. It was decked out with the bare essential condiments. The restaurant was packed. There was not a spare seat at any of the eight Formica tables in the shack. Everyone was here for the same dish. And, like a sixteen-year-old waiting for a favorite band to come onstage, I took my place at the front.

The wooden bench at the counter was my kind of seat. You were right in on the action and the noise, and half on the street. You were the target of any flying wontons or greens or a knocked-over soy sauce bottle. I was right in front of the

Torvill and Dean of the noodle soup world, the chefs, this elite group of ninja noodle nerds.

In addition, the ringside seat at this noodle wonton stall guaranteed a hot, foggy facial from the frequent blasts of sweet pork-scented vapors. At numerous points of any evening seated here, I knew that I would be completely submerged in the wet, hot aura of mì hoành thánh. I imagined a stall like this in China would be a fabulous gathering spot in winter, subsuming noodle munchers in a hot soup fog. With year-round heat, there was no way Sài Gòn could ever compete with Franz Klammer–friendly China. But, I could imagine it. Steam. Cold. Hot soup. Noodles.

In my experience, the mì hoành thánh served in some Sài Gòn restaurants could be a bit fatty, but not here, where it was light and slightly peppery, with an ever-so-slightly sweet pork stock soup. The fresh yellow mì noodles were quickly flashed in the pot at the front of the stall, followed by a few seconds in the main stall soup vat. The team threw in some hẹ (a kind of chive), a single green lettuce leaf, a greasy rice cracker, three or four thin slices of pork, and five or six wontons filled with seasoned minced pork. Within one minute of taking up position on the bench, I was served. Game on, bent forward, at the bowl.

It was not a soup that would blow your tits off. It wasn't a *revolutionary* dish. It was just very,

very good. Clean and simple. And therein lay its strength. Effortless simplicity, and the appearance of such. It was a no-bullshit number. I needed to know more.

On a subsequent visit, at around midnight, as the fog began to clear from his restaurant, I sat down with Mr. Huỳnh Thanh Sơn, head chef, the one with his belly covered, of Mì Hoành Thánh.

Like almost every soup seller with a popular shack that's successful without a lick of "eat me, eat me" neon flashiness, Mr. Sơn was equal parts humble and bemused — modest about his trade and his shed, and perplexed at my interest. The persistent feeling I got from these guys was "It's just soup, what's the big deal?"

I, on the other hand, recognized and reveled in my own foreign innocence and naive curiosity. Someone should document these people, this life, and this time. It felt critical. They deserved it. Whenever I looked at how the Vietnamese were "preserving street food" themselves, I'd get the urge to reach for my medication. The soulless, dead, lackluster night market around the central Bến Thành market. The "Bình Quới Tourist Village" that took street food and put it in a field: Field food, anyone? Then there were the proposals that would now and again gain traction in the local press for a "street food zone" here and an "ancestral foods preservation area" there. None of the artificial areas that had resulted from previous proposals worked. If history were to teach us anything, the likelihood of any new similar scheme working was less than zero. The street worked perfectly well as it was without top-down meddling from pen-pushing paper-clip counters. I wasn't sure those with a similar opinion to mine would win out. As I wrote and blogged, and watched this country develop at a scarily rapid rate, I did get the feeling that I was documenting something that would disappear one day. And within my lifetime.

Mr. Sơn was a short man with a full head of black hair. Any conversation at Sơn's front bench was conducted in saunalike conditions. I think he'd gotten so used to cooking in the steamy heat of his gurgling wooden kitchen that he didn't realize anyone else could possibly find it uncomfortable.

He was nothing if not polite. He answered my questions, no matter how tedious, simple, or random. I remarked that in Việt Nam, there was always something about a male chef busy digging into a vat of mì hoành thánh with a cigarette dangling between his lips that inspired my confidence. Mr. Sơn told me I was not alone in that.

"I don't know why, but it's usually men who cook mì hoành thánh," he said. "It seems to be more suited to men cooking it for some reason. Customers expect to see a man at a mì hoành thánh stall."

Just as I have never seen a man serve bánh cuốn, I think it would surprise and unsettle me to see a man slopping out the flimsy rice pancakes, not that it should.

There was one other constant at every mì hoành thánh stall. It was the stall itself, which was always wooden, and often decorated with Chinese paintings and calligraphy on mirrored glass that was embedded at the top of the wooden frame. Was it a reference to the origins of the dish? Mr. Sơn insisted that mì hoành thánh had transmogrified over the years into a truly Vietnamese rendition of a Chinese dish.

"I believe it did originally come from China, but now it's become more and more Vietnamese. How to explain what that means, I'm not sure," he said. "Here in Sài Gòn, the broth is more tasty than the way the Chinese do it, or even how they do it in Hà Nội. It's sweeter. Maybe it is just down to the sugar, but I think it's more than that."

Mr. Sơn learned how to make mì hoành thánh from his stepfather. It had taken him three years in all. This was clearly no simple broth to master. He'd set up soup stalls in four other locations before settling on this pad, in 1981. The 24/7 traffic on the clogged city artery that was CMT8 resulted in a persistent and voluminous number of customers.

Sơn told me that all cooking was to taste; Viet-

321

namese cooks didn't measure out ingredients to an exacting recipe. Again, there was that image in my head of the cookbook-free Vietnamese kitchen. It was the opposite of the glossy Sunday supplement spread, featuring the successful actor, author, or designer at home, holding a never-used Misono blade over an organic carrot, smiling into the camera, a library of recipe books lining the immaculate, crumbless, stainless kitchen. They'd have none of that in Việt Nam.

How can you teach something as innate as taste? I remember reading that when Gordon Ramsay decided to become a chef, the first thing he had to learn was how to taste. It was something he had never done. At least not properly. Whereas every Vietnamese person grows up learning to taste. Not just the chefs.

"To make the best mì hoành thánh, you really need to listen to the flavors and, obviously, the taste. That's the only way to make it special," Mr. Sơn said. "There are no magic ingredients. Sure, we use a bit of sugar. This is Sài Gòn. But it's all in the ingredients, and then it's in the quantity of those ingredients that you use."

It wasn't always like this. His early days in the food industry were at the beginning of the food chain, not the end of it.

"I used to be a rice farmer in Long Khánh province before I came to Sài Gòn," he told me.

"I miss that life sometimes, the peace and quiet and the fresh air. But after thirty years here in Sài Gòn, I'm pretty used to it. This is my home now."

In the morning, the restaurant was occupied by a phở seller who co-rented the place with Mr. Sơn. He'd arrive at 4 P.M., as the phở stallholder was going home, and he'd start prepping for the evening influx, which would run from 6 P.M. until just after midnight, seven days a week. It was a long day, week, month, and year, all revolving entirely around food.

"I get up at 8 A.M. and I go to An Đồng market. That's where I buy most of the food for the restaurant," he said. "After I choose what I need, they deliver it to my house in District 10 at about midday. From 2 P.M. I start to do the prep at my home and then I take everything over to the restaurant. By 6 P.M., we open for customers. After we close, just after midnight, we clean up and go home."

And the noodles. I wanted to know more about those noodles, which were cooked so that they popped like the skin of a small plum between the teeth. Al dente, on the edge of not cooked at all. Just perfect. I'd never had noodles like them before. And I never found them anywhere else in Sài Gòn. Mr. Sơn looked at me.

"Ah, yeah. The noodles. You like them, eh?" He smiled. "We have them custom made."

Cars, yes. Suits, yes. Whiskey even, yes. But noodles? Imagine that. Your very own custom-made noodles.

"My cousin makes the noodles. I showed him how to make them," Mr. Son explained. "They're not like the ones you buy on the market. They're much, much better. I can introduce you, if you want?"

Oh yes, I did want. How could I refuse an "in" with a custom noodle maker? Why would I refuse?

We stood at the threshold of the chef's domain. CMT8 was a lot quieter after midnight than at 6 P.M., but cubic capacity was of course still the dominant soundtrack on the streets. I looked back at the stall. The steam was still rising from the vat. It was messy, sticky work. I could see that.

"You know what you said about this being a man's job?" I asked. "I wonder, is it because it's so steamy? It's hardly becoming for any respectable woman, is it? I mean, look at you."

He was drenched in sweat. There was a reason that some of these guys cooked with their shirts off, and it wasn't that they were going for the Chippendale effect.

"No, I don't think it's that," said Son. "It's just, I don't know. There's no reason why a woman cannot cook this dish," he said. "But for me, if my customers didn't see me in charge, they'd

324

get worried."

And, there, just as I was leaving, I hit upon a Vietnamese truism, one I'd hear again and again from chefs and owners. They all had the exact same vision of what happened inside a customer's head if, for whatever reason, they failed to show up one night.

I tried to imagine an evening when Sơn didn't take center stage at his noodle joint. Would potential customers cower at the entrance, like frightened kittens, unsure whether or not to make the leap inside? Would they risk it without the reassuring presence of the captain of the stall? What fate would befall them on such a night? A soup other than what they had expected? A lesser soup? Some impostor, whose only interest was to stamp out all trace of the predecessor? I liked to think they would choose *not* to eat there, merely out of respect for their trusted noodle soup supplier.

I headed home. Sơn had promised to fix a date with the custom noodle maker.

CHAPTER TWENTY-FOUR:
BÁNH MÌ

Choosing what to have for breakfast was never easy. There was a vast array of affordable options. However, I'd become something of a regular user at the bánh mì stall directly opposite the café on Hoà Hưng. It was run by a sixty-year-old woman by the name of Mrs. Nguyễn Thị Cẩm. She was Toàn's wife.

She wheeled her stall out from her living room every morning. She sold Vietnamese filled baguettes, called bánh mì (pronounced "ban me" in Sài Gòn, "bang me" in Hà Nội), and fresh, unfilled baguettes, also called bánh mì (or bánh mì nóng when hot and fresh), from 6 A.M. until 9 P.M., seven days per week.

Bánh mì cupboards in Sài Gòn are like little pharmaceutical stands. There was always one nearby, whatever time of day you wanted one, always ready to dispense a snack or two. It's a truly Vietnamese prescription. The spring onion and coriander get caught between your teeth, and the mess of flavor is immediately identifiable as Vietnamese. The French may well have brought baguettes to Việt Nam, but the Vinas took the baguette to the bionics lab a very long time ago — "We can rebuild him."

And rebuild him they did.

The results were many and varied, and were almost all, bar one glaring exception, spectacular. It's time to forget about the French. Việt Nam moved the baguette along an eon ago.

From what I observed at many pavement corners in Sài Gòn, bánh mì stalls (like most street food stalls) appeared to be run exclusively by women. Apart from the mì hoành thánh and cháo lòng (rice porridge with offal) stalls, which were always run by men, a woman was in charge most everywhere else.

Bánh mì was a sandwich with no sell-by-date and came sans cellophane. There were options on what to put in and what not to, but normally I went for the works, which meant a smattering of chicken liver pâté, cucumber slivers, sliced red and yellow chilies, a sprig of coriander, spring onion, shredded carrot, chả lụa (a kind of Vietnamese pork luncheon meat), thin strings of dried, shredded pork, and a splash of hot sauce. As I took a bite, the bread crumbs would scatter. I needed a bib when I attacked this snack.

The veggies crunched and meats melded into one magic mouthful. The chilies the baguette sellers threw in were among the hottest I ever had in Việt Nam. There are baguette boffins bangin' out the bánh mì in fancy delis all over the United States, but I'd wager whatever snazzy American twists you might find stateside, none would match the Sài Gòn street original.

Following the unwritten law of the Vietnamese sandwich trader, Mrs. Nguyễn wrapped her goods in a phone bill, an electricity bill, a bit of newspaper, or sometimes a joint stock company sell order printed with orange type. The name, address, and phone number of the seller, and the amount of cash involved, were all clearly legible. The lack of personal privacy in Vietnamese life extended to street sandwiches.

Mrs. Nguyễn would seal the deal with an elastic band, pop the fresh bánh mì into the flimsiest of cheap plastic bags, and pass it to her customer in exchange for a few đồng.

After my snack, I settled in to chat with Mrs. Nguyễn, bearing in mind the four constants when talking to street food vendors:

1. They rarely knew how many bowls, sandwiches, wraps, drinks, or customers they served in a normal day. They could only ever tell you the bottom line. If it was a good day, they sold out. If it was a bad day, they didn't.

2. Many could not be very specific about

328

when they started their business. They'd say "Some years ago" or "More than ten years ago." And of course "I dunno, why do you even care?" was an ever-present undertone.

3. Those who *did* reveal that they had "secrets" in their cooking methods would never, obviously, tell me what they were. (Although they might hint at them.)

4. The street vendors I frequented for many years were mostly happy to talk about anything and answer most questions. All were happy that I was interested in their food. Although, I think, all were also bemused by me.

In order to understand how ridiculous I must have appeared to the street food merchants, I tried to imagine a Vietnamese guy, with next to no English-language skills, blogging fish 'n' chip shops in England. I'd see him taking photos of every backstreet health hazard chippy he came across, jotting down notes on the quality of the malt vinegar, ketchup, and salt cellars. Yeah, I'd think he was a bit of a weirdo, too.

Following rule number two and in the tradition of impreciseness, Mrs. Nguyễn told me she'd set up her stall sometime "before 2000." I'd eaten at hundreds of carts just like hers, but I'd never thought about where the carts actually came from. As if they descended from some street cart mountain on the whim of a fish-sauce-spattered street food god. So I asked her where she got hers. It turned out that she'd bought the cart on nearby Hùng Vương Street for three or four million đồng. She was as curious about my questions as I was about her answer: "Yes, they still make them over there. Why? Do you want to buy one?" she asked, half seriously, half joking.

The thing is, I kind of did want a cart, but where would I put it when I left Việt Nam one day? Sophie and I knew we wouldn't stay in the country forever. We both had the explorer's bug, and where would I put a bánh mì stall, anyway? In the living room, and use it to serve cocktails? It's a thought, I suppose.

She sold about one hundred plain, unfilled bánh mì per day, and "dozens" of the filled variety. But, really, she had no idea how many she sold each day. "I pay money to buy the food, and I see the money I get back when I sell the food. That's how many I sell," she said.

After grabbing my breakfast, I occasionally sat in her small front room, directly behind her stall, for a glass of tea.

There was a motorbike in the room, and a trestle table laden with a jug of green tea. Two chests of drawers were placed at right angles. Upon one was the family altar, on which two faded brass candlesticks sat on either side of the portrait of the deceased matriarch of Mrs. Nguyễn's husband's family. A tin of Nuvita whole milk powder was often the offering of choice to the ancestors, along with a packet of Thăng Long cigarettes, which were Toàn's preferred brand, as it happened.

The other chest of drawers was squashed between a washing machine and a tall fridge. It was stacked with empty 1.5-liter Pepsi bottles, a rice cooker, several teapots, a plastic vat of dubious home-brewed rượu, and a remote control, wrapped in plastic, used to power up the Sony TV that took center stage.

I sniggered at the sight of the TV. Sophie and I had bought our first-ever TV together a few weeks after moving to Sài Gòn. It was delivered to our front door on one of the all too common three-wheeled cyclos, hired by the TV shop owner. As the cyclo driver tipped the Korean goggle box from his transport onto the pavement outside our front gate, two old Vietnamese men walked past and eyed the telltale brand on the cardboard container. "Pah, Samsung. Very poor-quality electronics," said one. "No. Not good. Not like a Sony," said the other.

Toàn, Mrs. Nguyễn's husband, spoke some English. He had finished his senior high school education, which was not all that common back in his day. The couple had two daughters. One was already married, and the other was single and still lived at home. She was a skinny, smiley twentysomething who helped her mother between working shifts as a data input clerk at the local school.

I was always curious as to how people like Mrs. Nguyễn got involved in the street food trade. She was happy to tell me.

She had moved to Sài Gòn from Cần Thơ, Việt Nam's fourth-largest city, after spending a period in Sóc Trăng during the American War. When her sister got married and moved to Sài Gòn, Mrs. Nguyễn followed and lived with the newlyweds before setting up business as a hairdresser. After she got married and had her first child, Mrs. Nguyễn stopped cutting hair to take care of the newborn.

As soon as her first daughter reached tenth grade at school, Mrs. Nguyễn decided to start a new business.

At that time, a neighbor, a lady the same age as Mrs. Nguyễn, was running a bánh mì stall. It made little sense for her to set up a rival stall right next door, although the thought had occurred to her. The neighbor's business was already well established and successful. But then she fell on hard times.

"She had family problems, and decided to sell the business. So I bought it from her," explained Mrs. Nguyễn.

332

"Her son had a drug problem. He overdosed on heroin one day and died. She couldn't take the pain and so she sold everything and moved back to her hometown. He was her only son and only child. I heard that she died soon after. Everybody said it was from heartbreak," said Mrs. Nguyễn.

All of which added a certain ghostly air to the sandwich stall I called my breakfast bar.

At around 3 P.M., when the stall was quiet, she would pop out to the market to buy the ingredients she needed for the coming evening and the following morning.

The bread was baked just five hundred yards from her house and was delivered every day.

"Everything is fresh. I have no secrets to how I make a good bánh mì. The key thing is good ingredients and freshness. If Big C has a promotion on, I'll buy from there," she said, referring to the vast supermarket on Tô Hiến Thành Street, just a five-minute motorbike ride away. "Otherwise, I always buy from Hòa Hưng market on CMT8. Everyone knows that I never use any chemicals."

Here was yet another Vietnamese conundrum. No one admitted to using "chemicals," meaning flavor enhancers or substitutes of any kind. Chinese substitutes were especially suspect, as was anything Chinese, in general. And yet everyone said the practice was rife.

So who, I wondered, was doing it? The answer was everyone else, but not me, and not my family. Maybe that woman down the road.

"My customers are all regulars. They know I choose the best meat and it's always fresh and clean, and I only use pâté made by Vissan," she said, referring to the meat products company based in Sài Gòn's Bình Thạnh district.

From the living room, we had a clear view of the stall and the street, just a few feet in front of us. A customer arrived, put her foot on the curb, and yelled out her order. The mirrors of her Honda Dream were turned inward. She had a dark mark on her ankle, like a bruise, but it wasn't. It was a "Sài Gòn tattoo" — the telltale patch of flesh that had been burnt on contact with a motorbike exhaust pipe. A rite of passage for almost every woman in a hot country who took up motorbike driving for the first time, as they were more used to (a) showing their ankles and (b) taking the rear seat on the family runaround.

With the engine still on, the customer guided Mrs. Nguyễn in exactly how she wanted her meat cut, which sprigs of coriander and spring onion to add, just how much nước mắm to squirt in, and how to cut the red chilies to finish her order.

Like I said, everyone in Việt Nam has an opinion on food. A way to do things that "must be done right." And I saw proof of it every time a fussy customer arrived at Mrs. Nguyễn's.

"This job isn't too difficult," Mrs. Nguyễn told me. "The only thing is making sure you make ends meet. The hours are long, but you get used to that."

Taxis would grind past the stall, bumping along at 2 miles per hour in third gear. The cars with government plates would drive faster and press their larger horns louder and longer. Everybody hated the arrogance of it. I suspected the government cars of causing more accidents than all other vehicles in Việt Nam put together.

I wondered about the future of Mrs. Nguyễn's stall. I asked her daughter, Ha, if she would ever take it over.

"I may take it over one day. Maybe, yes. But I have my office job at the moment. I just help out here whenever I have free time and I'm at home."

Over the years of blogging in Sài Gòn, of all the thousand or more posts on the blog, it was the simple bánh mì sandwich that garnered the most response, on and off blog.

E-mailed tip-offs, blog comments, SMS messages, smoke signals, telegrams — I got them all.

I didn't realize just how passionate people were about their sandwiches until I blogged about them. At one stall, Thiên Phúc's, at the corner of Nguyễn Siêu and Hai Bà Trưng Streets in District 1, I gave the bánh mì business a bit more thought.

Phúc told me she had been slinging bánh mì from the same spot for eighteen years. The morning shift saw her at this location. In the evening, she wheeled her two-woman stall over the road and flogged from there. Unlike most sellers I met, she had a rough idea of how much she sold. On an average day, she'd sell three hundred filled bánh mì. At 5,000 đồng a sniff, I made that to be a daily turnover of around US $100 a day.

Hmmm, I thought. There must be well over a thousand of these stalls in Sài Gòn alone. Outlay is minimal: a secondhand stall would be adequate enough, ingredients are bargainsville, any hired help's a snip, and no doubt a street stall license is too. Buy three or four stalls, run a wee chain, and you've got yourself a nice little business with a potential turnover of . . . quick calculation . . . between $100,000 and $150,000 per year for the chain. Take out your costs and the view still looks pretty good in sandwich-land. I didn't know if there was a kind of bánh mì collective in Sài Gòn, but I was wondering, why wasn't there a plush chain of bánh mì parlors or swanky mobile merchants in town? I shuddered at the thought of it, and wondered what time and progress would bring to this country.

The attraction of the bánh mì, beyond the stupendous taste, was the anytime, anywhere nature of the breaded beast.

Sink your gnashers into a bánh mì pâté and you will experience a crust-cracking crunch alien to any brie, tomato, and basil muncher down at Pret A Manger. Bánh mì pâté was a breakfast, lunch, or dinner, anytime's-a-good-time kind of snack.

I became something of a bánh mì completist, always up for trying a new twist, looking for tip-offs, new places, and new ideas about the simple sandwich concept.

I succumbed to one of the simpler (but rarer) variants at the corner of Nam Kỳ Khởi Nghĩa and Nguyễn Đình Chiểu Streets in District 1, to one side of a branch of Lotteria, a Korean version of Burger King. Toàn took me there on one of his meandering tours of the megalopolis. This purveyor's stall was a morning-only deal, and she served something called bánh mì bi, which was a pigskin-filled baguette.

Toàn wasn't sure why this particular pigskin outlet was the famous one, but it was most definitely the best and tastiest, he'd assured me.

There was a single glass cabinet. On the left, there was chopped pork. On the right, shredded fried pigskin. A basket of baguettes on the floor to one side. And that was pretty much that.

For some reason this stallholder sold this sandwich using baguettes much smaller than your average street bánh mì, but she added the usual fixings: crinkle-cut, shredded, pickled carrot and radish, a dash of red chili flake suspension sauce, and a scratch of pepper.

It came wrapped in an old electricity bill, bound with an elastic band and handed over in a plastic bag. It cost a mighty 3,000 đồng, a couple of thousand less than the larger, more common version sold by the likes of Mrs. Nguyễn.

Looking inside the parcel, I could clearly see how the sandwich strata evolved from the bread base into pigskin, pork, and pickled vegetables. Fire, pigskin, pickles, and bread. It was another breakfast I would regularly grab as I sweated my way across town with a pram in the morning, trying to lull my child (or the toad, as we called him at that young age, due to his croaky laugh) amid the traffic din. A good proportion of my blog was researched and photographed at the next most convenient stall after he'd fallen asleep. I liked the randomness of it, although changing nappies under the gaze of a street vendor could prove alarmingly stressful. I never quite did it the right way for the vendor.

It was two years after our move from Hà Nội to Sài Gòn that the toad, our first child, arrived. He decided to come a little earlier than the doctors had forecast. It was just after I had filled the fridge with lobster tails, oysters, foie gras, and a bottle of Alsace that Sophie's water broke. It was Christmas Eve. We went to the hospital, although he decided not to show his face to the world until three days later. I was ordered out of the hospital, and spent a lonely Christmas Eve and Christmas Day with my head inside the fridge. A few short months after he was born, he started coming on blog research missions with me.

Occasionally the bánh mì tip-offs that came in sent me to somewhere else altogether on the street food scale, somewhere stratospheric. This happened one blustery day, as lightning struck, a bell tolled ominously, a cat meowed, and long-jawed anchovies turned over in their fish sauce tombs.

The e-mail read, "Another sarnie tip-off. A woman sets up (after 5:30 P.M.) a bánh mì thịt nướng stand. The thịt nướng are like little grilled sausages. Plus, she throws on some bbq sauce. Best sandwiches I've had in Sài Gòn. A real gem of a find."

I grabbed a camera, snatched the nearest notebook, powered out of the house, hailed a passing chariot, and headed out in search of this "gem." I alighted at the pavement stall at 37 Nguyễn Trãi Street in District 1. I was hungry. I had arrived. I grabbed the first plastic stool I could find and ordered.

Bánh mì thịt nướng translates vaguely as "meatball sub." It came wrapped in an electricity bill. The signs were good.

One bánh mì thịt nướng took less than a minute to assemble. There were two women working this stall, one grilling the thịt — the meat — and the other building the beast. Inside the baguette it was warm, snug, and saucy, filled with wee charcoal-grilled pork patties, pickled carrots, grated radish, fresh slices of cucumber, some chopped spring onion, fresh coriander, and a dash of hot sauce. Beams of steamy hot, sweet, meat-soaked vapors evaporated around me. It was seductively warm, a harlot of a hoagie. It had a confident aroma, the smell of a successful sandwich.

This was the best I had ever had in Sài Gòn.

Conversely, one evening, I dug out the runt of the bánh mì litter, opposite the Sài Gòn Tower on Pasteur Street. A half-Chinese, half-Vietnamese woman sold a challenging little number called bánh mì phá lấu.

As sandwich business models go, hers was ambitious. As I saw it, she had two main problems. First, she relied upon Saigonese to bother stopping their motorbikes or bicycles at the red light her stall was located beside. Never an easy task, but all credit to her for trying. Second, her product was not necessarily the most appealing. Once a potential customer saw that she was selling phá lấu, which is pig intestines, ears, tongues, scrotes, anal bags, and testes, all marinated in Chinese five spice and simmered slowly, they'd quickly move on.

Now, I knew that the Vietnamese weren't afraid to eat the lesser-explored parts of a pig's interior (and exterior). I hadn't forgotten my initial encounter with the Hà Nội uterus some years earlier. Still, when it came to bánh mì, I couldn't quite believe your average Vina-babe would choose intestines and sacs over, say, belly, chop, or cutlet.

This seller first smeared a baguette with some sort of brown, sweet, soy-sauce-based troweling. Tubes, entrails, and chitterlings went in next, followed by the standard pickled vegetable trimmings. It was postmortem porn. Nasty. Crunchy.

Bánh mì phá lấu made no sense to my mouth. I was forgetting those pesky Vietnamese taste buds. They had one helluva weakness for the crunchy animal parts that squeaked between the molars. That sensation repelled me, but attracted Sophie. She'd quite happily gnaw at a beef bone, and liked nothing better than spending an hour or more scraping away at a crab for every last hidden morsel of white flesh.

Try as I might, it was one section of the Vietnamese playbook I quickly decided to turn the page on, never to return. The same went for the tendons in meat. Not in my dinner. Tạm biệt. Cảm ơn. Good-bye. Thank you.

While I had become something of a bánh mì

explorer, willing to traverse town in all manner of traffic to sample a reputed and recommended subspecies, I realized that I had never seen a Vietnamese bánh mì bakery in the wild.

One day, Mrs. Nguyễn took the bánh mì by the crust and introduced me to the local baker. Duc Toàn Lo's bánh mì bakery was located at the far end of Hẻm Hoà Hưng, at number 83/27, past the parasols of the twenty or more stalls in the Hẻm, the floor-level fruit displays, the wriggling eels, and the bone-cracking thud of the blade at the butcher's stand.

Out front were five Honda Cub motorbikes. Six large wicker baskets sat on the patio. Just inside the front room was a nearly ten-foot-high electric oven. On the opposite side of the room were three glass-fronted metal cabinets containing rows of dough, waiting for their turn inside the oven. The roof was a mess of wires, fuse boxes, meters, and pipes. It was like standing in an oven, in a country that was already hot and humid.

A clock hung on the wall above a simple bright yellow drawing of flowers, etched directly onto the chipped and peeling white-painted walls. Next to the glass cabinets was an altar with two Buddha figures, a pot filled with burnt-out incense sticks, a packet of cigarettes, and a red and gold cylinder containing green tea. Under the altar, a small red generator sat waiting for one of

Sài Gòn's power cuts, at which time it would spring to life and save the baking bánh mì. Another cabinet, filled with seventeen rows of bánh mì dough, ten dough lengths per row, stood in front of the oven. They would be next into the fire.

"We used to be workers before, in a bread factory. We learned the trade there. When we spotted this opportunity, we went for it," said Hoa, the baker, who worked here with her husband, busy at the moment with a sack of flour behind the oven.

The old bakery ran on coal. It was dirty, smoky work. They decided to upgrade, and installed a brand-new electric oven to run the business.

They made two thousand bánh mì per day and delivered them to dozens and dozens of street stalls all over District 10. They worked through the night. Their motorbike delivery service started at 4:30 A.M. every day.

"We use two brands of wheat flour to make our bánh mì. This mix makes a better bread. We don't use rice flour. Foreigners think we use rice flour, but it's not true," said Hoa.

Bánh mì is the perfect term for this kind of bread, which is shorter and lighter than a French-style baguette. Each bánh mì took about fifteen minutes to bake in the tall oven.

"We have to work on the preparation during the night. First we prepare the flour," Hoa said.

"A machine kneads the dough. The hardest part is to make the bread, to take the dough, by hand, from the machine, and knead each bánh mì by hand. That takes time."

Two thousand bánh mì per day made the couple a living, but they were clearly not minted.

"We make enough to support us. We don't have any kids, so we don't need too much," said Hoa.

I felt like I'd discovered a hidden part of Sài Gòn. Where the bread comes from is just not something you think about much in Sài Gòn. You want bánh mì? It's there, if not in front of you, then around the corner, down an alley. But how many people outside of the trade, I wondered, had ever seen inside a Vietnamese bánh mì bakery? They're discreet, out of the way, not easy to find. More important, there was never a need to find them, as the products were delivered with such regularity to the streets. Did Hoa have any idea of how many clients they sold bread to?

"No idea," she said. "Fifty? Sixty? Maybe more." Her tone, to my ear, said something closer to "Who the hell cares?"

In retrospect, she was probably just tired. It was 2 P.M., I was a stranger, and I was poking around her oven, asking questions she'd never been asked before. Like all the other street vendors I ever talked to, she'd never really considered the questions I posed to her. This was simply what she did to make a living. That was as complicated as it had ever gotten inside her head. There were no romantic thoughts of keeping a tradition alive, painstakingly kneading bread and passing on her knowledge for the benefit of future generations. There was only the fact that people needed bread, she had the means to bake the bread, and she made money completing this cyclic relationship. And, she was knackered. Making and baking bread throughout the night, delivering and selling bread throughout the day, she was fast approaching a well-deserved nap-time.

One of Hoa's bánh mì clients hawked fried quails, called chim cút chiên, on CMT8, not five minutes' walk from the bakery. Mrs. Nguyễn Thị Linh, like so many street vendors, held a large chunk of financial responsibility for herself and her family between her two hands. It was her, the cart, and a wok of oil that brought home the fish sauce in her house.

From 4 P.M. every day, the quail ladies appeared all over Sài Gòn. I'd tried several, but settled on Linh's because (a) she was the closest purveyor to our home, (b) she was always such a cheery seller, and (c) she had the edge in the taste stakes. I visited her at least twice a month.

If Việt Nam's traffic sounds like a swarm of bees in the middle of a gaggle of geese, Linh's spot meant her head was firmly fixed inside the beehive. She was right out there, on the street. No cushy front room for her.

Her quails were marinated in a five-spice mixture, deep-fried in a shallow wok, and served with sliced cucumber, rau răm (Vietnamese coriander), a bag of salt and pepper, and a bag of chili sauce. The bánh mì was optional, and an option I always took. One order of quails cost nothing. A dollar. Linh's spot was noisy, polluted, and challenging, but like the spot occupied by the mì hoành thánh gang just up the road, it was also strategic.

"The traffic, well, you get used to it, and it is very good for business. This is a good spot," she said one night as she bagged up my order. "Though I must admit, the noise does give me a headache. It's never-ending."

She used to work in a clothing factory, but the hours were long and the pay low, so when her first baby arrived in 2000, she decided to follow her husband into quails. His family had been selling quails in the same district for twenty years.

Her day, like that of every other street food seller I got to know, was long. A morning-to-night shift, seven days a week.

"I buy ten kilograms of quails every day," said Linh. "I serve twenty or more customers every night. If there are one or two quails left over at the end of the night, it's not a problem. But, generally, I finish when I'm sold out."

It was after picking up a bag of Linh's quails one evening that Sophie and I made the decision that it was time. The toad was about one year old and had been on solids for months, but now was the time for him to begin the full-marinated carnivorous experience. He eagerly devoured a sliver of quail and moaned for more. It was clear that Linh would need to supply us with one extra quail from here on in.

Every morning, Linh headed to Nguyễn Văn Trỗi market to buy the quails and the pig's intestines she needed for the phá lấu, the fried offal often sold at stalls specializing in quails. (It's something I'll admit to never having ordered, given my previously stated feeling about the matter.) She picked up the spices in Chợ Lớn market, the Chinese quarter. Then she went home to begin her preparation work. At 4 P.M., she opened for business.

Beyond the noise, the headaches, and regular street hassle, Linh would tell me the only other thing that annoyed her was the hot oil splashes.

"It's pretty hard when I cook and I often get burnt. And dirty, of course, because of all the oil," she said.

I liked her confidence in her quails. It was a competitive business. CMT8 and nearby Tô Hiến Thành streets were lined with quail merchants every evening, but Linh insisted her offerings were the best. I asked her what made her quails so good.

"Oh, there are many secrets to making a good chim cút chiên, but there's no way I'm telling you them," she said. "There are many stalls like mine, especially further down Cách Mạng Tháng Tám, but they're not the same. They're not as good as mine."

I had to agree with her. I had tried three others, but it was Linh I kept going back to. For her quails. And her smile.

Chapter Twenty-Five:
It's the Chinese

Sài Gòn was like a pincushion, pricked with innumerable pins marking great places to eat all over the city. It was a map that I'd never have the time to fully explore.

One evening, I was back at a favorite old pin. While I was bent forward at Mr. Sơn's mì hoành thánh, two minutes' walk north of Linh's quail stall, he slipped me a piece of paper with a phone number on it. A contact.

"My cousin. The noodle maker. She says you can go along any morning. Best to arrive by 8 A.M.," he said. And off he shuffled, back into the steam, shirt off, familiar plastic flip-flops flapping, ladle in hand. The head of the Ninja Noodle Nerds of District 10 had work to do, wontons to deliver, noodles to wake up.

The following morning I found myself, with Huyền, my translator, on a worn wooden bench just inside the front shutters of the artisan noodle maker's factory at 387 Nguyễn Tri Phương Street in District 5.

The factory was sandwiched between a dentist and a bánh mì street cart. The noodle maker occupied a single room, approximately fifteen yards long by three yards wide.

Mrs. Huế introduced herself. She was a third-generation noodle maker. Her family had been making noodles from the same place on Nguyễn Tri Phương Street for more than sixty years.

I wanted to know everything about Mr. Sơn's custom-made noodles. Just the thought of it. Custom noodles. Imagine: it was like being at the engine manufacturer for James Bond's Aston Martin. How did she make those noodles so special?

"There are many secrets to making good noodles, but I'm not telling you any of them," she said. She wasn't smiling. She was setting out the ground rules for our conversation.

"It's basically a mixture of eggs — the whole eggs, not just the yolks — wheat flour, and water," she revealed. "But that's all I'm telling you."

She only made two kinds of mì noodles: thick, flat ones and the slim cylindrical ones ordered by Mr. Sơn to his own design — "a little bit of this flour, a little bit of that, not much of the other." They were used in mì hoành thánh, mì vịt tiềm (a duck noodle soup), mì xào (stir-fried noodles), and many other noodle soups and fried dishes across Sài Gòn. She also made the small square pastry packets used to encapsulate each wonton in sheds like Mr. Sơn's.

"The machine at the end there makes the dough," she said, pointing to a rickety-looking, mostly wooden contraption. "That second machine flattens the dough. And the third one in front of us here makes it into noodles. A long, long time ago, this whole process was done by hand."

She started making noodles at 6 A.M. and worked until 3 to 5 P.M., depending on the number of orders.

"We deliver most of the noodles ourselves, all over Sài Gòn, although some customers prefer to come and collect," she said.

And as for the standard response to my standard question:

"I have no idea how many noodles we make and deliver every day."

But how many sacks of flour do you get through?

"I've no idea. We make up the orders and they go out. I've never thought to count."

A staff of five people worked in the single slim room. At one end sat thirty-four white sacks labeled "Bột mì chuyên dụng đặc biệt" (special mì noodle flour). A radio with a separate speaker attached sat on a floury table next to the sacks. There were two fans in the room, both turned off.

Lining one side of the long room were the three noodle-making machines. On the opposite side was a long bench, staffed by three noodle arrangers, weighers, and baggers. At each stage in the process, flour was used to stop the raw dough blobs, and later the noodles, from sticking to each other.

Behind me, above the wooden bench at the entrance, was a whiteboard filled with orders written out in blue erasable pen, while on the bench were thirteen separate wonton orders awaiting the delivery boy. Six bags of mì, of varying weights, sat at the end of the bagging-up table, also awaiting delivery.

The first worker, a woman, would separate the noodles. The second, a man, with a Mandarin shirt, ponytail, and wispy long black beard, would organize them into small groups, weigh them, and pass them on to the final link in the chain, the bag lady, who would refer to each order pinned on the wall, weigh them a second time, and bag them for delivery. I imagined it would be a similar process at a diamond or gold dealer. Repeated weighing. Repeated checking. Quality assurance.

Outside the noodle factory was a row of motorbikes, some owned by those making noodles, some belonging to patients of the dentist next door, and some whose riders had pulled up to grab a bánh mì snack at the stall next to the noodle factory. It was easy to tell which motorbikes belonged to the noodle makers, as the front handlebars, seats, and rear wheels were all dusted with flour. A floury motorbike was clearly a hazard that came with the job.

"When it's the rainy season, we get fewer orders. People tend to stay and eat more at home during the rainy season. They don't want to get wet," said Mrs. Huế.

A single broom lay under the noodle-flattening machine. It was covered in flour. All five of the staff worked without gloves.

"Our noodles are really made for consumption on the same day, but if you put them in an airtight bag in the freezer, they will keep for up to one week."

Three low-wattage money-saving lightbulbs hung from the ceiling down the machine side of the room. Only one was turned on. Two opened sections of the corrugated iron roof let light in. If it rained, a small pulley could be used to cover the gap and protect the noodle-making area.

"I used to be an accountant before, but my parents moved to Australia to be with their own parents. I took over the business when they left," said Mrs. Huế. "If my children want to follow the business one day, then that's fine.

But I don't mind if they want to do something else."

"Our biggest problem is competing with low-cost, low-quality noodles imported from China. Some restaurants buy them because they're cheap, but they're not good quality, and they can be bad for your health."

I'd heard this line of complaint before. Everything bad in Việt Nam seemed to come with an adjective: "Chinese." The word "Chinese" was always present somewhere in the sentence. Crappy motorbikes were "Chinese-made." Economic woes were "the fault of the Chinese." Pollution was "bloody Chinese." Faulty condoms were "Chinese crap." Contaminated food: "It's the Chinese." The Chinese got the blame for the lot.

Historically, there was a racist undertone to this and a lingering postwar hatred of all things Chinese. It was the Chinese population of Việt Nam who were first persecuted by the Vietnamese authorities after the fall of Sài Gòn in 1975. They were labeled the "comprador bourgeoisie" and blamed for all economic woes. And it was the Chinese who tried to invade Việt Nam from the north in 1979. Later, it was the Chinese who claimed sovereignty over a group of minuscule rocks in the South China Sea called the Spratly Islands. The Vietnamese insist the rocks are theirs (as do Brunei, Malaysia, the Philippines, and Taiwan). And, the food. The hatred always came out in the food. The Chinese, it was oft-stated, made poor-quality, processed food and dumped it in Việt Nam.

There was a certain irony to the rhetoric, because if you ask any Vietnamese male what his idea of heaven is, he'll quickly relate the stock Vina-answer passed down through the generations: Vina-heaven is a French house, a Japanese wife, and Chinese food. Just to clarify that statement, that's a house from the colonialist, imperialist, pig-dog French, a wife from the country that invaded Indochina in 1940, and food from the eternally disliked Chinese.

If you can find a logical route through those space-time contradictions, you might be closer to understanding the Vietnamese mind than I am.

CHAPTER TWENTY-SIX: WHAT A VERY CIVIL CIVIL WAR

I was in a white Vinasun taxi, meandering through District 1 and enjoying the air-conditioned escape from the wet heat. I was hungry.

The driver spoke enough English to give him the confidence to spark up a conversation, but not quite enough to continue it at length. I reverted to type.

"Where do you go to eat phở?"

"Oh, many people like to eat phở."

"So I gather. Where do you like to eat phở?"

"Phở Hoa on Pasteur. Many people like it."

"Yes, many people do. I've eaten there. It's great. But what about you? Where do you like to eat phở?"

"Have you tried Phở 24? It's very near the Continental Hotel. Very good."

"Yup, I know that one too. But what about you? Where do you go? Where do you really go?"

"I like Phở Anh in District 3. Many people like it."

"OK. Let's go to Phở Anh."

On Kỳ Đồng street in Ward 9, District 3, there were a total of eleven girls on duty at Phở Anh. They were serving, sweeping, mopping, and washing herbs. One girl sat on a stack of stainless steel stools as she bagged up miniature plastic parcels of hoisin and chili sauce for the takeaway trade. Some of the girls had numbers written in yellow above the words "Phở Anh" on their T-shirts. There was one woman on beef-chopping and bowl-prep duties. The manager handled the cash and the phone, and held sole responsibility for barking orders at people.

At the back, twelve small baskets of basil and ngò gai (sawtooth coriander) awaited customers. Behind the two-shelf display, almost entirely hidden from view, I could see the motion of elbows and herbs and the sway of a blue shirt, where another girl was washing herbs. She replenished the empty baskets that would arrive at the rate of three per minute the entire time I ate at Phở Anh.

The soup arrived at my table, as it always did in a phở restaurant, rapidly. I spooned at the soup and smiled as I remembered the stark difference compared to the rendition in the north. A place I was about to return to. I was going back to Hà Nội for work. To write about food. *Would I still like the phở up there? Had the south made me soft?*

357

Had I changed?

What had surprised me and educated me in equal measure was how almost all of my income now stemmed from my blog. Not from advertising, or from the words written on it, but because of the editors, journalists, and others who had hired me because they had read my blog. This would continue to be the case long after I'd left Việt Nam and stopped blogging about food.

I became a journalism trainer for the BBC because of the blog. Reuters foreign correspondent — that'd be the blog. Consultant for the United Nations. Innumerable magazine and newspaper features and many, many media training sessions in Europe, Africa, and the Middle East — all because of the blog. This book, too, came about because of the blog.

Meanwhile, back in 2005, the *New York Times Magazine* was due to fly me to Hà Nội to write a feature on the food in the north. The commission had come as a complete surprise in my inbox one morning. I'd written for the *New York Post* several times before, but this was the *Times*. A whole other league. And the *New York Times Magazine* — of all things. "That's a seriously nice calling card. You need to shout about that one," said my friend Justin Guariglia, a New Yorker with whom I'd worked on a number of occasions, and who was a regular *Times* photographer. "Your byline in that outlet will open doors for you," he said.

Had Phở Thìn changed at all? It had been almost five years since I'd last supped there. Was it still the joint with the grimiest shed in the north, and the attitude to go with it? And would I still love it?

Here in Sài Gòn, Phở Anh was a well-staffed, well-organized, slick, clean, efficient engine, with fifteen tables and great phở. There was not one speck of filth on the floor for the eleven ceiling-mounted swivel fans to waft about. I almost felt sorry for them. It was a far, far cry from the municipal dump carpeting Phở Thìn's fine floor.

As I plucked at the bowl of blanched bean sprouts, delved inside a tub filled with quarter lemons and another with cut yellow chilies, and spooned from a jar of minced chilies in oil, I grinned again at the difference I could expect in Hà Nội.

Years ago in places like Phở Anh I'd come to ponder this world of work in which I'd improbably found myself. In this new media space, I was now a blogger *and* a journalist. I had turned down the opportunity to attend journalism school when I was eighteen years old, yet I'd somehow wriggled myself into it anyhow. Throughout all the years of pundits blabbering about "media disruption," one quote rang true and never left me. It was from an April 2004 interview with

"Internet technologist" Clay Shirky on the site Gothamist.com that I'd first read the very same week I started my blog, and it holds up as well today as it did a decade ago:

> So forget about blogs and bloggers and blogging and focus on this: the cost and difficulty of publishing absolutely any-thing, by anyone, into a global medium, just got a whole lot lower. And the effect of that increased pool of potential pro-ducers is going to be vast.

Increasingly, I was asked to write about this ever-changing world of new media. I was in-vited to conferences and offered "media con-sultancies." The contrast between my daily life inside the soup sheds of Sài Gòn and this digital media world I was expected to pontificate upon for much of my work was stark.

The *New York Times* put me up in the Hà Nội Hil-ton Opera Hotel. It was the first time I'd ever been put up in a decent hotel on a journalistic assignment. As soon as I checked in, I canceled my first appointment.

I was there, ostensibly, to draw up a "food map" of Hà Nội for the *New York Times Magazine*. A kind of top-ten, insider's hit list, if you will. I knew what I was going to write. I didn't need an hour-long schmooze with the hotel's marketing manager to guide me down blind alleys and horrendous wrong turns. I put my bags in my room and exited the hotel. I knew the way.

It was October 2005. Nothing had changed in the years since I'd left. The service. The decor. The cleanliness. I was back. Yes, the beef was still scraggy. No, there were no herbs. Not in that generous southern style, anyway. Yes, entering Phở Thìn at number 13 Lò Đúc Street still felt like getting a punch in the face, a knee to the balls, and an elbow in the stomach. And that was a good thing. I was back in the dugout, fighting the good fight for northern phở, after all those years of going soft at the hands of the southern chefs.

For four days in Hà Nội, I never once entered the hotel's breakfast buffet room. On two out of the four days, I got my pre-coffee start inside that gnarled phở den just ten minutes' walk south from the Hilton.

I was there to see Mr. Nguyễn Trọng Thìn, the head chef, owner, creative brains, and interior decoration expert behind Phở Thìn. I'd seen him before. I had just never known who he was. When my translator asked the soup controller if we could talk to the owner, he pointed to the guy on the street.

The unassuming phở master could often be found sitting outside the café next door, puffing

361

on a Thăng Long, nattering with the neighbors. And that's where I found him this time. I introduced myself as a fan. "Can we talk? I'd like to learn about your phở, about your restaurant."

He looked at me, puffed on his cigarette, put down his glass of tea.

"Sure, how long have you got?"

"How long can you give me?"

"However long you want. Come on. Let's go inside."

I had been expecting at least a grumble, a growl, and a sneer before an inevitable "go away." It was the opposite of the antiservice doled out during the more aggressive phases of the lunar month inside his soup shack.

"You know how I make my customers come back?" asked Mr. Thìn. "I put heroin inside."

I figured he was joking, but for one split second before he collapsed into guffaws, I did wonder if it was true. We were seated on the floor of a room above the restaurant, in the house his parents had bought sometime prior to 1950. My magazine assignment had nothing to do with phở. I was ignoring the other things I had to do. I had an audience with the Master.

He was a squat man, made rotund by his trade in delicious phở. He wore gold-rimmed glasses, a black T-shirt with the Nautica logo on it, and a pair of tartan-patterned shorts. He had a shaved, graying head, an unshaven gray mustache, and a slight goatee. There were three Band-Aids taped to his left shin: "An accident with a soup pot."

He told me that he used to be an artist and that he had once made wood carvings. And that he used to work for VTV, the state broadcaster. Then he'd opened a factory, producing chisels and other equipment for working with wood.

When he was young, he liked to eat good food. Not only eat it, but learn everything about it: "The animals, the cuts, the way to cook it. Everything," he said. He learned from people his parents' age. He had never cooked from a recipe book in his life.

"There weren't many shops back then, or restaurants. Most people cooked at home," he said, referring to the mid- to late seventies, the postwar era.

"For one thousand years we had the Chinese, then we had the French for one hundred years, then the Americans for thirty years. When the Chinese left they took all the knowledge. The French took the rubber and left us with Catholics, and after the American War, there were no good restaurants left," he said.

I was curious. How did a man with a career in TV, a sideline in wood carving, and a tool-making factory become a long-standing, successful phở shop owner?

"Did Shakespeare always write? No, he didn't. He acted and he did other things before he became the greatest writer of all time," he said, tapping one of three Thăng Long cigarettes he would smoke during our two-hour-long conversation.

Three fans hung from the ceiling. None were turned on. Three fluorescent lights lined the room. All were turned on and buzzing. Old plastic water bottles filled with ginseng rượu stood under a TV set and there were four bicycles at the far end of the room. Two filing cabinets and a cupboard lined one wall, while a jumble of stools, bags, a vacuum cleaner, and boxes were shoved to the very far end.

Nearest the door, next to where we were sitting cross-legged, were stacks of boxes with the label "Lisa cooking oil" on them. Under our legs was his bed, which consisted of two mats on the floor and a pile of pillows against the wall. He placed his ashtray, his cigarettes, a plastic blue lighter, and a fat leather wallet in front of him.

"Even Uncle Hồ worked the kitchens in London. There's a picture of him downstairs doing just that," he said, referring, of course, to Hồ Chí Minh.

I asked the Master about his trade, starting, as I so often did, with the basics:

"How many bowls do you serve a day?"

"No idea."

"How much beef do you buy a day?"

"No. No idea."

"How many eggs do you buy a day?"

"You've got me. I've no idea."

He had slightly droopy eyes that looked tired at the sides but brightened like a lightbulb experiencing a power surge when he spoke. His fingers were stubs of pure muscle. I could well imagine him using them to jab, prod, and hack at sides of beef at the kitchen slab, and to hulk bones over his shoulder past a line of customers, dripping blood through the restaurant, only to launch them like battleships into the vast black vats out front.

Those massive, blackened cauldrons fascinated me, the same ones I'd first come across stumbling home from the Lypse all those years ago. Cyclo drivers warming themselves outside were the first ones who drew my attention to Mr. Thìn's hole-in-the-wall full of delicious phở and a floor filled with dining carnage.

"Sometimes we serve cyclo drivers first in the winter," he said. "It is the phở shops that often keep these people warm in winter, you're right.

"The first pot I used was made of aluminum. It was trusty, but not such good quality," he said. "Then I bought an Inox pot. That's the pot you saw. I've used it for the last twenty years. It's half an inch thick."

You'd never know it to look at him, but Mr Thìn was probably very, very rich. And, like every elderly rich Hanoian I'd ever met, he hid

365

his wealth.

An old landlady I knew in Hà Nội owned three houses, including one on Hàng Bông Street, the capital's most expensive retail street, yet she looked and acted like a pauper. Only when you spotted the ring and the earrings did you know she had wealth. Understated diamonds and gold were the dead giveaway. Vietnamese women are addicted to jewelry, while the men go for gambling, cigarettes, and mistresses. A mistress in Việt Nam was often referred to, in a barely concealed code, as phở. The wife was rice, something you could have every day. Phở you got outside, somewhere else. It was exotic. More desirable.

Mr. Thìn's glorious pots were blackened hard because of the coal, he explained. And fat. Burning fat.

"Sometimes the fat spills over the top and sets fire to the pot. It brightens the kitchen up when that happens," he chortled. "It reminds me to spoon the fat off, too. You have to slow down the fire and make sure you skim it off. If you don't, then the taste is no good."

He passed me a photo album and pointed at two black-and-white photographs of himself. In them he was tugging on a thuốc lào water pipe filled with pure tobacco. He also had a few color photos of a trip to a restaurant in Seoul, "to show them how to make phở properly."

I always wondered if these guys ever thought about change. You know, cooking something else? Snazzin' things up a notch? Like Bob Dylan, 1965, Newport — surprise people and go electric?

"Never. I'm not going to change my recipe. Ever," he said. "Everything has to be original in the north. We're very difficult people to please."

Things at Mr. Thìn's were clearly set to stay acoustic. He'd stick to a strict regime of fifty-fifty cow bones and pig bones for his stock, and be done with it. This man was not for change.

"I only use the leg and the back of the animals. I take all the messy bits out of the back, and then it goes into the pot."

He cooked it for at least ten hours, making sure he didn't boil it too hard. Then he added spring onion, grilled dried shrimp, cardamom, cinnamon, hunks of fresh ginger, star anise, nutmeg, coriander, and onions. To serve, he added a mix of shredded spring onion, chopped basil, and chopped coriander sprinkled like powdered sugar onto the bowl as soon as the ladle exited from view. A second later, it was thrown in the direction of a waiting customer.

Ah, the matter of herbs. Not like in the south, I told him. Herbs-a-plenty on the plate down there, you know. Not like you stingy northerners, eh?

"They like it like that in the south. All those

greens on the table." He winced at the thought of it, his expression telegraphing pity. "That's not our way. It's not the right way. They're too influenced by Cambodia and Laos. They add a lot of sugar, too."

And there we had it. The age-old dig between the north and the south, and the south and the north. Northerners didn't like their nosh sweet, and southerners said there was no taste in the north. Rinse, repeat, and serve daily until death.

For the first three months that he was open for business, Mr. Thìn made no money at all.

"I made good food to encourage people to come. High quality, low price. No marketing, no advertising. That was my philosophy then and that's my philosophy today," he said.

His clientele were regular, numerous, and loyal.

"Some customers come every single day. Teenagers, young, old, all sorts. They haven't changed. The secretary of the Vietnamese parliament used to come here often."

I observed, as delicately as I could, that, like his clientele, the decor of his restaurant had not changed in all the years I'd been coming to eat his phở. Didn't he ever take a look around and think, *You know what, this place could do with a bloody good lick of paint*?

"I like to keep the old style," he said. "I don't want customers to think there's a new owner, with fancy new ways. We're very conservative in Hà Nội. Not changing anything is a way of keeping the old ways alive."

This I could appreciate. A stubborn stick-in-the-mud attitude. More power to his grubby elbow, I thought. But still, I wondered, was it just me and Mr. Thìn? Would the up-and-coming generation of Hanoians still choose to eat in a crumbling cabin, as opposed to a clean eatery with scrubbed floors and a kitchen sink that had more than a weekend-shag-type relationship with a bottle of dishwashing liquid? It was a question I put one day to my Hanoian friend Hương, the one with the American bar-owning husband.

"Everyone likes it like that in Hà Nội," she explained. "Look, we only care about the taste. We don't care what a restaurant looks like. The food is everything."

But still. Had they ever looked at the floor in one of these places?

"Don't you ever get sick of phở?" I asked Mr. Thìn. "Do you still eat it, after all these years?"

"Of course I eat phở. Look at me," he said, rubbing his belly. "I eat it every day. I thank Buddha for the good luck I've had, and for all the success of my restaurant."

I loved his phở. I loved the worn, uncomfortable wooden benches and the grime of the place. I loved my Sài Gòn phở, too, but there was that certain something about the Phở Thìns of northern Việt Nam that kept me coming back. The grit. The soul. The Sex Pistols–style service. It was something the southerners would never have.

Around the corner, back at Mrs. Ninh's tea stall, I met up with Chris, he of the scraggy-beef-eating wife, my original window into Vietnamese culture. A Yoda-type personality. This was our old meeting spot. Like Mr. Thìn's establishment, Mrs. Ninh's was also unchanged. I told Chris what Mr. Thìn had said.

"He'll never change. Not one thing. Not the decor. Nor the recipe. I respect that," I said, "and not changing the recipe I can understand, but don't you think that the inside of that place could stand a good scrubdown?"

"Hà Nội food is just basic. In a sense, it's pure," said Chris. "It hasn't moved on. Maybe that's the difference. The Saigonese push, change, adapt, and have fun. Hanoians are set in their ways. Stuck in this simplistic groove."

That said, there were the faintest of glimmers of innovation on the streets of Hà Nội, if you looked for them. Phở cuốn, a beef and herb noodle wrap, first started appearing in the nineties. Phở gà, the chicken version of the classic phở noodle soup, apparently first appeared during wartime when food shortages were the norm and the Hanoians were forced to adapt. And

there are pockets of cross-pollination of northern classics. One seller sells a hybrid bún chả
pork and herb noodle number crossed with bún
riêu, the tofu, crab paste, noodle, and tomato
soup. Today, the "bánh mì kebab" — basically
a Vietnamese doner kebab — is everywhere.
With development, the Vietnamese are changing, despite the older generation's attempts to
keep things the same. These departures from
tradition are evidence of change happening at
street level. And change at street level is more
fundamentally Vietnamese than any foreigner-
filled, trend-focused "fusion" restaurant in Hà
Nội — those also began to appear in the late
nineties, but their faddish appeal quickly waned.

"But there's more to it than that," added Chris.
Like a bowl of phở, there were many layers under the veneer in Việt Nam.

"Together with that kind of yearning to keep
things the same, there's that born right to believe
it is they, the north, who unified this country," he
said. "It is *they* who are the strongest. The ones
who should be respected the most. That they are,
essentially, right in everything, including the
food."

I looked at him with a smile. "Yeah, but it's all
better in the south, no?"

"That's the north-south paradox, laid out in
food. In Hà Nội, the food has zero imagination.
And they don't want imagination. They reject it.

They simply don't want change."

That mind-set is real and should not be underestimated. During the Japanese occupation, from 1940 until the end of the Second World War, the north experienced a famine in which up to two million people starved to death. Food shortages were the norm during the American War. Communism eventually spread south, and by the time it did, perhaps a certain gray austerity due to wartime sacrifice had become a fixture upon the northern palate.

And yet, there remained another paradox: it was hard to find southern dishes in the north, at least southern dishes done well. However, in the south, there were plenty of Hanoian restaurants, tons of them, especially around the airport in Sài Gòn.

Hanoians I spoke to over the years took this as proof of not only their military victory over their southern cousins and American backers in 1975, but of a kind of tandem culinary victory, too.

"If you travel from Sài Gòn to Hà Nội, you cannot find Saigonese food," said one Vietnamese colleague at the British embassy. "But there are many Hà Nội restaurants in Sài Gòn and they're always busy. People from the south eat there too. Everybody knows Saigonese people prefer Hà Nội food."

I repeated that rather bold claim to the Saigonese I got to know over the years. The Saigonese never laughed, scoffed, or shouted back at these claims. They'd only ever give a slight smile, a tired sigh, and a "Yup, that's Hanoian-speak" look. None agreed with the statement. Not one.

Hanoians were far more aggressive in defending their food. It was personal. It was an insult to call their cuisine basic, unsophisticated, or bland. It was as if to say such a thing suggested you were missing the point entirely. Hà Nội was the traditional home of language, learning, and culture, which, by implication, included Vietnamese food. Therefore, Vietnamese food from Hà Nội was pure Vietnamese food, was the barely hidden refrain.

The truth, if you can call it that, was always a little bit different, depending on who you talked to. And I talked to many people about it over the years.

"Of course there are a lot of Hanoian restaurants near the airport in Sài Gòn. That's where they all live. That's where the military base was after the war. They wanted their food. Not our food," said one southerner.

"Southern food has more sugar, but I still find it better in the south. Maybe I just got used to it," said another, from the north.

"I can't eat anything when I go to Hà Nội. I eat Western food instead," said many southern visitors to the north.

"Everyone knows Hà Nội is the cultural home of Việt Nam. The home of phở. The original phở," said northerners.

It was an eternal battle. Forget about the Americans, the French, and the Chinese. The Vietnamese had their very own civil war, without foreigners, without ideologies, and *still* without end. For the most part, though, at least as it played out on my blog, what a very civil civil war it was. Or as journalist Helen Clark commented on my blog, "I think the great north/ south phở debate comes down to which city you call home first. Expat Hanoians generally sneer at the south's sweet broth and say the city is too big and has no soul. Expat Saigonese complain northerners are grumpy ripoff merchants and you can have more fun in a morgue most Saturdays."

As for me, I sat with one cheek on either side of the fence. I liked the herbs, abundant variety, and rocket-propelled flavors of the south. But the teenage punk in me could never quite give up on the two-fingered salute and stapled-together soups served inside the bloodstained hovels of the north.

I was a Hà Nội expat. Living in the south and in denial. Probably.

CHAPTER TWENTY-SEVEN: ALL VIETNAMESE LOVE BÁNH CUỐN

I found another voice of the north-south schism in Bến Thành market, in Sài Gòn. It was inside this covered cathedral that I got to know Miss Lan Huệ. She sold bánh cuốn at stall number 1006.

Bến Thành was Sài Gòn's largest central market. If you had to put a pin in and say, this is the geographic center of Sài Gòn, the likelihood is you'd plant it on the roof of Bến Thành. The food court occupied one corner of the market, taking up less than a quarter of the market's space. The rest was taken up with vegetables, dried fish and meat, clothes, watches, toys, tea, coffee, and decorations. The outdoor sections were filled with meat, fish, shellfish, poultry, flowers, herbs, vegetables, and fruits.

It was here I first made the mistake of buying frog meat. I had an urge to make Sophie garlicky French frog's legs — you know, for a taste of home. The problem was that, technically, the meat was still inside the frog's skin, which still encased the frog, which was still hopping, if struggling, inside a large hessian sack, jammed in tight with several hundredweight of his kin.

I ordered three from the frog woman, who was crouched next to the sack on the wet pavement. She told me to come back to pick them up after I'd done my other shopping. I hadn't realized that buying frogs meant waiting for them to be slammed against the pavement and roughly skinned while stunned or recently deceased. I saw the frog woman's skills at work as I mooched over the herbs in the stall opposite.

Farther along was an offal stall. It was laid out like a mortician's confectionary store: hearts, lungs, pancreases, lumpen blood clots, and uteruses snuggled up against trays of pig's breasts, esophagi, and ears. In front of this offcuts business was the cow's-tail stall.

The deeper I'd gotten into the "noodle" end of my blog, the more interested I became in the "pie" side, as in, traditional British food. I needed oxtails to make stews and soups, British style, only the tail flogger wasn't too keen on how I liked mine prepared. Horror flushed her face as I asked for my tail to be rendered virtually fat free. It was as if I had asked the woman to turn sound upside down. It was an impossible task. "Fat? Off an oxtail? There won't be any taste. It's . . . destruction," I read on her face. To the Vietnamese, the fat is a sodding great part of the flavor, not something you sling in the bin. Regardless, I'd get my tail the way I needed it — ignorant of the fatty flavor enhancer so beloved by the Vina-chefs the length of the country.

Miss Lan's stall was located inside, away from the frogs and the offcuts, in a corner of the food court. Vendors sold a plethora of Vietnamese soups, noodles, sweets, and grilled dishes. If you wanted a crash course in Vietnamese food, this was the place you wanted to come crash.

Unlike almost every other offering on the market in Sài Gòn, bánh cuốn is a northern dish, credited to the Thanh Trì district, on the outskirts of Hà Nội. Miss Lan was originally from the north. She was the third generation of her family to make a living from bánh cuốn, although she was the first to sell it in Bến Thành market.

The original market, near the Sài Gòn River, dated back to the early seventeenth century. It got its name from the wharf on the river. "Bến" means "wharf" in Vietnamese. The French moved the market to Gia Định Citadel in 1859 and renamed it Les Halles Centrales. The thatched roof of the building caught fire in 1870, and the market burned to the ground. It reopened in its current location in 1912. Sellers started hawking food in Bến Thành market in 1979. The building was renovated in 1985, but the food section proper only opened much as it still is today in 1987. Miss Lan was the only bánh cuốn seller in the market.

"To make a good bánh cuốn, the first thing you need to get right is the batter. It can't be too thick," she said.

It sounds like a simple enough dish: mashed-up minced and fried pork, mushrooms, and prawns, wrapped in a flimsy rice film. It comes served with sliced cucumber, chả lụa (Vietnamese pork roll), and bean sprouts, sprinkled with deep-fried shallots and chopped mint, with a nước mắm dip alongside. Simple though it may be, it takes a delicate touch and deft chopstick skills to replicate this dish in your scullery.

You'll also need a double boiler, a ladle, and a bucket of ready-made rice flour mixed with water. A splash of the white mixture is spread across the skillet of the double boiler, completely covering the surface. It's then covered with a lid and cooked for thirty seconds or so. So far, so good. The tricky bit is the transfer of the cooked noodle pancake onto a clean surface to stuff with the meat. Miss Lan's helper was slick and moved the film to the prep surface with ease, like slinging a net onto a lake to catch fish. I've tried doing it. The gloppy sheet either ended up an unusable blob or, more commonly, on the floor.

"The second thing is the nước mắm. Get those two things right and the rest is easy," Miss Lan said.

The dish itself is one of the lightest on the Vietnamese menu. In the north, it's a breakfast or evening dish, but there's something about thin rice flour pancakes that never appealed to me first thing in the morning. I needed a few hours before I could attack anything with the thin, filmlike texture of bánh cuốn. And so, for me, bánh cuốn was almost always a lunchtime indulgence.

"In Hà Nội, maybe they use too much batter, as I hear it's quite thick up there. It has to be very thin to be delicious," she said.

Miss Lan had no idea how many customers she served a day. "I've never kept count, but probably a hundred or more, I suppose."

She woke up at 4 A.M. every day and opened the stall at 4:30 A.M., seven days a week. She bought all the ingredients she needed in Bến Thành market and prepared everything, bar the batter, the night before.

"It's a big market. There are plenty of customers. It's easy to earn a living here," she said.

It was also Sài Gòn's most aggressive market. There were women whose sole job it was to manhandle you to a stall. Of the fifty or sixty stalls in the food hall, not one was staffed by a man.

"But what about the regional appetite for such a thing?" I asked her. "You're selling a northern dish in a southern market."

"I think all Vietnamese love bánh cuốn regardless of where they come from," said Miss Lan.

Unlike many other northern dishes, for example the northern version of lẩu, a heavy winter offal-, fish-, and frog-filled hot pot, and some of the blander northern soups, bánh cuốn was a countrywide hit. And, unlike many other transplants to the south, Miss Lan had always held onto her northern taste buds.

"I prefer northern food, because that's where I come from. My taste is more oriented to the north than the south. It's just the way I grew up," she said, before adding a common refrain. "Sure, in the south we use a little bit more sugar, but it's nothing compared to Laos or Cambodia."

Compared to the sellers back on the Hẻm, Miss Lan had a good spot, right on the corner of Sài Gòn's busiest food court, in the city's busiest market, with no shortage of customers, locals and tourists alike. This was as prime a food-selling spot as you could get in the whole of Việt Nam.

"There are a lot of competitors on this market," she said. "You can see everyone fighting for customers. But I'm the only one who sells bánh cuốn, so I do pretty well. It's a good business. Plus, my stall is right on the corner of the market. It's a good place. It's much harder to sell in the center of the food court."

I always wondered whether, given the chance, people like her would ever want to change their job. A spot of accountancy, computer programming, or filing, perhaps?

"No, not really," she said. "But if I did ever do something else, it would still be something to do with food. I love cooking."

CHAPTER TWENTY-EIGHT: BÀ SÁU BÚN MẮM

Of the twenty or so street food stalls along the Hẻm near our house in Sài Gòn, just one had a sign. It belonged to the sixty-year-old bún riêu lady whose stall was nearest the main road, and who only sold her tofu, crab, and tomato noodle soups on the weekend. She had made the minimum effort needed, and applied felt tip pen to a brown piece of cardboard box. None of the other stalls had any identifying features beyond the food in the pot or what happened to be spread out on the table. You either knew what the hell it was, or you didn't.

And, in the case of the next item, I did not know. Sophie, the toad, and I were seated under a parasol at a stall near the entrance to the Hẻm. It was a drinks and chè — Vietnamese desserts — stall. We'd been offered something cold and black to try, called nuốc đậu đen. From what I could gather, it was made of black bean juice, water, and sugar. A fabulous chance find, earthy and refreshing, ideal on a hot day. I was reminded of my time in South Korea.

I had a theory as to why Koreans were slimmer than Westerners. The secret was in the ice cream. Koreans loved ice cream, but eschewed sugar and chocolate for . . . beans. The most popular ice creams in Korea were made of beans. And beans were good.

The next item on the day's menu was of another space-time continuum altogether.

I'd already tried bún mắm twice. After remembering the repeated recommendation of Bà Sáu Bún Mắm from the other traders, I'd asked Loan, our housemaid, to snag me a bowl on one of her morning walks with the toad. Having been utterly blown away by it, I'd decided to make a visit in person stallside. And Bà Sáu had ripped me off.

Not by much, but I was sensitive to being treated differently purely because of the color of my skin. Bún mắm cost 7,000 đồng. She'd stitched me up for a mighty 10,000 đồng (just over a dollar). I had an unwritten rule that I never revisited street vendors who ripped me off. In almost one decade, Bà Sáu was the only chef who got a waiver on that rule.

On paper, her bún mắm is a noodle soup. In reality, it resembles a miniature muddy mangrove swamp, a microbiosphere with its own climate, featuring both arid and damp regions.

Hell, maybe there's a fully functioning government in there, too.

I'd previously told Sophie about the mythical Bà Sáu Bún Mắm, and I guided her and the toad down the alley to her lair.

Finding this place felt a bit Indiana Jones, like I'd waded through reeds, traversed gorges, and cut my way through thick vines to reach this point, this stall, to quaff from this chalice on this stainless steel tabletop down the Hẻm. After nearly ten years of street food, I'd found Bà Sáu.

Bún mắm is from Sóc Trăng, nearly 150 miles south of Sài Gòn in the Mekong Delta, a mostly flat agricultural part of Việt Nam known for growing half the country's rice. It's also home to nearly half of the nation's fishing boats.

There was a lot going on inside Bà Sáu's bowl of bún mắm. It was absolutely rammed full of goodies: prawns, pork, fish, eggplant, squid, and hẹ, those Chinese chives again. Then there were the noodles. In this case, the bún were of the thick vermicelli variety.

The bún mắm sideshow consisted of the ever-present Vietnamese herbs. Ten different leaves, sticks, roots, and bushes in all. I will attempt to describe them:

Bông súng — the purple stem of a water lily.

Cù nèo — a soft, spongy fella, called variously yellow sawah lettuce or, technically speaking, *Limnocharis flava*. It looks a bit like celery and is a must for the fishy, tomato-y, pineapple-y canh chua cá southern megasoup.

And then there's bắp chuối, or banana flower.

Along with coriander.

Rau dắng, which doesn't really have an English translation. It's sometimes called bitter herb, slender carpetweed, or *Glinus oppositifolius. Yeah, I know.* What it *does* have is a strong, bitter flavor, and it is often served with cháo cá (rice porridge with fish). It is apparently useful if you're suffering from a stinking cold.

We also have raw bean sprouts.

Rau muống curls — morning glory or water spinach in its raw state, served in curly threads that have been hand-pulled from the main stem.

Rau thơm — sorrel.

Rau quế — basil.

Diếp cá — a powerful and unusual "fish

mint," so called because it tastes *rather* fishy.

The soup is a slightly sweet, complex, miry Mekong flood of fermented prawn paste and chili lathered into a thick, earthy stock. The eggplant has had time to soak the soup up, and each velvet bite squeezes soup juice from the veggie core. It's an unlikely sounding hit, but this gob-fillingly gorgeous soup is of another place and time. I didn't know this was something humans had the capacity to engineer.

Two Vietnamese visitors to my blog summed it up far more succinctly than I can:

"You who can eat bún mắm are happiest people in the world" and "I admit that I don't like bún mắm but the rest of my family is addicted to it."

Another reader emphasized the importance of having a good tongue if you dared to try to replicate this impossibly complex dish at home:

"The ratio of pork broth and fish broth depends on your taste, so don't add all of the strained mắm liquid in at once."

Ah, the mắm liquid. The source of much stink in many a Vietnamese kitchen. As I've mentioned before and I'll mention again, get beyond the stench and you, too, will discover that mắm tôm is a supercharged, high-octane muscle car in a jar. It deserves respect. Once converted to its charms, you will submit to Vietnamese food forever.

Bà Sáu earned her moniker because she was the fifth child in her family. ("Sáu" is the Vietnamese word for "six.") The Vietnamese number their kids, with the firstborn being called number two. The father always holds number one status. The locals on the Hẻm called her Bà Sáu or Bà Sáu Bún Mắm. Imagine that, being identified throughout your neighborhood solely by the name of the soup you produce and your birth order.

There was some method in the name-calling madness. Bà Sáu had been making the soup and selling it in this same spot on and off for fifty-five years. First with her parents, then on her own when she was old enough. She was sixty-five years old when I first met her in 2002.

I was a huge fan of the many and varied Vietnamese soups in Sài Gòn. Something of a soup stalker, even. But what, I hear you ask, was my *favorite*? That was a tough one, right enough. Don't think I haven't mulled it over. I've thought of little else for the last fifteen years. But, if I had to commit to a soup, it would be easy. Without even the merest flinch of indecision, I'd say bún mắm.

In my experience, it was never as ubiquitous a soup as bún riêu, phở, bánh canh cua, or hủ tiếu on the streets of Sài Gòn. I was never quite sure why that was, but I got the impression that bún mắm was not held in such high regard by

387

the Saigonese. It wasn't one of Việt Nam's supersoups. It was "too regional," I was once told.

I put it down to the healthy splosh or ten of mắm tôm, that purple prawn paste I so loved, down in the depths of the vat. That's the one providing the punch and the pong here. It must be said, once again, that bún mắm does reek.

And then there's the soup stock, the essential key to the explosive device, which is a pork bone–fish combination. Bà Sáu also made sure she threw in a no-nonsense, roughly chopped-up bag of fresh lemongrass as she commenced the countdown to soup liftoff.

"I started bún mắm here a very, very long time ago. Before the revolution," she said, referring to the French colonial era, which finally ended in 1956.

She rented the six-foot-by-six-foot box room where she sat and served. She lived at the back, down an alleyway, in the same place she had lived since she was six years old.

As we took a pew, I surveyed her tabernacle.

To the left of me, two stainless steel containers held wooden chopsticks and spoons. There was another container, a red plastic one, to my right, in which three pots of minced red chilies panted impatiently. There were two small plastic decanters with nước mắm, one on either side of the stainless-steel-topped wooden table.

A stack of thin toothpicks leaned inside a small

red plastic holder with an odd stand in the shape of a six-toed foot. An old ice cream container held the ever-present toilet roll. Four small white dishes, a cheaper version of what you might find in a Japanese restaurant to pour soy sauce into, held quartered lemons.

By 9 A.M., the floor was strewn with toilet paper, toothpicks, and wrung-dry lemons. It was the kind of bomb-site aesthetic that never lost its appeal for me. The utter lack of pretension, the focus entirely upon the food, and that it appeared to go against the grain of everything I had been brought up with were the strongest attractions. However, there was, at a stretch, a comparison to be made with the old English pubs I adored and missed. Those battered, crumbling, ancient coach houses, with sticky floors and nicotine-stained ceilings, were just as lived in, in their own way, as Bà Sáu's joint. And if life revolved around the pub back in England, it most certainly revolved around street stalls in Sài Gòn.

But there was more to it than that. These Vietnamese street stalls punched you in the face with something real. There was no turning back once you'd tasted their offerings. A street stall was like an old vinyl LP, picked up in some secondhand store, filled with liner notes, messages from the band and producer in the runoff grooves, names of the previous owner of the LP written in pen on the inner sleeve. You could touch it, smell the life it had lived, pass it between friends, and watch the needle track the grooves in it. Street food stalls in Sài Gòn are like vinyl, as spick-and-span, sterile, soul-sucked restaurants are like MP3s. The fun with vinyl happens before the music starts* It's the same with Vietnamese food on the Vietnamese streets. It's not just about the food.

Behind Bà Sáu was a squash of bags, bottles, plastic buckets, a clock that kept precise time, saucepans, and an extra parasol, for days when it was too sunny or it rained.

Inside a two-tier glass cabinet to her left, she kept the fresh products: the mysterious, unique, amazing Vietnamese herbs, along with plastic takeaway containers and two more toilet paper rolls.

Despite the clock kept for cooking, and like many street vendors, Bà Sáu's sense of time was somewhat imprecise. She simply could not remember exactly when she started working in this spot. It wasn't important to her. She'd been doing the same thing, in the same place, for a very, *very* long time. For her, that was enough.

For me, it was unimaginable. I'd escaped a

* Inspired by David Hepworth, in discussion with Fraser Lewry and Mark Ellen on *The Word* podcast 158, "Is Rock Dead?," January 14, 2011, between the 18 minutes 38 seconds point and 20 minutes 50 seconds.

job I saw as soul destroying at twenty-five years old to go in search of my own personal monster. Not because I had to, but because I could. I had that luxury of choice. And I'd managed to find employment that could take me anywhere in the world. Bà Sáu would never travel anywhere outside southern Việt Nam. Yes, she was proud of her soup. Everyone told her how good it was. How could she not be proud? But pride didn't pay the rent. Bà Sáu did what she did because it was the one thing she excelled at and could support a family by doing. She'd been born with her monster chosen for her.

After helping out her parents for a number of years, she originally got started on her own in the street food business by selling the sweet Vietnamese desserts called chè. They came in many shapes, colors, and sizes, but were mostly made of rice, corn, tapioca, beans, banana, and coconut milk. And they could be hot, warm, or cold. "But," said Bà Sáu, "that was a very hard job." She made the full-time switch to soup when she started renting the box store by herself on the Hẻm.

In later years she added bánh canh cua and bún riêu to her repertoire.

And, for a day or two at the beginning of the lunar month, like everyone else on the Hẻm, she cut out the meat and sold only vegetarian dishes: spring rolls, noodles, and rice. It's a Buddhist thing: Vietnamese Buddhists do not eat meat on the first, the fifteenth, and the thirtieth day of the lunar month.

A gas bottle burner sat in Bà Sáu's pantry and storage area. The gas was connected to the single-burner stove next to her on the floor. A brick, cut into four pieces, held the heavy cooking pot over the gas burner.

"I started cooking with my family," she told Sophie and me. "They had a business just like this. They used to cook and sell all kinds of food. I learned just from being around them and by doing. I had to help out from when I was young. You just pick it up. It's just what you did back then."

Unlike the youth of today, I thought. How many of them would know how to cook a soup like Bà Sáu's bún mắm from scratch? Fewer than in Bà Sáu's day, of that I was sure. I wondered, did she know the story behind bún mắm? Its origins?

When a neighboring fruit seller heard the question, like a competitive TV quiz show contestant, she couldn't resist, and barged in with a finger-on-buzzer response. "It's from Sóc Trăng province," she piped up. "I read about it on the Internet."

Bà Sáu feigned interest. It was not a question she had ever asked herself. Quite frankly, she couldn't care less.

"It's just Vietnamese food, that's all I know," she said.

Sóc Trăng, in the Mekong Delta, was an area that had been heavily populated with a mix of Vietnamese, Khmer, and Chinese for centuries. That offered one possible explanation as to how this soup had originally been forged from the muddy depths of mixed-up nationalities. Maybe it was true. It was "too regional" for younger Saigonites.

I never did get to visit the province to try this soup there, although one blog commenter did urge me to go, suggesting that bún mắm was the staple dish in the Mekong Delta and that another, less pungent version of it called bún nước lèo was even more delicious.

And for that missed opportunity, I have regrets. But, after almost a decade of eating in Việt Nam, I saw regrets on every street corner. There are hundreds of dishes I never, ever got to try. This was one more to add to the list.

I'd barely sniffed at the "Imperial cuisine" of Huế and was largely ignorant of a vast number of regional specialities that had never made the journey into either northern or southern megalopolis, plus I had only ever attempted to cook Vietnamese once. In truth, such is the variety in this small country — and a single lifetime would not have been enough to explore it fully.

Bà Sáu sold her soup until the vat was clean and empty, and by around 10 or 10:30 A.M. every day it was all gone. Sometimes, if I was unlucky, it was bone-dry before 9 A.M. One thing never changed: Bà Sáu sold out quicker than *anyone* else along the alley.

She bought all of her ingredients on the much larger Chợ Hòa Hưng, a few hundred yards away at 539A Cách Mạng Tháng Tám Street, as it was less expensive than buying on the Hẻm, where she worked and lived.

She was married and, like her mother before her, she also had five children: four boys and a girl. They were all still in Sài Gòn. The daughter sold coffee from a stall next to Bà Sáu's. Her sons all worked in the painting and decorating business.

"Mostly the outsides of buildings. They do all sorts of jobs. Anything to earn a bit of money," she said.

She started preparing her soup at 3 A.M. and she served the first customers from 6 A.M. Sometimes she'd have to serve particularly keen diners while she was still setting her stall up. She performed the same ritual seven days a week.

"It's the mắm tôm that makes bún mắm delicious," she said. "Plus some of my own little secrets."

She wouldn't tell me all of her secrets, but she did, finally, after years and years of my eating at her stall, let me in on one of them.

She used something called ngãi mắm.

"It's expensive," she told me. "It's really important to know how to choose the right one."

Ngãi mắm, it turned out, was called Chinese Keys in English. An aromatic root, it's a member of the ginger family, with long thin, orangey brown fingers and a yellowish interior. It is known as krachai in Thailand, where it is a kitchen staple. Bà Sáu always bought her mắm tôm from a specific mắm tôm purveyor of excellence on Chợ Hòa Hưng.

What did Bà Sáu think of the skills of her compatriots in the kitchens farther north?

"I've got no idea about the food in Hà Nội. I've never been there," she said. "All I know is, the food that I serve is one hundred percent traditional. It's the food I grew up with. Nothing's changed."

In that, she was an exact mirror of the stubby-fingered soup maestro Mr. Thìn, of Phở Thìn on Lò Đúc street in Hà Nội, and the queen of the noodle, Cô Ba, of Highway 22. A strict adherence to tradition, unwavering until death do them part. This was a commitment I was not confident that the youth fully appreciated, or had the inclination to continue. Would KFC, Pizza Hut, and the Korean fast food chains continue their march into the Vietnamese stomach? Or would the nation resist, as it had all the other invaders?

If everyone, including me, thought Bà Sáu

produced the best soup on the market, who then, I asked the soup queen, did *she* think was the best chef on the street?

Before the gray-permed cook could answer, a conical-hatted chè seller who'd taken up a breakfast pew next to me answered for her.

"Everyone knows," shouted the seller, "that Bà Sáu serves the best soup in this district."

Bà Sáu had clearly heard it all before. She didn't flinch or smile at the praise. There was no ego at play here. But she pointed over the alley, to the other side, next to a small front-room-meets-minimart that seemed to stock everything from toothpaste, diapers, and chocolate bars to cooking oil, stockings, umbrellas, and rice.

"Mrs. Linh's phở," said Bà Sáu. "It's very good. But she took the day off. She doesn't have enough money to cook today. It's a hand-to-mouth existence down here."

Bà Sáu had the same problem, one exacerbated by changes in the market. Another seller, Mrs. Văn, a sixty-year-old woman who made tofu-stuffed bún riêu in front of her house on the alley, told us one day, "The people who live down the alleyway complained about the noise and the lack of access to their homes," she said. "It was very difficult to ride a motorbike down here and impossible to get a car down. Plus, they built the office building at the entrance to the alleyway, and it just wasn't practical to have a market down here every day, like before."

The resulting slump in traffic had affected trade and the life of the street.

"If I can't sell enough, I can't make a profit. And then I can't buy the ingredients the next day," Bà Sáu explained. "I usually get the most customers on this market, but today, I only made a little bit of money. These days, life is very hard."

It was an ongoing complaint all over Việt Nam in the early part of the twenty-first century. The economic gap between the pure street vendor and the established restaurant owner was often vast. Years later, in 2013, I discussed this with Hà Nội street food blogger Mark Lowerson of the *Sticky Rice* blog over tea one morning at Ninh's stall in Hà Nội. He elaborated, "Visitors just don't realize that these street food sellers aren't necessarily doing this out of a love for the food. It's economic necessity. So, when you ask questions about the history of the food, the taste, and whatnot, they don't know how to respond. It's just what they do to make ends meet."

But in reality, it wasn't just about making ends meet. The Bà Sáus of Việt Nam were the ones keeping Vietnamese food and street culture alive. And they manage to do that despite the incursions of the fast-food chains and the arrival of massive supermarkets that threaten the very existence of a hundred local markets like that on the Hẻm. If Bà

397

Sáu and the thousands like her decide that it just isn't worth making their soups every day, how do you calculate the cultural loss to Việt Nam? The streets might end up safer, quieter, cleaner, but where does all that food go? Behind closed doors? Into expensive restaurants? This isn't just about the food. It's about history, culture, people. It's about a way of living. Street stalls are the pulsing corpuscles of the city, and what makes it breathe. And the authorities seemed dead set on ripping out the city's respiratory system.

Bà Sáu made a soup that would fetch big bucks in the right space in New York City. A soup that, if it was possible to export in the same way Việt Nam exports clothes, shoes, plastic goods, rice, and fish sauce, would have set her up for life. But no. How could a street stall owner in an obscure corner of Sài Gòn be aware of market forces and sales potential for her soup half a world away?

At around 10 A.M., Bà Sáu started to pack up the stall and stack her things back into the lockup she served from. The four small blue plastic chairs were the last to go in.

"I don't see my job as being difficult. It's not a difficult thing to do. I just worry about how much I sell," she said.

But what, I asked her — refusing to let the romantic notion of her soup, her stall, and her recipe disappear into Sài Gòn's fume-filled ether, never to be heard from again — what would become of her soup? Her recipe?

"When I decide to stop working, it'll be up to my children," she said. "If one of them wants to carry on, I'm ready to teach them, but if they don't show an interest, then that's fine with me, too."

There's a sadness that comes with this notion, but it was a blasé attitude I respected: that her soups might only ever exist in this form during her lifetime. And then, in a puff of smoke, they'd be gone. The soups wouldn't be gone, but her versions of them would. Like the difference between those who were at Andy Warhol's Factory in New York in 1966 and saw the Velvet Underground play their version of rock 'n' roll, and those who decided to stay at home on those nights. The latter group of people can listen to the recordings, watch the videos, read the interviews of those who were there, but they'd never really be able to replicate the experience of the former group of people.

The future of these soups rested entirely on the next generation. Anyone who has had a glance at Vietnamese TV cooking shows on YouTube will know there's little hope there. Soulless, catastrophic cooking lessons delivered in an alien environment of pristine cutting surfaces, immaculate cookware, and tarmacadam makeup.

Respect for food is wrought out of cast iron in Việt Nam. That will not change. But, in my lifetime, the street soup vats as we know them today may well dry up for good.

Laws may suck the street food air from the streets. Rapid economic development combined with an educated workforce may make the street food lifestyle choice less attractive, less of a choice made of economic necessity as it was for the Bà Sáus of the street.

There are signs of what might happen.

Not unlike in Brooklyn or London, there is the beginning of a popular movement focused on traditional food in Việt Nam. Craft beers and down-home eateries selling simple, homemade food. A number of top Vietnamese fashion models, including Trang Trần and Thu Hằng, have even opened fried-tofu diners in Sài Gòn, selling the same dish I used to eat from Nhung's pannier on the streets of Hà Nội. Spruced-up street food has become trendy among the young middle class. Food is fashionable. But fashions change.

Whether or not this new generation will stay the course like the Bà Sáus of the street is a very big question. The food will survive, and it will endure, but much of the life found on the street, the fun before the food and before the needle hits the groove, is destined to disappear along the way if the streets eventually succumb to the government's scorched-earth treatment of street vendors.

"I don't have any plans to write down my recipes," said Bà Sáu. "I'm ready to teach anyone who wants to learn how to make my soups, but I won't be writing anything down. It's best to learn how to cook with a hands-on approach. That's the only way. You don't need books."

I never asked her if her kitchen at home was lined with recipe books and food magazines. I really didn't need to. I already knew the answer.

The wall next to her cooking pot was the corner to one of the dozens of alleyways on the Hẻm. It was also the entrance to her living quarters.

The wall was blackened with years of soot, a combination of fire on the soup vat, shoulders and legs rubbing its curves, and hands, feet, backs, bums, and knees using it to lean against. The off-white pillar on the other side of the stall had a single band of dirt across its vertical length, like a lonely zebra stripe across the midriff.

"I don't mind any changes in the market," she said. "The only thing I worry about is selling my soup. If I sell more, I'm happy."

Another one of those low-wattage lightbulbs hung on the dirty wall at the entrance to the alley. It was attached to a piece of cardboard with two mobile phone numbers, written in red, under the words Mắm Châu Đốc, indicating that a salted fish specialty from the southwest of Việt Nam was sold somewhere down this passageway. Just call the number. This single lightbulb helped Bà Sáu to see as she began her work well before the sun had come up.

A large, strong padlock dangled off the gray grill, ready to secure her store as soon as her belongings were inside. She'd open up tomorrow, and again the next day, the same as she had done, almost every day, for over fifty years.

"Back in the old days, before the revolution, the market was very, very different down here," she said. "It was ten times more crowded than it is today. I miss those times, the market back then. I don't have as many customers as I did in those days."

Those who visit Bà Sáu, at 83 Hẻm Hoà Hưng, are truly happy people. Here is her weekly schedule, and her original advice to me:

Monday:	Bánh canh cua. "Get here between 7 and 8 a.m."
Tuesday:	Bánh canh cua
Wednesday:	Bánh canh cua
Thursday:	Bánh canh cua
Friday:	Bún mắm

Saturday:	Bún mắm. "Come before 9 a.m."
Sunday:	Bún mắm

Chapter Twenty-Nine:
A Northern Soup in a
Southern City

Sophie and I had decided to leave Việt Nam. We'd never envisioned living in the country forever, and in the end, it wasn't a question of when, because we knew that already; it was a question of where to next. We had concluded that 2006 would be our final year in Việt Nam. With the toad approaching preschool age, burbling in three languages — sometimes simultaneously — and Sophie's career in a rut, Việt Nam was beginning to lose its appeal. While the decision to leave was difficult, primarily because of the food we knew we would miss and be unable to replicate anywhere else, we still felt we must leave. We had spent long enough on the other side of the world.

The decision to leave spurred an urgency to try more, eat more, explore more. It's no exaggeration to say that it felt like a clock was ticking over every meal during our last year in Việt Nam.

If Bà Sáu had taken me on a trip deep into the southernmost regions of the Vietnamese palate, the next place I discovered, a twenty-minute walk away from Bà Sáu's knee-high table, took me for a nostalgia trip back up north.

I landed at Mrs. Thanh Hải's front door in District 3 like some lost orphan inquiring after a bed of straw and a little something to stave off the chill. I had been guided to the entrance by a blog reader, tempting me with the cook's northern dishes in a quiet part of Sài Gòn. He'd told me there was a bún ốc (snail noodle soup) shop down an obscure alleyway not far from where I lived. I decided to pay a visit.

There was no sign to greet me the first time I arrived there. On the right of the alleyway entrance was a very popular hủ tiếu noodle shop. A woman in a conical hat sat on a stool, washing, cutting, and laying out all the herbs in large plastic bowls, preparing for the lunchtime service.

I walked down the alleyway, past a fine array of shabby lean-to joints selling beef, pork, and chicken stir-fried noodle dishes, until I reached a right-hand junction at a motorbike mechanic's shop.

I followed the turn into a communal-style courtyard with trees, concrete, and quiet. Yes, I know: quiet in Sài Gòn. How odd. *Good* odd. I'd forgotten what it could be like to sit in a bare-bones restaurant and not suffer motorbike fumes, parping car horns, the shouting, and the grime.

Within the courtyard there were no billboards indicating Thanh Hải's restaurant. From my experience, as you should know by now, this was a very, very good sign. It meant everyone, i.e., local folk, knew where Mrs. Thanh Hải worked and what she served. There was no need to show off with a big, snazzy, shouty, "choose me" sign outside. This was word-of-mouth marketing in its purest form.

I did a quick scan of the courtyard, joining the jigsaw pieces together once again, and calculated that snails were probably to be found at the joint on the right-hand side. I asked if this was the snail shack. It was.

Mrs. Thanh Hải, who had been selling snails from here since moving to Sài Gòn from the north more than twenty years before, very kindly gave me a tour of her kitchen, which was located at the rear of the small, eight-table restaurant, and told me about her cooking.

She repeatedly apologized for the mess, the number of snails lying around in buckets, steamers, and basins, the heaps of cleaned greens, and the baskets of fresh noodles. Like that concerned me? *I think not.*

Between ladling out the crab, tomato, noodle, and snail–stuffed bowls, Mrs. Thanh Hải told me about her life. How did a woman from the north of Việt Nam wind up here in Sài Gòn, down an alley, selling northern food that her customers, both southern and northern, were lapping up?

"My husband moved here near the end of the war," she explained. "He was a soldier. This area was controlled by the government, and the rooms and houses were given to soldiers."

As she talked and worked, she'd occasionally gaze out at the quiet courtyard, where washing hung out over the balconies, a few birds tweeted, and a mechanic could be heard bashing a sprocket at the shop down the lane.

In 1980, Mrs. Thanh Hải arrived with her two children. This was almost six years after her husband first landed.

"I didn't know what to do when I first arrived, so I sold lottery tickets," she said.

When she served her soup to my table, I was shocked at the size. It was big. It was in a big bowl. It was a big soup.

I just knew I was going to like it. The place, the host, the soup, that look I'd grown to recognize after all these years. After a while, eating out in Việt Nam, you just knew when something was right.

Mrs. Thanh Hải, unsurprisingly, told me that she served the best bún ốc in Sài Gòn. As if to emphasize this point, she told me she'd had customers from Germany and Sweden "and now you," from Britain. We get everywhere, us heathens.

There were no strong flavors to her bún ốc, no southern sweetness either, just fresh, hearty, yet light, scoff. It was staggering. I was sold.

After packing in the lotto game, she had switched to selling fruit.

"Like the woman down the lane there," she said. "Just the same as her, except I only had a couple of baskets back then."

The woman down the lane in question sat in her conical hat behind a mobile glass cabinet that was filled with cut mangoes, rambutan, and papaya. Three plastic stools, each with a basket on top, held more mangoes, more papaya, and the green, sour, crunchy fruit called trái cóc, much loved in season by the Saigonese, who dabbed it in chili salt.

In 1986, Mrs. Thanh Hải switched from fruit to soup, and started selling her home-cooked soups on the streets of Sài Gòn.

"I've always cooked northern food at home. I thought, why not sell the same soups I cook for my family to people on the streets?"

With that belief, she set about carting her soups around the streets from early morning until she sold out.

"Very few people were selling northern dishes at that time. I was worried that nobody would want to eat them. My husband asked me, 'Why are you doing this? No one's going to buy it.' But I stuck to my idea. And I didn't change the way I cooked at all."

I was only halfway through my lunch. Ốc xào chuối xanh (fried snails with green banana) was the next number.

It came with a wooden stick like a toothpick, to pick up the snails, and chili and nước mắm dip. To my surprise, the freshwater snails, the ốc, were not at all chewy; my teeth simply eased through the flesh. The green banana, chuối xanh, was almost potatolike in flavor and texture.

The deal was sealed with a handful of fried purple perilla, tía tô. It was simple, no-nonsense northern grub. Unspiced, unadorned, unrefined, and bloody *great*.

Lý, Mrs. Thanh Hải's daughter, joined me at the table. She spoke English and wanted to practice on me. She went on to explain what made their soup dishes different from all the others in Sài Gòn.

"In the north, they just take out the snail and throw it into the soup, but that's not the best way to get a good taste," she explained. "Whenever I see bún ốc cooked like that in Hà Nội, I have to take each snail out and dip it in nước mắm. Otherwise, there's just no taste."

"Here, we fry the snails in oil and garlic first. It adds far more to the flavor."

Indeed it did. Mrs. Thanh Hải's bún ốc riêu

cua (freshwater snail and crab noodle soup) was packed with phenomenal flavor. The big soup came with a large plate of fresh herbs for starters, topped with beautiful thân chuối, or the white banana stem shavings, bean sprouts, more tiá tô, húng quế (basil), and crunchy raw curls of rau muống (water spinach).

The broth was fished from one of two large vats in the kitchen and was made predominantly, Mrs. Thanh Hải told me, from freshwater crabs. She had long since ditched the ancient and secret family recipe handed down and carefully guarded through generations since the Trần dynasty, in favor of the more readily accessible Knorr stock cube option. She added tomatoes, along with chopped spring onions, fresh vermicelli noodles, crabmeat, and the snails.

Lý went on to tell me that they bought snails only from An Giang province, in the Mekong Delta.

"They're the best. Big and wide. You get a real fat snail down there. Same goes for the freshwater crabs," she said, laughing at the thought of the fat things she had seen pass through her front door every day since she was a kid. A hundred kilograms of snails and forty kilograms of crabs, every single day.

The restaurant was open from 6:30 A.M. to 9:30 P.M., and fed an estimated six hundred or more people per day.

Each morning, they would send three staff to the market to buy live crabs. Lý insisted that they paid a higher price for their snails and crabs, because they only bought the best quality.

Once purchased, they paid someone to kill and clean the crabs, and then brought them to the restaurant in large hessian sacks.

"My mother says she never changed anything in her recipe, but she did," Lý confided in me. "When she was selling on the streets, she had to listen to the feedback from her customers and, step by step, she changed it. She improved it."

As the restaurant started to do well, Mrs. Thanh Hải acquired some land outside Sài Gòn and began to grow bananas, coconuts, and herbs there, to supply her kitchen. She still bought some select ingredients from the markets in Sài Gòn.

Mrs. Thanh Hải's restaurant was such an oddity: a North Vietnamese bolt-hole in the 'burbs of central Sài Gòn nestled amid a bún mắm shop, just up the road on Kỳ Đồng; a bánh canh cua crab noodle store on Nguyễn Thông Street; and two whole streets nearby given over to southern-style snails, grilled and steamed in coconut, that came out to play after 6 P.M. Mrs. Thanh Hải had thrived in the most unlikely of locales.

"I'm the only cook in my restaurant, even to this day," Mrs. Thanh Hải told me. "It's difficult to get these dishes right. The techniques are complicated, so I'm always in charge of that.

You can't skimp on quality and experience."

Mrs. Thanh Hải used to catch crabs and snails in the rice paddies she tilled in Thái Bình province all those years ago, during wartime.

"That's where I learned my craft, and how to cook these dishes, in those rice fields. It's all done by memory, what my mother showed me, and what her grandmother showed her. What you're getting here is the *real,* northern bún ốc."

I turned to her daughter, who was slowly and silently shaking her head at me, out of her mother's sight. Once her mother went to tend to a customer, Lý explained, "She had to add a few things and change the way she cooked slightly down here. The southerners wouldn't put up with a bland bún ốc like you find in Hà Nội."

It was here, at this restaurant, that I saw for the first time the two Việt Nams colliding under a single roof. The two sets of taste buds: one for those born and bred and developed in the north, and another set born in the north but steadfastly nurtured in the south, where they were corrupted by sugar, Cambodia, and Laos, as I was repeatedly told (by northerners).

"I love southern food," said Lý. "There's more variety. More ingredients. A more developed taste. The Saigonese take a dish and play with it. They make it better."

Lý put this to her mother when she returned to the metal table under the minimal, wall-

412

mounted menu.

"No. My taste buds remain rooted in the north," her mother blasted back. "It's where I grew up. It's the food I grew up with and the food I learned to make. I haven't changed anything and I don't add any sugar to my bún ốc."

I turned to Lý. She smiled at me. There was that little shake of the head, just visible once again.

As ever, I learned more about bún ốc by blogging about it than I did by merely eating it. I had no idea what the white banana stem shavings were at first. One commenter, Robyn Eckhardt of the Eating Asia blog, told me, "Banana stem (the white stuff) — stem of the banana tree. It's quite common in the north, but seen less often in the south, in my experience. A friend who journeyed down from Hà Nội to Sài Gòn to show me how to make bún riêu cua at home actually carried some banana stem with her on the plane — she said 'true' bún riêu simply must have banana stem."

The banana stem was rare. I'd never seen it before. In fact, as I continued munching my way across Sài Gòn like an uncontrollable bundle of Pac-Man pixels, it was the leaves, twigs, branches, and herbs that beckoned with increasing urgency from every table. "Look at me. I'm important. Take note."

413

CHAPTER THIRTY:
MY SHIFT IS UP

It is always sad to leave a place to which one knows one will never return. Such are the *mélancolies du voyage:* perhaps they are one of the most rewarding things about traveling.

— Gustave Flaubert,
Flaubert in Egypt: A Sensibility on Tour

Sophie and I sat down in the spacious but basic kitchen in our rented house and looked over the options, both those that had passed and those that remained. Sophie had lost out on a job opportunity in Bucharest. Although she had initially seemed like a shoe-in, an incoming French diplomat's wife had subsequently put her own name in the Romanian hat and Sophie, the far better, far more qualified candidate, had been ousted from the running.

A chance for Sophie to take up the reins of the Moldova branch of her NGO, in the capital, Chişinău, had also fallen through. Perhaps it was for the best: one expat who had been quite unhappily based in Moldova later told me, "Think yourself lucky. That was very fortuitous."

We were down to option number three, the last one on the table, which would also have us going back to Europe, but with no jobs and few immediate prospects, to take our chances. Specifically, we'd move to Toulouse, in the south of France, where Sophie had, for the most part, grown up, and where, five years earlier, we had been married.

It was ironic that during the last month of our stay in Việt Nam, as things were sold, boxes packed, shipping arrangements made, and every soup supped felt like it had a very final aftertaste of "never again" to it, my blog exploded.

Since the beginning, many popular Web sites, blogs, and newspapers had linked to it. These links are the oil that propels the Internet, that juice that makes the popular *more* popular and the unlinked invisible. Without links pointing to your blog, you simply do not exist. When a writer for *Tuổi Trẻ*, Việt Nam's second-largest newspaper at the time, with a print circulation of 400,000, wrote about and linked to my blog on its site, my traffic went supersonic. That one link from *Tuổi Trẻ* brought in more visitors than the *New York Times*, the *Guardian*, Radio Singa-

415

pore, the BBC, Nick Denton, Jason Kottke, and Gapingvoid combined. I earned more in advertising clicks in that one week than I had done for an entire year. I was big(ish) in Việt Nam.

In that last month, the decision to leave began to look dumb. What were we leaving for? For the chance of picking up interesting work, for both Sophie and myself, in France? When we had all of this around us? I began to think that I could make a living out of this blog. I could see a way for me to harness my own entrepreneurial streak upon the street. That I could run street food tours, hold street food evenings and slideshows, link up with a cookery school, write a book, sell photographs. It was all there, up for grabs, and I was turning my back on it. For France.

Don't get me wrong — I have zero regrets about leaving. Change is good. But, in the years since boarding that plane out of Sài Gòn, don't think I haven't stepped back and occasionally thought, *You bloody idiot.*

At some point in the late nineties, I was interviewed by a Vietnamese newspaper about tourism in Việt Nam.

The general thrust of the discussion was "What can Việt Nam do to encourage more tourism?" In sum, I replied, "Việt Nam can't compete with Thailand on beaches or islands, nor with Cambodia on monuments, nor with Laos on tranquillity. However, it can totally compete on the food front, and that is where I think Việt Nam should put its efforts."

Little did either of us know at that time the changes that lay ahead.

CHAPTER THIRTY-ONE: APOCALYPSE NOW

As early as 2001, I'd heard that there was a desire within government to pull a Singapore, to ring in street food and sanitize the streets. Soon I began to see the most obvious signs of change: the bling-bling bars and the fast food chains selling pizza, fried chicken, and burgers.

The first flashy Vietnamese diner, Bún Ta, opened on Nam Kỳ Khởi Nghĩa Street in 2005. It took street food off the street, gave it colored noodles, and served it up on heavy ceramic plates in a swinky-swanky, whitewashed, air-conditioned joint. It rapidly became a lure for Saigonese of every shade of "LOOK AT ME, I'VE GOT CASH."

In more recent years, after we had left the country, the government enacted laws.

In July 2008, street vendors and sidewalk traders were banned from operating in sixty-two streets in Hà Nội and forty-eight public areas. Sài Gòn began requiring a license to operate on the sidewalk, and banned street food traders from fifteen downtown streets in 2009. The government said this was to "beautify the city" in Hà Nội's case, and for "city aestheticism" in Sài Gòn's — a result of the state discourse around "modernization" and "civilization."

Despite the rollout of new laws, one study shows that the number of sellers has actually kept on growing. If that is really the case, more power to them. However, the legal edicts keep on coming, too.

January 2013's Circular 30 from the Ministry of Health required street food sellers to attend food hygiene training classes and to possess a certificate. The law, like all the others before it, is probably unworkable. Just ten days before the circular took effect, most owners of "sidewalk eateries" were apparently oblivious.

"Most street food sellers said they are not aware of the new regulations, and that they would move around to avoid inspections," reported *Vietweek* in January 2013.

So, now, as the food fight grinds on, there are misguided plans afoot that I fear will destroy and have already begun to destroy the very thing that the government purports to want to save.

Take the plan to "preserve traditional gastronomy" in Hà Nội, via a highly regulated "food area" that raised its ungodly head in the summer of 2013. One of its prime goals was to "prevent any bad impressions for foreign tourists," the developer said, according to *DTINews*.

Bad impressions? Have these guys ever *visited* their revamped disaster zones and surveyed the damage done? Because I have, and it was utterly heartbreaking.

In 2013, I went back to Việt Nam. I visited Hàng Da market in Hà Nội, where I used to shop for fruit and flowers every Saturday morning with Sophie. The renovated 2013 version of Hàng Da was an object lesson in how *not* to redevelop a market. It had been moved underground. It was empty, stalls were partitioned, and there were no smells, no noise, no smiles, and *no customers*. It was beyond soulless. What greeted me in that subterranean car park would have been more appropriate in Pyongyang, not buzzy, busy, brash Việt Nam. Hàng Da today, in the centre of Hà Nội, is an utter disgrace.

Equally disgraceful is the unfathomable shambles of Việt Nam's airport food offerings. If there were one place you'd want to leave a good impression of your food, it would be at an international airport. But instead, both in Hà Nội and Sài Gòn, it was all racks of instant noodles, nasty, cheap sandwiches, stale French fries, and hot dogs. Where there should be the glittering nymph who sprinkles magical street food fairy dust across the land, instead there's

the impish cousin with her sack of kitchen horrors. Việt Nam, you should be ashamed of yourself for the awfulness of your airport offerings.

There are other causes for concern. Diên Biên
Phu Street in central Sài Gòn is named after
the historic battle that saw the end of French
colonization, a battle in large part bankrolled
by the United States. It's therefore with some
irony that the street that bears the battle's name
should now be the new frontline in a U.S. fast
food giant's battle for the hearts, minds, and
cholesterol levels of the Vietnamese, a nation
with rising childhood obesity, diabetes, and
heart disease.

After two decades of speculation, and following KFC, Pizza Hut, and Burger King, on February 8, 2014, the Golden Arches finally arrived in
Việt Nam on Diên Biên Phu Street. The McDonald's franchise is owned by the son-in-law of the
current prime minister of Việt Nam, a man with
plans to open one hundred branches throughout
the country within a decade.

Fast food giants, street food laws, and vendor crackdowns. Is this, to borrow a well-worn
phrase, apocalypse now?

I remember strolling through the kimchi-strewn
back alleys of my local market in Iksan, South
Korea, in 1996. I was with a Korean colleague,
Mrs. Hong, one of the teachers with whom I used
to share Korean eating adventures on a weekly

basis. She pointed at the female sellers squatting on the floor with their roots, berries, dried mushrooms, red chilies, and persimmons laid out on a tatty piece of cloth in front of them.

"Do you have that in your country?" she inquired, shaking her head, tutting with a sharp intake of breath at the squalor of it all.

"No, we don't. Even if anybody wanted to do it, it probably wouldn't be allowed," I replied. "Health and safety, quality assurance, regulations, and all that."

"One day, my country will be like yours and we won't have this," she fired back.

In her eyes, "this" was a bad thing. She was expressing the same yearning to somehow clean up, make it *better,* and "fix" what, in part, attracted people to the country in the first place. The old adage "If it ain't broke, don't fix it" is anathema.

So, what is the future for street food in Việt Nam, under this self-imposed pressure to "fix" it, to keep the food but lose the street, or at least sanitize it? An eventual cleansing of the streets to keep up appearances would seem to be inevitable. It's an outcome that no one, not even the soulless bean counters, will ever enjoy, especially if no one visits their underground markets and "designated street food zones."

I reconcile this vision with the fact that, to the Vietnamese, the food is the most important thing. It always will be. Fast food outlets will be a welcome novelty, but they won't become the country's default dining option. I trust in the Vietnamese inability to change on that front. But just *try* eating bún chả off a sprayed-clean formica table in a restaurant with suited waiters and Muzak, just as my South Korean colleagues thought that was the way their food should be presented to me all those years ago, when I first traveled overseas. Yes, it's still food, but that's not enough.

The MP3 is an inadequate replacement for vinyl. Like McDonald's, the MP3 file is convenient, fast, cheap, and easy, but it's worse than second rate when it comes to quality of experience on every single tangible level. Eating in Việt Nam shouldn't be like listening to an MP3 file. It isn't *just* about the food. You could eat Bà Sáu's soup in a silent, sterile, hospital-like environment. You could, but you wouldn't enjoy it. Vietnamese street food starts with noise and ends with taste, with plenty of other things going on all around you at the same time. You see, the street is the extra condiment. The one not listed on the menu. It's the one you'll never find inside the Metropole, where Graham Greene clinked cocktails, or in the fancy fusion restaurant in central Sài Gòn, but it's the one inherent to your enjoyment. Take the street out of street food and you just have food.

I've corresponded with many Việt Kiều who claim that the renditions of Vietnamese dishes served up in Orange County, California; New York City's Little Sài Gòn; and elsewhere are far superior to what you can find in Hà Nội or Sài Gòn. They may be right, but to me, that will always be second best, like airbrushing a Rembrandt, taking out all those nice wee bits in the background and replacing them with steel-gray blank spaces.

The street chefs told me the food will never change. And I believe them. My legs get creakier but the stools stay stubbornly low. Laws may chip away at the streets like misguided jackhammers, but up until now, there's been enough resistance to every authoritarian stroke in the form of Vietnamese mettle. The food in the street may keep the legal jackhammers at bay, but can it last? As the travel books say, go now. You know, before it's too late.

LINER NOTES

It was in 1992 that I found myself in the bedroom of a psychedelic rock legend. Pete "Sonic Boom" Kember of Spacemen 3 was born and grew up in the same town as me. I was in his room in the village of Dunchurch to interview him for a fanzine I was writing. Since my sixteenth birthday in 1985, I'd seen his band play Rugby's pub back rooms a ton of times. Spacemen 3 had recently split up. Following on from a solo album, under his Sonic Boom pseudonym, some years earlier, he'd just released his second single under the moniker Spectrum. It was a reworking of Daniel Johnston's classic "True Love Will Find You in the End." As I started browsing through Sonic's extensive record collection, it occurred to me.

"I can see why you chose your band names," I said. "Spacemen 3, Sonic Boom, Spectrum. All the records you've ever made segue into one another inside your record collection under the

427

letter 'S.'"

He didn't let on if he'd done that on purpose, but he laughed as if to indicate that it had indeed been planned all along.

It was an attention to detail I appreciated. He dominated the letter "S" within his own record collection. There was another detail Sonic was careful to include within his recordings — liner notes. He included these on the inner or outer sleeves of his records.

I've always been a fan of the liner notes that came with the vinyl records I used to buy in the 1980s. Liner notes began to die out with the advent of the CD. It was with disappointment that I'd buy an LP that had nothing in the way of liner notes, no details of the circumstances of the recording session on the inner sleeve and no thought to scratch even the most perfunctory message to listeners in the run-out grooves. I took a liking to the bands that cared enough about their craft to include these details.

Given the opportunity to write a book for the first time, I wanted to create my own liner notes. And here they are.

It was late 2011 when I received an e-mail from Anthony Bourdain, asking me if I wanted to write a book. I was working as the Reuters foreign correspondent for Rwanda in Kigali, the capital. The news agency's in-country bureau was less than lavish. It consisted of my laptop upon a eucalyptus table in the dining room of a former diplomat's bungalow in Kiyovu, Kigali's leafiest district.

I reported inflation figures, bank rates, grenade attacks, refugee crises, diplomatic shenanigans, prison biogas projects, and foreign direct investment. Việt Nam was a fond, but distant, memory.

My head was firmly in Rwanda. I let the idea of writing a book slip until the following summer. I was at home in France for two months when the book idea, and Anthony's offer, started to nag at me. But what would I write? What could I write?

It was on the plane back to Kigali at the end of August 2012 that I decided I would like to give it a go. I didn't know if I was up to the challenge, but the two-month break in France had cleared my head. I was no longer working as a full-time correspondent. I had time.

I dropped Anthony an e-mail to see (a) if he was still interested and (b) what it was he saw in me. I needed an outside eye. He wrote back, "Who are you? Why did you dedicate time to documenting street food? Story of Vietnamese food culture as you know it — who, what, where? Who the hell were you when discovering it? Make the case that others should find it important (too)."

The e-mails traveled between Rwanda and

New York, and the same day, sitting at the same eucalyptus table, I replied to say I would write ten thousand words by the end of September. If he liked what he read, we'd push on. If not, then we'd forget about it.

I thought and planned for a week before I wrote anything. I was astounded at how much detail I could remember. I began to write the very first section on paper in late August of 2012. The first sentence of the book is the first thing I wrote and it is probably the only sentence in the entire book that has remained unchanged throughout the many edits.

Fortunately, Anthony liked what he read.

"Thrilled with how it's going. Very, very pleased and excited. It's great. Proceed."

It was Friday, October 12, 2012. My wife, our son, and I celebrated the best way we could in Kigali: we bought two takeaway pizzas from the New Cactus restaurant and a bottle of cheap red wine from La Gardienne on Avenue de Kiyovu — a street that journalists had referred to during the 1994 genocide as "Machete Avenue."

For much of the next year, I kept a sticky note on my laptop with the essence of what Anthony had e-mailed me. During this stage of writing, it felt like I was regurgitating the lot onto the page in a rather unstructured way. At one point I did mention to my agent that I seemed to be writing a series of thousand-word short stories that I didn't quite know how to knit together. It also felt odd to have a head full of Việt Nam while seated at a desk in Central Africa, enduring power cuts (which reminded me of Việt Nam) and water shortages (which didn't). Fortunately, a good friend of mine, Anjan Sundaram, was also living in Kigali at the time and was just finishing his own first book, *Stringer*. We had plenty to talk about and learn from each other. As he was further into the process, it was mostly me learning from him.

I continued planning and writing in Kigali, but not full-time. Family life and other work got in the way. I finally signed my book contract with Daniel Halpern at Ecco in May 2013. My manuscript deadline was March 4, 2014. As soon as I signed the contract, I stopped work on the book altogether.

Part of the writing process, for me at least, is having time to let the thing settle. Get some distance from it. I'd written approximately seventy thousand words at that point. A good half of those words got the chop from me or my editor.

I needed to come back to it with a fresh eye. I picked up the paper pages again during one intense week in late August 2013, on the dining room table at home in the Gers, France.

At the end of that month, we moved as a family to Dakar, Senegal, for my wife's job. I continued writing, this time on another dining table and at a desk in the bedroom of our new temporary home in downtown Dakar.

In September, I was able to go back to Việt Nam for almost one month. I wrote more than twenty thousand words in-country. First in room 401, VietFace Hotel, Hà Nội, and then in room 306, Minh Chau Hotel, Sài Gòn.

The first rough draft of the book was completed on November 22, 2013, in Dakar.

Meanwhile, in New York City, Laurie Woolever had already edited the first fifty thousand words — the "Hà Nội section," as I referred to it at that point. It was now time for me to work through her very thorough edits and follow her superb guidance, while she attacked the "Sài Gòn section."

We worked this way, back and forth over e-mail using the shared document features in Microsoft Word and Apple's Pages application, until the beginning of February 2014. When we were both happy, we agreed it was time for my literary agent and Anthony to get a look.

It was then I began to work with Ryan Willard, assistant editor at Ecco Books, who pushed me to look at the book again from different angles, sand down the grain, tighten up the bolts, and lay down the varnish.

My biggest concern during the writing and editing process was whether I was succeeding at bringing the street onto the page. I wanted fish sauce to drip from every page, for star anise and beef bones to waft up as the reader flicked to the next chapter, for the smell of stale beer and cigarettes to permeate every paragraph. Well, okay, every other paragraph. My editors squeezed me dry, but it's probably the writer's disease that I'm still not confident that I've managed to achieve these lofty aims.

Having said that, one other thing I've learned from writing a book is that, even when you've finished it, copyedits are over, and the book has officially been "signed off" for publication, you still look at it and think, "Hmmm . . . if I could just rework that paragraph. And that transition could be done better. I'm not sure I described that well enough." Ad infinitum. That's why we need editors: to tell us when too much is too much and when enough is enough.

The other thing I learned about writing is that ideas are great, but writing really is all in the rewriting. And there is no such thing as "writer's block." You pick up a pen and you write. What you write will be better on some days than on other days. But there is no "block."

I originally planned the book on a Bur-O-Class eighty-page graph paper notepad. I plotted the book's narrative arc on a sheet of large flip-board paper. The bare bones of those original ideas and plans survive in this book. A lot of the fluff fell by the wayside, as I now understand is the way with these projects.

To write, I used Rotring Tikky 0.3 and Rotring Tikky multiple pens, and Artliner 0.3 and 0.5 black pens. Additional stationery supplies were purchased from Chez Mon Ami in Dakar. Later, I used a black and silver Gillio Firenze fountain pen Sophie bought for me in Belgium.

I typed the book into an eleven-inch Apple MacBook Air using Pages. Over the year, I printed out various draft stages in Kigali, Toulouse, Dakar, and Hà Nội.

For note taking, I filled two red Moleskine (140 mm x 90 mm, 192 pages) pocket ruled notebooks. I know Moleskines are seen by many as the height of pretension, and some foreign correspondent friends chide me for using them. But, in my experience, they are extremely robust, given the battering I tend to inflict upon my notebooks in the field. Unlike other brands I've used over the years, my Moleskines have never fallen apart.

I filled notebook no. 1 between September 11, 2012, and August 7, 2013, at the following locations:

Kigali: at home, mostly in the kitchen while cooking or on the patio while waiting for takeaway food orders on Friday or Saturday nights at either the New Cactus or Zaffran, both in Kiyovu.

UK: I wrote in the notebook in Bristol; Tunbridge Wells; the Cranford Arms near Regent's Park, London; on a bus on Oxford Street; in the bar at the Anchor Hotel in Kippford, Scotland; and while waiting for a flight at Terminal 5, Heathrow Airport.

France: I wrote in it on Grande Rue Nazareth, Toulouse, and at home in the Gers.

I started notebook no. 2 on August 8, 2013, and had filled it by October 27, 2013, writing at the following locations:

France: at home.

Dakar: From September 5, 2013, I wrote in it on Rue Jules Ferry.

The sky: over western India on Emirates flight EK392 on September 28, 2013.

Việt Nam: in Hà Nội, Sài Gòn, and Tây Ninh during October 2013.

I wrote over one hundred notes in the iPhone 5 Notes application totaling several thousand words; many of these notes ended up in the book. I drew all the sketches from photographs I took in Việt Nam. The only exception is the sketch of a Hà Nội street scene opposite the title page. I drew that from an image by Flickr user Vincent Casey.

The German poet and essayist Heinrich Heine famously once said, "Where they have burned books, they will end in burning human beings." I had the notion to completely reinvent this idea and burn my own book. With cigarette ends.

I wanted the book to feel as if a tile of life had been peeled from the Vietnamese street and landed into the lap of the reader. A plastic tile that accurately resembled a table from the streets of Vietnam. If the designers couldn't realistically emboss cigarette burns into the design, I told my publisher, I would personally burn the first few hundred copies of my own book with strategically placed cigarette burns (I don't smoke). Call it a limited, handcrafted edition. If they had the budget, I wanted that look, and I was prepared to smoke for my art. In the end, unsurprisingly, the designers took a more practical route.

I am indebted to more people than I can remember, especially the hundreds of named and nameless street stall vendors whose stalls I ate at over the years. Long may you rule the Vina-streets.

When I lived in Việt Nam, I regularly went out eating with a number of people not mentioned in this book. In no particular order, thanks and xin chàos are due to Channing,

Thomas, "Dirty" Batman Ben, Dave "the Rave," Jon, Heather, Jenny, and the Gentlemen of the Commonwealth Club. Finally, I could not have written this book without the help of everyone who interpreted and translated for me over the years, particularly Lý, Huyền, and Trân.

ABOUT THE AUTHOR

Graham Holliday grew up in Rugby, England, before moving to Iksan, South Korea, in 1996 to teach English. He relocated to Việt Nam the following year to teach English to senior government officials. He started working as a journalist in Sài Gòn in 2001. He is the author of the "almost award-winning" *noodlepie* blog about street food in Sài Gòn. He has written for the *Guardian*, the *New York Times Magazine*, the *South China Morning Post*, *Time*, the BBC, CNN, and many other outlets. He went on to become a foreign correspondent for Reuters news agency in Rwanda. He now works as a journalism trainer and media consultant for the BBC and other organizations, and is working on a novel. He is currently based in Dakar, Senegal. This is his first book.

Web: noodlepie.com
Twitter: @noodlepie
E-mail: graham@noodlepie.com